W9-AFV-224

Arcadia

MARK LANE

ARCADIA

Holt, Rinehart and Winston
New York   Chicago   San Francisco

First Edition

Photographs by Carolyn Mugar

Designer: Bob Antler

SBN: 03–081854–0

PRINTED IN THE UNITED STATES OF AMERICA

Contents

v

4. The Trial 55

5. The Investigation 230

*Eight pages of black and white photographs
follow page 146.*

Prologue

Late in October, 1967, I read a newspaper account of the death of seven young children who had apparently been poisoned. The Associated Press story began, "The last of James and Annie Mae Richardson's seven children died today—poisoned by an agricultural insecticide." Newspaper coverage of the event persisted for the next several days, featuring photographs of the parents, of the funeral in Arcadia, Florida, and educational inserts about the history and deadly propensity of parathion, the insecticide that evidently had caused the seven deaths. One newspaper reported, apparently not tongue in cheek, that "Parathion, one of the deadliest chemicals ever used to kill insects, is so dangerous to human beings that some Florida citrus growers have given up using it." Larry Nipp, head of the Florida Pest Control Commission, was quick to respond, "Citrus people and

big farmers want it. It's an excellent product for them." One
magazine reported that the popular insecticide was "developed
by the Nazis prior to and during World War II when Hitler
was considering chemical warfare. It wasn't quite ready for
use when the war ended and German scientists completed
the research."

Within a week the controversy about the merits of parathion and despair over the seven deaths gave way to new
horror as James Richardson, a black American citrus picker,
was charged with murdering the children. The story blos-
somed on the front pages again as the De Soto County Judge
and the County Sheriff provided what appeared to be ample
evidence of Richardson's guilt. "The motive was remunera-
tion for life insurance," reported Sheriff Frank Cline at a
press conference. Cline explained that the very night before
Richardson poisoned the children he had taken out an insurance policy on each of their lives. He added that five other of
Richardson's children had also died "over the past few years."
Lie-detector tests also corroborated Richardson's guilt, Cline
revealed. The case seemed almost conclusive, but when it
soon appeared possible that Cline had overstated various aspects of the case, I proposed to take a trip to Arcadia and look
around a bit. Other events disposed of my well-intentioned
intention, and I soon forgot my resolve.

One year later, almost to the day, just after I had lectured
at a university in northern California, I decided to drive down
the coast toward Los Angeles, as I had two free days before my
next engagement. I stopped for the night at the Big Sur Inn,
rented a small and antiquated room, and before going to sleep
rummaged through some old magazines. The most recent one
was the November 13, 1967, issue of Newsweek, and it contained an early article about the Richardson case. I was to
lecture in a few days at the University of South Florida in
Tampa, and suddenly I wondered how far Arcadia was from
Tampa, if Richardson had been acquitted or, if convicted, if

he was still alive, Florida being a state that takes its capital punishment very seriously.

The day following my lecture at the University of South Florida, I participated in a seminar with the Dean of the school, Margaret Fischer, and a Pulitzer Prize-winning journalist for the Tampa *Tribune*, John Frasca. At lunch I asked each about the Richardson case. Both were aware that he had been convicted, but unaware of the sentence. I later found out that he had been convicted of murder in the first degree, that the jury brought back no recommendation for mercy, and that he was therefore given the mandatory sentence of death in the electric chair.

Both Dean Fischer and Mr. Frasca volunteered the opinion that the case against Richardson had seemed flawed in some way that neither was able to clearly articulate. But that both had doubts about the case was certain.

My year-old resolve to look into the matter was reinforced or perhaps reborn. During the next eight months I conducted more than one hundred and fifty interviews in fourteen cities and towns in Florida, traveling many thousands of miles on Florida's fine highways and dusty back roads. Before my journey had ended I knew a great deal more about how the seven children died and how justice functions in part of America. This book is a report upon what I discovered.

We begin when the first local police officer is informed that the children are ill and end with Richardson on death row in Raiford, Florida. There are many stories and as many themes that run through them as we search for the facts. There is the black illiterate farmhand who finds that he is opposed by Arcadia's white establishment and proscecuted by Florida's leading State's Attorney. Yet as soon as the racial line appears to be set, we find a young, white, southern lawyer, John S. Robinson, defending Richardson and receiving some encouragement from the local police department and animosity from the local sheriff. Just when it appears that the case against the defendant is about to fall as a result of its own very frail construction, a Negro prisoner, Ernell Washington, materializes to give the Sheriff's charges the appearance of some substance.

There exists a legal fiction that a defendant must be presumed innocent unless his guilt is established beyond a reasonable doubt. Many experienced defense attorneys will contend that the notion is inoperable in highly publicized cases, where news reports tend to reflect the view of the prosecutors. When the trial is set in the Deep South, and the defendant and his witnesses are black, while the judge, jury, sheriff, and prosecuting staff are all white, the presumption of innocence plays but a small part in the deliberations. Richardson was required to prove his innocence to the satisfaction of the jurors. This, in the circumstances, he was unable to do at that time. In his path were placed many obstacles. Political considerations intrigued some, greed purchased another, resentment still another, and through it all many others sat, some shaking their heads in sorrow, some in sympathy, but most doing no more than that.

There are many stories here, and they are told through two sets of mutually exclusive facts. First there are the legal facts: witnesses who testified in the presence of the jury, physical evidence introduced at the trial, rulings by the judge. Never mind that the relevant witnesses were not called, that the jury never learned that the properties of the poison precluded the possibility that Richardson did what he was charged with doing. That which was not presented to the jury was beyond the scope of the legal facts and cannot be considered as part of the legal body of truth. Therefore we present the trial scenes in great detail and with maximum fidelity. It may be said that portions of the trial record are set forth in more than sufficient detail, indeed to the point of boredom. Portions of all trials are too methodical to sustain interest, let alone to create excitement. That too is part of the legal truth to which I have tried to be faithful.

The careful reader may complain, as did an editor who read the manuscript for my publisher, that some facts are established out of chronological order. "One of the deceased Richardson children is referred to as Betty Jean Bryant, and it is not until much later in the trial that the reader learns that some of the seven children were Mrs. Richardson's by a previous marriage." Some degree of patience is required of the reader if he is to experience the development of the evidence as did the jurors. Others may briddle at the inconclusive answer given by a witness or be frustrated by the failure of the inquiring attorney to ask the relevant and logical question. These too are normal jury reactions. For my part, I can only assure the reader that the evidence is presented fairly and in context.

I assume greater personal responsibility for the chapters that precede and follow the trial sequences. Here too I have primarily recorded the words of others, but the questions that prompted the responses are my own. In these portions are found the facts that contend with the legal truth. Here are the witnesses who have never testified, except to you—through these pages. You will hear the facts that for various reasons were not fashioned to reach the jury through the proper legal exemplar. In a sense you will occupy the position of an appellate court with original jurisdiction. Unlike the real courts, which generally cannot look at the facts except as they were presented to the jury, you may see the entire picture unrestricted by legality. You may then judge the action of the jurors. And of yourself as well. If you do conclude that an innocent man sits on death row, will you shake your head in sorrow or in sympathy?

M. L.

September, 1969

ARCADIA

1. The Deaths

It WAS WEDNESDAY, OCTOBER 25, 1967.

Just after twelve noon, teachers began to bring Negro children into the General Hospital in Arcadia. The little town in south-central Florida feared that a school-cafeteria poisoning case was about to erupt into epidemic proportions. Lt. Joseph M. Minoughan of the Arcadia Police Department hurried to the hospital. "I was at home eating lunch when I got a call to report at once to the hospital. All they said was that it was some kind of poison case. When I arrived at the hospital there was general confusion, approaching panic, there, and I just could not get any relevant information at the time. My first thought was that this might be a ptomaine case and that it might effect all of the children who had lunch at the school. In Chicago I investigated over twenty-five ptomaine-poisoning cases, and if I had just been able to see the children brought into the hospital that day, I would have known at once that this was no simple ptomaine case."

Minoughan was the first law-enforcement officer to arrive at the hospital. He quickly determined that some of the poison victims were pre-school age and that all seven of them were members of the same family. "It was clear that they may have been poisoned at home. I secured the address of the family, Richardson, 131 Watson, and rushed over there. The door was unlocked; I opened it and made a quick search to determine if anything was there that might have been responsible. If so, I didn't want anyone else to get into it, and I was anxious to report to the doctors what I might find to help them in treating the children."

He found a can of insect spray. "I didn't think that was it, but it's all that I saw. Then I saw a young woman standing there. Her name, Dorothy Bracey. She lived next door. I told her to make sure that no one got into the apartment while I was gone, and I rushed back to the hospital."

At the hospital Minoughan was informed that some of the children had already died and that others were suffering from convulsions and were foaming at the mouth. "That wasn't ptomaine. I was sure of that. I rushed back to the apartment, and as I got there I saw the Chief [Arcadia Police Chief Richard Barnard] and Cline [De Soto County Sheriff Frank Cline] coming out of the apartment."

Barnard was at Smith's Feed Store when he heard the police radio in his automobile begin to crackle. "I called in and was informed that some children had been poisoned and that they were at the hospital. This must have been about fifteen minutes after twelve. I went to the hospital at once, of course. Joe [Lt. Minoughan] had been there already and had just left. I established immediately that they had not eaten at the cafeteria at the school. I talked with the teachers who had brought them in. A little later Cline arrived,

and together we went to the apartment. The door was unlocked, and no one was there. Joe had just left to return
to the hospital before we arrived at the house. There was a
very strong smell in the house. So strong that you could
almost feel it in the air. It smelled like a bitter metallic
taste, perhaps like alum. We searched the apartment thoroughly for any trace of poison, but we found nothing.

"As we left the apartment, Joe arrived back there. We
searched the little shack behind the apartment house, but it
was empty. I saw Bessie Reese outside there—she lived
next door—and I interviewed her. She told me that she
had prepared the food for the children, that she heated it up
and dished it out to the kids. I thought that if there was
going to be any case at all, she would be the most important
witness. But of course there was no evidence of any crime at
that time. Poisonings are often accidental, and so far there
was no indication that this one was not."

The County Sheriff has primary jurisdiction over all
felonies committed within De Soto County, including those
that take place in Arcadia. The Chief of the Arcadia Police
Department investigates misdemeanors committed within the
city limits and assists the Sheriff in investigating felonies
committed within the city as well. The one Negro police
officer in the area was Will Clemmons, who worked for
Chief Barnard and assisted him in the investigation.

Sheriff Cline was the last law officer to arrive at the hospital.
"We went over to the apartment, I forget who I was with,
Judge Hayes or somebody, and I smelled that poison. I
smelled it twenty-five foot from the house. Did you ever put
a penny in your mouth? Well, that's what it smelled like,
so I said to myself, 'By golly, it's got a parathion smell to
it.' I wondered how many people are going to get it. I knew
it right away that it was parathion, even though I didn't say
it out loud to anyone. I went out of the apartment and

looked into the shed. I was looking for the poison, but it wasn't there. Not in the house, not in the shed."

Before long six of the Richardson children were dead. Betty, age eight; Alice, age seven; Susie, age six; Dorreen, age five; Vanessa, age four; and James, Jr., age two. Dianne, age three, was dying.

The parents, James and Annie Mae Richardson, had been working some sixteen miles away since early that morning. They had been picking fruit in the groves outside of the city. Early that afternoon a message was sent to them. They were informed that one of the children was ill and that one of the parents could leave the field and return to town. The couple was inseparable, however, and together they returned by truck to Arcadia. At the hospital Cline began to question the parents, who had not yet been informed that their children were dead. Cline asked for the keys to the apartment. Richardson gave him the key to the door and the keys to the locks on the refrigerators. There were two refrigerators in the apartment. One functioned; the one that did not was used as a cabinet for tinned goods and household cleansers.

Eventually the Richardsons were informed of the tragedy. Mrs. Richardson became hysterical, and sedation was required. Her husband stared with unbelieving eyes and insisted that it could not be true. When he was assured that all the children but one were dead, he became silent. He then began to pray quietly.

Reporters from throughout the State began to converge on the little town. Barnard later commented, "Why, they had so many television crews and wagons and reporters that I was unable to get into Cline's jail. He was holding press conferences with Judge Hayes, and the reporters were taking down every word."

Reporters asked Barnard and Minoughan for statements, but both replied that it would be improper to make public comments about the deaths. Each also declined to have his picture taken or to appear on television.

Richardson was repeatedly questioned by reporters. He said that he did not know why his children died, and added, "But the Sheriff better find out. That's his job." That comment, when published, earned Richardson the Sheriff's enmity. Frank Schaub, the prosecuting attorney for the area, quickly made an on-the-spot appearance. Fresh from his widely publicized victory over F. Lee Bailey in the Coppolino case, his personal examination of the apartment was a major news event. Investigators also arrived from the State Attorney General's office, the State Agricultural Department, and the State Health Department. Cline, nominally in charge of the investigation, had all the help that he could use. Before long De Soto County Judge Lee Hayes, Schaub, and Cline were holding press conferences and relating to the reporters what little evidence there was. Barnard offered to assist in the investigation and to make his staff available to Cline but he disapproved of the public-relations aspect of the investigation. Cline spurned Barnard's advice as well as his offer of help, thus eliminating him from the investigation and the one Negro officer in Arcadia as well.

The next morning the last child died.

The only witness to the fatal meal had been Bessie Reese. At a press conference Cline said, "The children became ill after eating a noon meal of beans, rice, and grits which their mother had prepared the night before and left in a refrigerator for them." Cline also told the press, "It has not been established if anyone was caring for the younger children nor if there was an adult present when the meal was served."

During the same morning a two-pound sack of parathion was discovered in the shack behind the apartment building in which the Richardson family had lived. It contained enough poison to wipe out a good-sized city. Cline, Barnard, their staffs, and Schaub all agreed—that bag had not been there the day before. Someone had placed it there after the premises had been searched five times. An Associated Press story that asserted that it relied upon Cline and his staff, reported that the bag of parathion had "mysteriously appeared" on "the steps" of the Richardson home. The appearance was mysterious enough, although it was in the shed, not on the steps of the building that the family had occupied. Cline told reporters, "It wasn't there yesterday. The house was examined very carefully then." Later that day Cline conceded that the bag had been found in the shack. At a press conference he said, "I haven't found out who put it there, but I will." He added, "It was a suspicious appearance."

Later Cline said that whoever put the bag of poison in the shack probably also murdered the children. Cline told the press that Charlie Smith, a black resident of Arcadia's Quarters, had discovered the parathion. "He had some woman call in my office, and I went right over and found it there." However, Lt. Minoughan was the first police officer to arrive on the scene when the poison was discovered. When he arrived at the shed he was informed by Bessie Reese that Smith had found the poison. Minoughan then called the Sheriff's office to report the discovery of the evidence. Minoughan had been on duty early that morning. "I received the call over the radio in my car between seven-forty-five and eight-oh-five A.M. I patrol the school crossing at five past eight, and I had not gone there yet when the call came in. I was told that Smith found the poison. He led me to it, picked it up, and showed it to me. I told him to put it down immediately and to wash his hands. When Cline arrived I showed him where the bag was."

Minoughan did not know who had called in the discovery to the police station. I asked Barnard, and he said that he had been informed that it was an anonymous male caller.

THE CHARGE

The next day Cline and Schaub's local assistant, John Treadwell, III, told reporters that Richardson had "discussed insurance policies for the children the night before their deaths." Treadwell told the press that he had received "conflicting statements" from Richardson and from the insurance salesman as to what had transpired during those discussions. At the conference Treadwell noted that the salesman, to whom he referred as "George Purvis," his given name being Gerald, talked with Richardson "just a few hours before" the children were stricken. The Associated Press story carrying Treadwell's observations also reported that a funeral for the children was being planned for Sunday at the high-school gymnasium. It concluded, "Authorities found the bag of poison at the Richardson home."

The following day Treadwell said, "Until we find out whether the poisoning was external or internal, we can make little progress." He said that the State pathologist was examining remnants of the lunch and blood samples from the children's bodies. He added, "We also are trying to determine whether a bag of parathion mysteriously found in an outhouse at the home was the same type of chemical as that which killed the children." He repeated that he had uncovered a conflict between Richardson and Purvis as to the insurance conference.

On Sunday the funeral took place in the gymnasium. The funeral director explained, "There's not a church in town big enough to handle the crowd." More than one thousand persons attended the event. The Reverend C. S. Elder officiated. As the seven white caskets were formed into a crescent at one end of the gymnasium, a student sang a hymn, and Richardson collapsed in tears. His wife appeared to be calm throughout the major portion of the services, but before they had concluded she too collapsed. Elder was more outspoken than he had been in the past. "These children will never have to walk in anger or despair again and never will be subjected to sin. These deaths are God's way of saying to Arcadia, 'Put your house in order.'" As the bodies were taken to the cemetery, Richardson's mother cried out, "Good-bye, little darlings; good-bye, little darlings."

National news magazines covered the funeral, as did the television and radio networks. Never before had one man in Arcadia, Sheriff Frank Cline, been the center of nation-wide scrutiny. Chief Barnard later told me that, "Cline saw the chance to make a big name for himself. He needed to make an arrest real bad."

Two days after the funeral Cline charged Richardson with seven counts of murder in the first degree. Richardson was booked as a defendant in seven murder cases. Evidently Cline had acted without adequate consultation. Police Chief Barnard said, "There just is no case against that man." Treadwell, speaking for the State Attorney's office, charged with the responsibility of actually prosecuting the case should it come to trial, was inclined to agree with Barnard. Suddenly the murder warrants were dropped, and both Annie Mae Richardson and James Richardson were formally charged with child neglect. Cline then found a stalwart local ally, as Judge Hayes, who served as both county judge and coroner, announced to the press that, "We're going to issue murder warrants tomorrow." Hayes added that both he and Cline felt there was "enough evidence to file murder charges," but he complained that both Schaub and Treadwell did not con-cur. Both of those men would be forced to support the charges after a local hearing, Hayes reasoned. "That's why I am summoning a coroner's inquest," he said, "to sub-stantiate evidence already on hand."

The news services asked Cline for the basis of the charge

against the Richardsons. Cline replied that he "would not give details of his investigation" at that time.

The next day Cline held a press conference and announced that Richardson had had five other children who had died under mysterious circumstances in another Florida city and that the motive for the crime in Arcadia was Richardson's desire to collect fourteen thousand dollars in insurance money. At the conference Judge Hayes said that both Richardson and his wife had taken lie-detector tests and the results showed that Richardson had "guilty knowledge of the poisoning." Hayes was to conduct a Coroner's jury the next day. He was empowered to pick his own jury. Hayes and Cline then led the reporters to the Richardson house, where they posed for photographs and granted television interviews.

THE CORONER'S JURY

The coroner's jury held a hearing on Thursday, November 2. The press was invited to attend, and cameras were encouraged. In many respects the event was probably unique in recent American jurisprudence. The presiding officer had previously announced that the prospective defendant was guilty and that he would be charged with murder.

Before the hearing began Hayes said that, "We will meet today to instruct Frank Cline to file murder charges against Richardson." The effect of that statement could hardly be lost upon the citizens of Arcadia and upon his handpicked jury. *The Arcadian*, the local weekly publication, described Hayes as "unquestionably one of the most influential and most powerful men in De Soto County." He had been on the bench for more than thirty-one years.

The archaic rules of that court did not provide for a stenographic record of the witnesses' statements. It is, therefore, necessary to rely upon the recollection of reporters and others who were present in an effort to reconstruct the testimony. The most sensational development came during the testimony of Cline. He said that he had evidence "that at least three children have died in another county" and that in addition to the three who died "there was three more who became sick of household things like potash, but did not die." He explained how he had uncovered that "evidence." "Detectives in Duval County [Jacksonville] related the evidence to me over the telephone." Judge Hayes, it cannot be said, runs a very tight courtroom when it comes to the rules of evidence.

The school principal and one of the teachers testified that the children became ill after the luncheon recess. Bessie Reese said that she participated in serving the food to the children. They had returned from school, she said, at "about five minutes to twelve." Then she proceeded to "divide up the rice" in seven equal parts.

Treadwell, who conducted the examination, established that Mrs. Reese was then on parole but failed to ask the witness about the charge on which she had been convicted. She said that she and her daughter, Dorothy Bracey, had taken care of the Richardson children in the past and that her daughter and other members of her family had gone to Sarasota that morning. As they had not returned by lunchtime, she said, she was alone with the seven children. Had Mrs. Reese heated and served the food, as she had told Barnard? Treadwell did not inquire. Did she not smell the poison odor while in the kitchen preparing the poisoned food? Treadwell did not inquire. How could she have given the children food from which such a powerful smell emanated? Treadwell did not inquire. Richardson, of course, was not represented at the hearing and therefore was unable to question the witnesses.

Treadwell quickly moved from the death scene to the discovery of the sack of parathion the next morning. Here Mrs. Reese was most specific. She recalled that Charlie Smith walked up to the building that she had shared with the Richardsons. According to Mrs. Reese he said, "Bet there was some of that parathion around if we'd just go look for it."

Then Smith "walked straight as an arrow to the shed in the back yard. He walked up to the window and asked me to help pull a board off the window, so he could look in. After we did that, he reached in and asked me to give him some light. We used a cigarette lighter, and then he looked down and said, 'There's something here.' He pulled up the sack and gave it to me. I could read part of the warning and what it was."

Mrs. Reese said that a woman saw them with the sack and called the Sheriff. Smith then put the bag back into the shed. Smith was present in the hearing room but was not asked to testify at that time.

Three doctors and a nurse who had attempted to treat the children at the hospital testified about symptoms that they had observed. All believed that the children had been killed by an organic phosphate, possibly parathion.

The next witness was Gerald Purvis. He began, "I called at Richardson's house on Tuesday, the 24th, about 7:30 or 7:45." Treadwell did not ask Purvis whether Richardson had invited him to the apartment or if he was soliciting from door to door. The witness continued, "We discussed insurance. We talked about a family group plan." The ordinary application of the rules of evidence would have prevented such vague testimony. The conclusions offered by the witness did little to inform the jury of the relevant facts. There may be sound reasons for departing from the strictures imposed by the rules, but in this instance, as in too many others, Hayes showed no desire to see the full facts developed. "What did Richardson say to you and what did you say to Richardson?" are the obvious questions to be put to the witness. In this case, since only one of the two was charged with the crime, the sum of the conversation was distinctly of less value than an examination of the separate parts. Purvis continued, "He said that there were ten in his family. I remember that his wife came in a couple of times and another lady, Bessie Reese." Purvis said, "When the time came to pay the premium, he didn't have it. I asked if he could borrow it from someone. He tried to borrow it from the lady who came in. But she said she didn't have it." Purvis testified that he finally told Richardson that, "I'll be back next week." Treadwell then insisted that Purvis had left Richardson with the impression that there was a valid policy. Purvis strenuously denied that he had intentionally created that impression but conceded that it might be possible that Richardson had not understood him correctly. Purvis then said that there was additional discussion about doubling the amount and that he then left the premises. There was, of course, no cross-examination, since the defendant was not represented. The searching questions for the crucial witness would have to await the trial.

A pathologist testified that the children had died as a result of organic phosphate poisoning. A chemist said that parathion was found in the stomachs of the children and in certain utensils taken from the Richardson home. Dorothy Bracey testified that she had told the Richardsons that she was going to Sarasota on October 25 and therefore would be unable to care for the children that day. Several law-enforcement officers, including Barnard, Cline, and Minoughan, testified that they had searched the shed and had not seen the bag of parathion there on October 25. Charlie Smith also testified.

The Arcadian sought to dismiss Smith as a man "who by his own admission has a fondness for cheap wine." I interviewed Smith three times, and he informed me that he really preferred excellent French champagne but that his budget unfortunately permitted the acquisition of only inferior local brands of wine. He was questioned very briefly by Treadwell, who led him through the testimony. He explained that he saw Bessie Reese on the morning of the 26th, walked to the shed with her, and with her ripped a board that had covered a window opening from the shed. There, just inside the window, was the parathion. He was excused with alacrity. Just half an hour after the jury had retired to consider the evidence, it returned with a unanimous verdict: "Death with premeditation at the hands of James Richardson and party or parties unknown." Hayes immediately ordered Charlie Smith arrested and held as a material witness. He set bond at two thousand dollars. No other witness was placed in the Arcadia jail.

No new evidence had been divulged at the inquest. James Richardson's name had hardly been mentioned by the witnesses. The status quo had been preserved regarding the facts. When the hearing was over, the evaluation of the evidence by the Chief of Police was still valid. At the time there remained no case against Richardson. Yet the hearing had brought about the change that Hayes had intended and virtually predicted. The hysteria against the defendant had mounted considerably. The one new fact was the verdict by the coroner's jury. In the face of that charge, Schaub and Treadwell were brought into line. Both men were dependent upon the population of Arcadia for votes, and neither ever again said publicly that no charge should be made. Although no one ever prosecuted a case more vigorously than did Schaub and his assistant, the feeling persisted that they had been trapped prematurely into a case neither wanted to try. The State Attorney's office was placed in the position of a girl who discovered that she was pregnant and quickly decided that she had better fall in love.

2. Arcadia

AN UNPUBLISHED HISTORICAL WORK ON FILE
in the local Chamber of Commerce office refers to the
Arcadia area as "a vast wilderness where panthers, bears,
wolves, and wildcats abound" and where the rivers contain "great numbers of alligators." The 1967 Progress Report
of the Chamber of Commerce refers to Arcadia as "South
Florida's most friendly community."

The truth lies somewhere between these two extremes,
unfortunately, perhaps a bit too close to the former.

The name conjures up pastoral innocence, a contented,
simple people. Unconflicted Arcadia, nestling along the
Peace River, will impress the casual observer as a beautiful
antebellum town. Huge live oaks reach from the fine homes
across the old streets to touch each other; the Spanish moss
sways gently in the southern breeze. Just plain folks, in-

14

formally dressed, greet each other with smiles and waves. One community leader commented, "Wear a coat and tie in this town and people ask if you're going to a funeral or something." A peaceful, tranquil, all-white town on the surface. Yet the statistic that insists that one of three is black alerts the visitor to the degradation that rests beneath the veneer of middle-class respectability. In Arcadia the blacks are truly not visible. Housed in the Quarters, they journey by day to the citrus fields to pick fruit or the plains to pull stumps. The fruits are processed and packed by Sorrell Brothers in Arcadia; the stumps are worked for pine oil, resin, turpentine, and dipentene by Gulf Naval Stores in nearby Nocatee.

Black poverty in Arcadia is like an iceberg. It is massive, awesome. Yet not until it is examined more closely can its depths be comprehended. The shacks that line the roads appear to rival those anywhere for degeneracy.

They crumble, they sag, light pours through them. All that seems remarkable about them is their evident denial of gravity. Yet they are sound and impervious structures when compared with those whose view they block from the roadway. For behind many of the rotting shacks are chicken-coop-like huts, each inhabited by one or more persons, although there is not enough room in them for both a pallet and space to turn around.

Kerosene lanterns light them and, in the winter, kerosene stoves heat them. There is no running water. But tourist stop at the gracious, white-pillared homes, watch the elderly folks play shuffleboard in the sun or the younger ones tennis at the clean, white, municipal courts, walk up on the green-carpeted entrance to the historic court building, and you will just know that you are in a friendly, happy, uncomplicated city. For Arcadia, in the great Peace River Valley, is the home of southern hospitality, southern cooking, and southern justice.

It was not always this way in Arcadia; one time it was almost worse.

The town's history reveals its name and the name of its river to be misnomers as well as accidents. Peace River was originally called Peas Creek, then Pease Creek. There remains some dispute regarding the origin of the name for the town previously called Tater Hill Bluff. Many agree, however, that one Tom Herndon, the town's first postmaster, was offended by the odd and longer name. One day, it is said, he received a letter from his brother who resided in Arcadia, Louisiana, and forthwith changed the name of his town to Arcadia, Florida. Life was plainly less complicated in those days of little government.

Yet the tranquillity promised by the new names was illusory. The area was nationally famous for strife. During the last quarter of the ninteenth century, the hostility between the homesteaders and the illegal activities of the politically well-connected land-grabbers erupted into war. Some twenty land-grabbers, known locally as the Sarosota Vigilantes, murdered two of the prominent settlers. The homesteaders rose up in anger and demanded justice and a trial. The existent power structure, although inclined to support the murderers, granted one of the demands, and a trial was had.

The setting was a small wooden courthouse, overwhelmed by reporters from places as distant as New York and Chicago. The reporters were more than a little surprised to discover that the last thirty miles to the courthouse had to be traversed on horseback.

Having made the ride into the town once, most of the city reporters were reluctant to make it again, except for leaving the town never to return. Yet there were no telegraph facilities available. Accordingly, expert horsemen were very much in demand, and they were hired by the newspapermen to carry dispatches to Tampa and file them by wire from there.

Justice had its limitations even in those days. Of the twenty men accused of the crime, only five were indicted. Two were sentenced to life imprisonment but they "escaped" from jail soon after the trial. They had been given official, albeit furtive, permission to leave, and they did. The two felons were never caught. Actually they were never really sought. One of the five had been sentenced to death by hanging, in response to the demands of the settlers, and in the somewhat imprecise application of the spirit of an eye for an eye. The local law enforcers arranged for him to flee as well, but he was adamant. He demanded a full pardon. A compromise was arranged; first the sentence was commuted, he left jail, and then a full pardon was granted. In the meantime, the other two who had also been convicted were quietly released from custody. Frontier justice had its therapeutic effect. Confrontation with a tense and highly volatile situation had been avoided and the close working relationship between the land-grabbers and the local political leaders managed to remain intact. Today no remnant of the courthouse remains, and grass grows and cows graze where it once stood.

The avoidance of confrontation is not the resolution of conflict. Before the turn of the century, cattle ranching began to play an important part in the economy of the area. In 1895 the infamous Cattle War began. Before it ended six years later, thousands of head of cattle had been stolen, gun fights had become daily events, and ranchers were shot from ambush. Professional gunmen were brought in by various cattlemen, and violence became part of community life—and death. A local publication complained, "No one is safe outside of his home after dark." Another added that, "Not even the Indian wars compared in violence" to what was then taking place. The reference reminds us that the settlers who resisted the unlawful encroachments of the land-grabbers had themselves wrested the land from the Indian tribes with

available for improvement. Arcadia spoke of its proximity to the Panama Canal, its enviable interior location, which provided protection from a naval assault, and of its prairie landing areas, thirty miles by sixty miles. Merchants spoke of a new Arcadia, of a boom that would not fade. The Air Force base was established near Tampa, however.

The two abandoned airfields were purchased by the State, and in 1949 a state mental hospital was established there. Today that institution, the G. Pierce Wood Memorial Hospital, is by far the largest employer in Arcadia, with a local payroll of 863.

The Chamber of Commerce boasts that "with the establishment of the Gulf Naval Stores Company and then the Central Transformer Corporation in De Soto County during the past ten or twelve years, De Soto County is becoming an industrial county as well as an agricultural one." Yet in its inventory of resources for industrial development, the Chamber of Commerce reveals that after more than a decade of operation, Gulf employs three hundred, and those not on a regular basis, and Central Transformer but seventy-five. The economy remains centered upon the black workers in the citrus groves and a large part of the white working force in the mental hospital.

It was a warm December day in south-central Florida as I drove to the Arcadia cemetery to visit the graves of the seven small children. The cemetery is an impressive part of town, more majestic and more lush than the Arcadia Country Club with its rolling green lawns and more tastefully landscaped than the grounds of the fine old homes in town. Cypress trees ladened with the ever-present Spanish moss abounded everywhere, as did graceful palm trees. Underground pipes with sprinklers kept the grass and bushes a moist and brilliant green. I asked a bystander if he might direct me to the graves of the seven children, and he answered with a laugh, "Well, you sure won't find them here." He pointed beyond the outer boundary of the cemetery and said, "They're over there in the nigger cemetery." The cemetery reserved for the remains of Negroes was a large, sandy field on which some grass had evidently previously grown but now was burned a light brown and bore close resemblance to the sand. There were no bushes and there were no trees, and many of the graves were just a pile of sand with little aluminum signs four by seven inches bearing the name, date of birth, and date of death. In the circumstances, the Richardsons' graves were relatively easy to locate, as all seven were distinguished by small granite markers.

As I stood at the graves, a truck with two men approached. A short, squat, black man in his early thirties said, shaking his head sadly, "Well, ain't that a shame. Seven little children killed like that." With him was a white man, probably in his twenties, who appeared to be his helper. The white man spoke, "Well, you know Richardson didn't do it. Everybody knows that." The Negro cautioned him, "Don't say today what you can't face up to tomorrow."

I asked them both if they felt that the Sheriff had presented the evidence fairly and had conducted a fair investigation. The white man answered, "Of course not. Cline is sneaky." The Negro quickly interjected, "Just remember, he said it, not me." And then added, "Mister, this is the South. You asked me about Cline. Them people can just kill you without giving it a thought. This is not just the South, this is the *Deep* South. I know James didn't do it, but I have to live here after you leave." We began talking about conditions in the town. The Negro worker told me that the movie theater had been torn down when it "had been ordered to integrate." After talking for a few minutes, we parted, and the Negro, after looking quickly around for a moment, said, "Ain't that a shame. You know, there is no way that man could have done it."

THE NAACP

From the cemetery I drove over to town to interview William Burton, president of the Arcadia branch of the National Association for the Advancement of Colored People. Burton is the barber for the black community in Arcadia. His barber shop is directly across from the Sorrell Brothers Packing Company, which provides many seasonal jobs for the community.

Burton's dark-brown face was framed with silver hair. He is sixty-eight years old. He smoked an ancient pipe, so worn that half of the bowl had been smoked away. He wore a frayed blue work shirt and an equally battered pair of slacks. His manner was cautious. The shack which held his single barber's chair was as old and as dark and as worn as everything inside of it. Burton lives in a small room behind the barber shop.

I spoke to him of my interest in the Richardson case and did not indicate to him my feelings about the jury's verdict. I asked him what his position was regarding Richardson's guilt. He replied, "Well, this branch of the NAACP did not take any position in this case. My branch did nothing. All that I know about the case, I read in the newspaper." I asked Burton if he thought that Richardson was guilty. He answered, "Well, I am neutral. I just can't get off the fence on this one." I told Burton that Sheriff Cline had informed me that he had offered to help in the Sheriff's prosecution of the case. I asked Burton if he had made such an offer to Cline. It was at once plain that while Burton had not told Cline that he would help prosecute Richardson, he was unwilling to indicate that Cline was either lying or mistaken when he had so characterized his meeting with Burton. "Well, in a sense I did offer to help after the babies were found dead,"

Burton said. He went on, "But there are hundreds of us here taking the same steps. We just didn't know who did it, and we all would have liked to know who did do it." Burton explained that before Richardson's arrest, he and others in the Negro community had indicated a willingness to make available whatever evidence they might uncover so that the guilty party might be apprehended and prosecuted. Burton said that he did not present any evidence to Cline indicating Richardson's guilt. This much was also clear—the local NAACP and its leadership, both mired in fear, had taken no action in defense of James Richardson.

The subject shifted to the rights of blacks living in Arcadia. I asked Burton if Arcadia was an integrated town. He replied, "I'll give it to you like this. I think that, noticing the actions going on, that the majority of us is mostly satisfied with how it's going. It's not fully integrated, but we are not putting forth no efforts to make it integrated, because most of us is satisfied with how it's going. You got to understand that as much as the law makes 'integrated,' it means that the colored must implement the move getting that to be done. I don't stick my neck out to say that I can't go into that place or any other place and that I want to. Arcadia is not so big a place. It could be integrated overnight. But we all seem to get along fine together as it is. I don't try to force my people to go no farther than they want to go. It's not fully integrated, but it's mostly integrated, and we are satisfied." I asked Burton to comment upon the allegations that none of the restaurants in Arcadia are integrated. He looked up at me in surprise. I felt that he was not surprised to hear that the restaurants were segregated but that I would raise the question so bluntly. He answered after a moment's pause, "I heard that one restaurant, the De Soto Restaurant, serves colored. Yes I heard that there's a white folk's restaurant on De Soto Street that serves colored." I asked him if he had ever eaten there, and again he paused, and slowly he shook his head and said, "No, I haven't tried to test it." I asked him if he could provide the name of a single Negro who had ever eaten at the De Soto Restaurant or any other "white" restaurant in town. He lit his pipe, looked up at the ceiling, and then looked directly at me and said, "No, I sure can't." I asked him if the movie house in town was integrated. He said, "Well, we don't have a movie house anymore. It got closed down. Now, there is a drive-in theater outside of town." When I asked if Negroes had been permitted to enter the movie theater when it operated in Arcadia, he said, "There was no rule against it, but not many wanted to go anyway." I informed Burton that I had been told by several persons that the theater was closed because Negroes demanded that they be allowed to purchase tickets. He responded quickly, "Did you get that from white or colored?" I said two people at the cemetery had just told me about it, and he answered, "Well, I have heard that statement, but I wonder, would a man tear up his own business for a thing like that? Remember, that theater was doing fine when they closed." When I asked him why the theater would close when it was doing so well, he said, "I just don't know." I asked him if he had visited the cemetery where the seven Richardson children are buried, and he said he had been out there. I asked him what he thought of the conditions at the cemetery. He replied, "Well, our folks are mostly poor."

We discussed the average income in the black community in Arcadia, and Burton said, "Well, this is seasonal work in the fruit belt. Some of the boys make pretty good money. Some of them do pretty good." When I asked him to place a figure upon that evaluation, he said, "Well, some of the boys make almost two thousand dollars a year." I asked Burton if any Negroes are employed in Arcadia in the De Soto National Bank or any of the major stores or restaurants in town. He said, "Well, not as cashiers or bookkeepers, if that's what you mean, but several places have them as janitors." I asked Burton if there had ever been protests or demonstrations in Arcadia sponsored by the NAACP. He said that there had not been any. I asked for the reason. He replied, "We are mostly satisfied. I don't believe in pressuring nobody in doing something when I am not willing to implement it. We don't see where it is going to be beneficial."

When I inquired if Burton thought there might be any danger in protesting against conditions in Arcadia, he said, "Well, first you have to find something to protest against." I told Burton that I had traveled around the country a bit but that I had never seen conditions more worthy of protest than those that existed in Arcadia. Certainly I had never seen housing conditions to compare with Arcadia's black slums. Burton said, "Yes, but those people seem to be satisfied. I am trying to get our folks to get in shape to implement these things. Well, I am putting myself on the spot now, but I will be willing to tell you that one of our jobs is to get our pastor to step forward in these things, and that's hard to do. Our people will listen to a preacher before anyone else. I suppose there is lots that could be done here if we tried."

We talked for a few minutes about Sheriff Cline, and Burton advised me that he felt that Cline "was a very fine sheriff." He added that Cline "got most of the colored votes when he ran." I inquired if Cline often visited the black community. "Yes, he comes in here at night. You might see him at any time during the nighttime." I asked Burton what Cline did in the black community at night, and he said, "I don't know," and said that Cline had "lots of friends in the colored community." I asked if he visited his friends at night, and Burton said, "Yes, he does." I asked if Cline's father had a good reputation in the black community, and Burton said, "I would rather not make a comparison between the two." I posed this problem for Burton. If the development of the facts regarding the Richardson case revealed that Richardson was innocent and that he was discriminated against because of his color, is it conceivable that the Arcadia branch of the NAACP might enter the case? Burton replied, "I don't see how there could be any discrimination in this case." I asked Burton if he knew Bessie Reese's daughters. He said that he did. I asked him if he knew if Frank Cline knew them. He answered, "He knows much more about them than I do." I asked Burton if the NAACP was concerned about the sign in the Trailways Bus Terminal Café which proclaimed the management's right to refuse to serve anyone and to prosecute anyone who might create a disturbance after being denied service. He looked quietly down at his feet for a few moments, then looked up at the door and said, "Well, that doesn't mean nothing."

I asked Burton if it was true that he was a "special deputy" for Sheriff Cline, and he said, "Yes, that's true all right." My last question required him to determine whether there was the possibility of a conflict in interest in serving the NAACP and the white sheriff in a bigoted and thoroughly segregated town. "I just don't see no problem there," he replied.

THE CHURCH

I interviewed the Reverend C. S. Elder at the Negro cemetery in Arcadia. "I deposited them there," he said, indicating the seven small graves. "I gave the eulogy at the funeral, even though I didn't know that man [James Richardson] from Adam's cat." He said, "I was the one, with a small committee, that went into the jail to ask Richardson if he wanted to have a lawyer. Mr. Atkins, the head of the Florida NAACP, asked me to see the man, so I did. That's when he picked Mr. Robinson to be the lawyer."

Elder said that he helped to get the NAACP charter re-established in Arcadia. "There are about sixty or seventy members now. But I will be frank, I've been here four years now and I haven't heard of a single thing that they have done in that time."

I asked about racial problems, and he replied, "We have no real problems here. Things are improving, perhaps a little slowly, too slowly for some, but there is improvement." I asked if the schools were integrated. "Oh, yes. They sure are." I said that I had heard that the high school was integrated but that there had been considerable hostility toward the Negro students on the part of some white students. I told Elder that I had heard that a number of young Negro boys and girls had been beaten. "Well, yes, there has been some trouble, but no more than you usually expect in this kind of thing. Boys and girls do fight." I asked if the elementary school had been integrated or if Arcadia really maintained separate black and white schools.

The reverend answered, "I don't know about the grade schools, but I can tell you that the high school is integrated." Why did he not know what kind of school his parishioners attended? "Well, I haven't had any complaints from them about the schools." Were there Negro teachers? "Yes. At the Negro school, all of the teachers are Negro."

Are the restaurants integrated? "There again, no one has complained to me about anyone being barred. None of my parishioners have complained." Had he ever seen a Negro eat at any restaurant in Arcadia? "No, I have not. But I have not heard that they are barred."

We spoke about justice for the Negro resident of Arcadia. I asked if Cline was a fair sheriff. "That is a very hard question to answer in a community like this one. Very hard indeed." I asked him to try. He contemplated for a moment, looked at me, at the small graves, back at me, sighed, and began. "There are two kinds of 'fair.' A man may be able to analyze evidence properly, but, on the other hand, when it comes to justice, the man may not be fair about that, under certain circumstances. Do you understand what I am getting at?" I said that I thought I knew what he meant but asked him if he could be more specific about the Sheriff. Does Cline care about justice for the black man? "I think that I have gone far enough. This is Arcadia, my friend. Any further would be pressing it."

We spoke of the man on death row. Do you think he is innocent? "Well, most people are talking about that now since that magazine article. Many people think that maybe they did get the wrong man. But you see, I am no lawyer, so I don't know."

I asked him to sum up the relationship between the white and black communities in Arcadia, and he said that he was unable to do so. I asked, "Is everything just fine in Arcadia?" He replied, "Just fine? That would be pressing it. But we are not disturbed about the situation. Let me put it that way." I told him of the housing conditions, of the take-home pay of the Negro workers, and asked why he was not disturbed. "Well, I understand that they are talking about a new housing project for Negroes, but I'm no housing expert, so I don't know."

The "magazine article" was a letter that was published in *Playboy* magazine in March, 1969. In the letter, I described in outline form the case against Richardson. The story was carried by the wire services and widely published in Florida. *The Arcadian* replied with a bitter editorial, and the subject was again on the agenda in that town.

THE PRESS

Arcadia is very sensitive to unkind remarks. The observer who probes may get the impression that just beneath the conscious level Arcadia is trying to suppress reality. That effort, not as pronounced as the citizen response in that excellent work of fiction *Bad Day at Black Rock*, *is*, for all its subtlety, nevertheless present. Richard Nellius was sent to Arcadia by the St. Petersburg *Times* to cover the Richardson case. He stayed to write a feature story about Arcadia, which was published in the Sunday supplement *The Floridian*.

In it Nellius noted, "Arcadians are suspicious of strangers and sensitive to outside criticism. They're still smarting over a story in a Miami paper that called Arcadia 'a dusty little town on the edge of the Everglades.' Actually, Miami is a lot closer to the Everglades than is Arcadia. But there is a world of difference between Miami and Arcadia. And the better part of a century."

If the Arcadian power structure was "smarting" from the reference to dust and the proximity to the Everglades, it was enraged by the Nellius piece. The natural vehicle for the response was *The Arcadian*. The weekly newspaper generally confines itself to local affairs. A feature story reported that the DAR chapter was served "delicious refreshments of 'Tassie Tarts,' coffee, and salted nuts." Another disclosed that "Kayo Keen celebrated his 12th birthday with a Sock Hop Saturday night" and that "games and dancing were enjoyed by all." The day after the children were poisoned, *The Arcadian* reported that two men "brought in a 12-pound snook last week and released several smaller ones. They went back out a few days later and returned with a couple of nice reds and a bass."

Near Christmas time, as is the case with many journals, a touch of sentimentality was observed creeping into the stories. "On December 25, many youngsters will experience the ultimate in Christmas joy when they find a long-awaited gun under the tree." The story suggested that the parents should be responsible in supervising the use of the present and also reminded the readers that, "Private ownership of guns is the historical birthright of all Americans and the first gun can represent a memorable occasion for a boy."

The Arcadian supplements its income by selling "No Trespassing" signs for fifteen cents each.

On occasion the newspaper took positions on larger questions also. It consistently supported the most conservative candidate in either party, viewed Robert Kennedy as half-devil, half-Karl Marx, and attacked persons it most despised as "like Robert Kennedy." It opposed "welfare" and gun-control legislation, favored the "unconditional-surrender" approach to the war in Vietnam, and called for the elimination of the "doves" in an editorial titled "War Without Doves."

The Floridian article was attacked in a column written by *The Arcadian*'s publisher, Bill Hackney. He denied that the Sheriff and the School Superintendent would have made the comments credited to them, since "Both face what could be tough reelection campaigns this year."

Hackney said that the "dead giveaway on Mr. Nellius is his comment that political philosophy here ranges from conservative to ultraconservative." This makes it appear, wrote the publisher, that "his political philosophy is closely allied with that of his boss, *Times* publisher Nelson Poynter, and Nelson is far enough left to make Robert Kennedy and Hubert Humphrey look like Barry Goldwater."

The First Federal Savings and Loan Association located in Arcadia placed an advertisement in *The Arcadian* to dispute the *Times* article. It featured the argument that Arcadian children are independent and responsible since they are "exposed to the outdoors, and come naturally to hunting, guns, animals, fishing and camping."

The Nellius article stated that violence prevailed in Arcadia, that justice was imperfect there, and that Negroes were frightened. The bank responded that "our community may not be perfect" but "why not take stock and be conscious of our blessings." The tendency of the advertisement may have been commercially sound, it may even have encouraged Arcadians to open accounts at the bank or to take stock there, but it did little to assist the residents to face the distressing facts of life in that small town in south-central Florida.

I have no doubt that the white middle-class Arcadian will not recognize his city from the description given in this chapter.

The Chamber of Commerce, speaking for the business and social leaders, proclaims Arcadia to be "a friendly, growing, and progressive community." The same report finds the Chamber failing even to list the NAACP as an organization that exists in Arcadia, while the De Soto Gun Club, the Sheriff's Possettes, the Saddle Club, and the Daughters of the American Revolution are prominently presented.

"Progressive" being a relative term, it might be best to examine the context of Arcadia's politics and the tendency of the voters on national questions. While most of Florida and the rest of the nation were participating in choosing between Richard Nixon and Hubert Humphrey in 1968, a sign outside of Arcadia stated with admirable candor, "This is Wallace Country." Another succinctly advised, "Put Your Heart in Dixie or Get Your Ass Out—Vote for Wallace."

The suggestion was largely heeded by the voters in Arcadia. They went strongly for Wallace. The only suspense that year revolved around the question of who would come in second.

Given the circumstances, the Arcadian response to an outside analysis does not tend to invalidate it. Rather it serves to reinforce the suspicion that there is a banality to evil. The degradation of the black residents of Arcadia is a continuing process, yet, it is not a daily event. Each day hundreds return from the groves to substandard housing, each day they are excluded from the life of the white city, from the restaurants, from the bars, from the social affairs. Their children are poorly educated each day. Many are ill-fed each day. Many are illiterate and remain flawed by the inability to read or write each day. Charles Dickens is not for them;

neither is the daily newspaper. It is the regularity with which the evil is practiced that makes it appear invisible to those who wish to avoid the fact and the consequent necessity of enlisting in the uncomfortable war against it. More odious crimes have been committed during our lifetime. They too were unnoticed. In beautiful, highly cultured Heidelberg the citizens never noticed that Jews were rounded up and sent to concentration camps. In the village near Dachau housewives flicked the ashes from the bright and newly laundered clothing hanging from the line. Lawyers, doctors, publishers, and judges all went about their business, and they, all of them, would have bridled at an uncomplimentary treatise about their home town. It is now too late for the burghers to act; the crime has been completed. There is yet time in Arcadia.

Quite literally the signs of discrimination are all too apparent to avoid. The facility with a restaurant that most closely approximates a public enterprise is the Trailways Bus Depot, with its café. Behind the lunchroom counter a framed, glass-enclosed sign reads, "This is a privately owned business. It is not based on municipal, county, state, or federal property. It is not a public utility, school, church, or polling place. We received no grants or subsidies from any city, county, state, or federal funds. We reserve the right to seat our patrons or deny service to anyone. Any person creating a disturbance on these premises after being denied service will be prosecuted. The Management."

The café in the bus depot serves passengers in interstate travel and cannot lawfully refuse to serve persons because of race. Yet, if the sign had read, "Niggers Stay Out," its meaning could have been no better appreciated by the residents of the Quarters, just a very short walk away.

Arcadia, surrounded by cattle, the headquarters of the Cattlemen's Association and the All-Florida Championship Rodeo, takes on the appearance of a western town, one hundred years ago, on Saturday nights and during the rodeo days. Cowboys in big hats and Levis ride into town carrying rifles. Pickup trucks have replaced the horse, and the rifle racks across the rear window of the cab are more the rule than the exception. Arcadia has managed to combine the hospitality of the Wild West with the sense of ready justice of the Deep South. It might be unfair to say of Arcadia that its major industry is mental illness, its history is marked with constant community rejection and violence, its cancer is almost total black degradation, and many of its white residents have guns. Unfortunately, it would not be that unfair.

3. The Defense

JOHN S. ROBINSON

The events in Arcadia were widely reported throughout the nation. In Florida the coverage was so intensive and voluminous that the press ranked the deaths and the subsequent charges as the number-three story in the State for the year, following the election of Governor Claude Kirk and his marriage. The divulgence of each new particle of evidence was cause for front-page headlines and another interview for the evening television news programs with the redoubtable Judge Hayes in his capacity as County Judge, on-the-spot investigator, presiding officer at the coroner's jury, County Coroner, or leading citizen of Arcadia.

One could hardly accuse the Sheriff of hoarding his evidence, either; he too granted interviews to the press and openly proclaimed his belief in Richardson's guilt. On one occasion Cline said that Richardson had "twenty or twenty-one children, and half of them are now dead." On one statewide television program the Sheriff said, "James Richardson is guilty of the crime." On another appearance Cline said that Richardson had "failed to pass the lie-detector test," thus appearing to corroborate a previous assertion made to the press by Hayes. Hayes showed that his personal involvement was so great that he had decided not to permit the law to interfere with his actions as County Judge. While the Richardsons were held on child-neglect charges with bail set at five hundred dollars each, Hayes said, "We're not going to let them go even if somebody posts the bond."

When Cline was asked why James Richardson would kill his own children, he replied to the reporters that the defendant "was a psychopathic miser." Cline then confided that Richardson had probably poisoned "three of his children" on a prior occasion. Later he said that five might be a more appropriate number, still later that three may have died of poisoning but perhaps three others survived, and still later that "two or three" had been poisoned. If the pretrial comments made by the responsible officials now seem ludicrous as well as repugnant, at the time they appeared to James Richardson to be more than just a little unfair. Alone, without a single influential friend and with no access to the media for reply, the almost entirely illiterate farm worker heard of the stories that were circulating about him, with increasing incredulity. He paced the ancient Arcadia jail cell, protesting his innocence. As panic rose up in him, he prayed, his deep belief in God being all that saved him from giving himself up to hysteria. A more astute assessment of the situation might have convinced him that he had been defeated already, that court-appointed counsel would reach him eventually but in all probability too late to undo the harm.

Perhaps even by then the trial had been transformed from a classical search for the truth into a ritual with a predetermined conclusion.

Across the State a white, thirty-year-old, successful lawyer, who specialized in domestic-relations cases, returned home for dinner. The television set was on and running when he arrived. With a dry gin martini in his hand he settled down to watch the evening news broadcast. Cline and Hayes were reporting on the latest developments that continued to convince them anew that James Richardson was a mass murderer. John Spencer Robinson put the glass down, paced his well-appointed living room, set in a fashionable section of Ormond Beach and quietly said, "Damn it." His wife called in from the kitchen, "Did you say something?" He almost shouted back, "Yes, I said, 'Damn it.' "

He walked toward the telephone, hesitated a moment, and then called Jack Young. Young was responsible for garbage collection for Daytona Beach. Robinson had negotiated various contracts for him, and he knew that James Richardson had worked for him at one time. Young was in, and the lawyer asked him what he knew about the defendant. Young answered, "Well, I know one thing—I can't believe he killed the kids. He loved those children. He was a good family man, a fine worker who never missed a day's work. I don't care what the papers say, I know I don't believe it."

Robinson made the next call without hesitating. It was to Joel Atkins, president of the NAACP in Florida. In 1964 and again in 1966 Robinson and Atkins had worked together for Robert King High, a Democratic candidate for governor. Robinson had served as a campaign manager. After exchanging greetings with Atkins, the young lawyer said, "I'm real concerned about what's being done to this man Richardson. Everyone is talking about how guilty he is; it's in the newspapers every day. I just saw those two clowns on television again tonight. The trial may just come too late for him." Robinson added that he had no idea if the defendant was innocent or guilty, "although it looks like they have a good deal of evidence against him." Robinson said, "Joel, in either event, he needs a lawyer, and he needs one now. I just called to find out if your organization is planning to do anything in this case."

Atkins responded that he too was deeply disturbed about the fashion in which the case was being presented. "I agree with you, of course, John. Guilty or not, it's a shame what they are doing to him. I plan to contact our NAACP man in Arcadia and get a small committee in to see him. That way we can ask him if he wants counsel, and if he says he does, we'll submit a few names to him. I don't suppose he'll have any real basis for making a selection, but nevertheless, the choice will be his."

Atkins then asked Robinson if he would be willing to have his name added to the list. He said that even if he were chosen, he would be obligated to serve only temporarily as counsel, "until the court appoints someone for the trial or the plea. So is it all right if I submit your name?" Robinson answered, "It certainly is. If he wants me, I'll do what I can for him."

Not many hours later a committee met with Richardson in his jail cell. He listened intently as names were read off and then said that he wanted John Robinson.

Robinson had been born in Kingsport, Tennessee. His father, Amos, was the sheriff of Sullivan County there. His ambition was for his son to be a lawyer. The older son had become an accountant, his daughter was born deaf, and John wasn't quite sure what he wanted to do with his life. At sixteen he began driving trucks. He hauled chemicals in tankers from Tennessee to the West Coast during the summers and went to high school the rest of the year. Later he attended Florida Southern College in the mornings, securing the requisite funds for an education by working as a disc jockey for radio station WYSE in Lakeland for four hours each afternoon. He majored in speech and English, and, determined to earn his B.S. as soon as possible, carried a full load of courses through the summer months. One summer, being too low on funds to be certain that he could register for the fall semester, he returned to hauling acid across the country. He graduated in three years, and quickly was appointed the program director of a radio station in Ocala.

When he met Clark Davis, a brilliant comedy writer, he decided to try a new career. They formed the team of "Davis and Spencer" and worked the major nightclubs of the South. Robinson was the straight man, who also sang and played the baritone ukulele, as the team moved from Shreveport, Louisiana, to Baton Rouge, to Miami and Atlanta. The duo appeared on local television and radio shows, and their closest call to fame came when they auditioned for the Jack Parr program. They were not accepted, however, and finally the team broke up. Davis went on to become a prominent television executive.

Robinson enrolled at Cumberland University Law School. He graduated first in his class. The graduating class of seven probably made Cumberland the smallest law school in existence. Robinson moved to Daytona Beach and began a teaching career, instructing in law for the layman and a course in citizenship at the Daytona Beach Junior College.

The citizenship course was particularly popular with those born abroad who wished to apply for United States citizenship. Robinson also formed an association with W. W. Judge, who was one of the foremost defense lawyers in the State. Judge had been the state's attorney for the Seventh Judicial Circuit, which included the Daytona Beach area. Two years later Robinson opened his own office and began a general practice of the law. He specialized in all aspects of domestic-relations law, including divorce, separation, custody, annulment, and adoption actions. "I suppose my practice developed along those lines quite naturally," he said, "since many people do move to Florida in order to secure divorces." In a very few years he became one of the busiest and most respected attorneys in the field. Before long lawyers from other states began referring matrimonial cases to him, and his practice began to swell. At about the same time a graduate of a licensed embalming school became a client. Robinson, who had recently read *The American Way of Death*, a humorous and scathing analysis of gouging in the funeral business, wondered if some local attempt at reform might be successful. He formed a partnership with his client and opened the Hannah Funeral Home with an investment of one thousand dollars. To the astonishment of the established parlors, he began advertising inexpensive funerals, and to their decided discomfort, the response was unprecedented.

Within four years the Hannah establishment was valued at $175,000.

Once he was financially secure, he turned to politics and community work in earnest. In 1964 he had been High's campaign manager for the county that included Daytona Beach. That year High was defeated in the Democratic primary. Two years later, he tried again, and with success. High won the Democratic nomination and announced that Robinson would be given a cabinet appointment if he was elected governor. High was one of the most liberal candidates for statewide office in the South, which made him particularly vulnerable in those areas that other southerners refer to as "redneck." In southern political parlance a "Nigger Sheet" is disparaging campaign literature designed to be circulated in those areas inundated with white fear or hatred of Negroes. Such literature was published and distributed, charging High with being endorsed by Dr. Martin Luther King, Jr., and sundry other and similar acts of misconduct. High was defeated.

Robinson's political and community activity continued. He was elected president of the Young Democrats of Volusia County and vice-president of the Congressional Young Democrats. He served on the board of directors of the Guidance Center, a federally supported program to assist those who were mentally ill. He helped to organize the campaign for funds to eliminate tuberculosis. He served on the board of Open Forum, the Daytona Beach platform for distinguished guest speakers, as well as on the board of the Big Brothers Association and the Children's Aid Society. He became a member of the first Interracial Board established in his city.

Its purpose was to ferret out discrimination in public accommodations or restaurants in Daytona Beach. The board solicited complaints, and Robinson and others personally investigated them.

Robinson was arriving on the legal and community scene. In 1966 he was selected as "one of the outstanding personalities in the South" by a newspaper poll and that year was also listed in *Who's Who in the South*. He became a member of the proper social and country clubs.

That year he also negotiated a contract for the former Yankee baseball pitcher Don Larsen to take a team of American baseball players to Brazil. After most of the arrangements were made, including contracts for a touring team from Japan as well as one from Panama, Larsen demurred. The Brazilian officials were understandably upset until Robinson agreed to lead the team himself. The team consisted of a number of famous professional ball players, but on occasion not quite enough of them. Once Robinson played right field, as his colleagues did everything in their power to discourage any balls from being hit anywhere in his vicinity. The tour was a triumph, with a trophy being presented to Robinson, on behalf of the Brazilian government, for having been the first American to bring a professional baseball team to that country.

He lectured at the Bethune-Cookman College in Daytona Beach and was later presented with the President's Award by the college for chairing the United Negro College Fund for the area. He then convinced his mother, a native of Tennessee, to enroll at the almost all-Negro school. She did, and graduated from there in 1968. She now teaches fourth-grade classes in an elementary school in nearby Port Orange.

I asked Robinson what accounted for his approach to the racial question, which would have constituted scandalous behavior in the Old South a very short time ago. He said, "When I was working for the radio station in Ocala, I delivered newsgrams to various places where people congregate, at restaurants and clubs, for example. At the golf club, I met a young man who worked in the pro shop. He was a music major with a degree from Florida A. & M. He was the first Negro I ever really knew, and in a short time we became friends. We were both bachelors, and I invited him to have dinner with me in my apartment.

"It was clear we were committing the crime of talking to each other as equals as we entered my apartment building. If he had been carrying my luggage, I guess everything would have been all right. A neighborhood character saw us go in, and about six men and a girl were at the apartment door a little while afterward. One of them wanted to know, 'What's he doing here?' and I answered, 'He's having dinner with me.' That hardly ended it. The next question was 'Why?' And my answer, 'It's none of your damn business!' didn't end it either. I was warned that I'd better get him out of there right away. It was an ugly scene, worse than it seems on retelling. We went to his place for dinner. I knew then that I would never really know what Negroes have to go through, probably every day, in this, their own country. It was embarrassing and then some. This, probably more than anything that had happened before or has happened since, made me realize that to some people just being black or brown is being inferior and that other, and valid, distinctions are meaningless to them. I decided then that I would never be influenced by anything that anyone ever said about another man due to his color. It was sort of a personal and private declaration of independence from bigotry."

In 1966 Robinson entered into a law firm with Richard H. Whitson. Whitson was born in Birmingham, Alabama, and practiced law there. In 1958 he moved to Daytona Beach. For seventeen years he had handled every job in the insurance-claims business, from street investigator to head of the home office. He later formed his own adjusting firm and met Robinson on a case which he was investigating. Robinson had never been too fond of handling the rather lucrative personal-injury aspect of his practice, and Whitson was an expert in the field. Within a short time they became partners. The breakdown of work assignments was almost preordained. Whitson spends eighty percent of his time processing and trying the personal-injury cases, while Robinson concentrates on matrimonial and defense work.

I asked Robinson why he had called Young and Atkins. "I was incensed by the denial of Richardson's rights. It represented the most extreme annihilation of a man's right to a fair trial that I had ever seen in this state. The Sheriff and the Judge were condemning the defendant every day, it seemed. A headline a day, a news break in the evening for the television audience. Where could he get impartial jurors? Frankly, I thought that they had a pretty good case against him, but that was not the issue. But when I talked to Young, who presented the very first indication that the man might be innocent, I knew that I had to call Atkins at once. I had just talked to my father about the case the day before. Everyone in the State was discussing it. My dad said that if one of his deputies said half the things about the guilt of a man in his custody that Cline had already said, that he would fire him on the spot. He said that custody is a responsibility, not a license."

Robinson never knew why Richardson had chosen him as counsel. They had other matters to discuss first. "I saw him in that broken-down jail just after the coroner's jury had met under the leadership of its impartial Coroner. I told him that I had just come to try to protect his rights at the early, pretrial stages, and that the court would appoint another lawyer to represent him later. I just wanted to try to preserve his rights so that the trial could have some meaning, although I suspected that maybe I was too late for that even then.

"He was so grateful to me for just being there to talk to him. James made some very religious and mystic comments about the Lord sending me to him. He tended to interpret events in that fashion all the time that I knew him. I asked him what had happened, and he said, 'You won't believe what's happened. They are trying to say that I killed my own children. I loved them children.' He said that they kept telling him that if he admitted that he did it, they would go very easy on him. He told me that Cline was pushing him around and calling him a nigger, and questioning him 'in a very mean way' every day. James told me that Cline kept on telling him that he had killed five other children in Jacksonville. He denied that he had ever harmed any child."

Later one of the other prisoners, Ernell Washington, told Robinson that Cline placed an eavesdropping device in the cell each time that the lawyer was about to talk to his client. Robinson told me that Washington had told him that the bug was behind the radiator. The third time that Robinson interviewed his client in the cell, he looked behind the radiator and found a very small microphone there. He picked it up and spoke into it very clearly. "Hello, Sheriff Cline. This is John Robinson. I am taking your bug with me." He then disconnected the microphone and placed it in his pocket. Robinson said, "Until then my relations with Cline, whom I had reason to believe was terrorizing my client, had never been overly cordial. After that episode, however, he just refused to talk to me."

I asked Robinson what impression his client had made upon him at the first interview. "I believed James. There was no doubt in my mind after talking to him, nor is there now. He is incapable of killing anyone, let alone his own children. I never have believed that there is such a thing as a 'born murderer' or even a 'murder type.' I have tried too many cases and represented too many different kinds of people to accept that easy explanation of nonconforming human behavior. But each of us knows one or more persons who is so gentle, so kind, and so committed to life that we can feel certain that they do not possess the capability to commit murder. James is one. I would have no fear if he and his wife were to baby-sit for my daughter or cook for my family.

"In the course of my practice I have talked with a number of people charged with various crimes. A lawyer develops the ability, almost an extra sense, to make a soundly based judgment as to his client's guilt or innocence. All defense lawyers have been lied to by their own clients on occasion about essential elements of the case. If the lawyer is unable to distinguish between a truthful client and one who is less than frank, he is going to be a sorry defense lawyer during the trial, and the client is going to be badly hurt.

"Sure, I've had the experience that every lawyer who represents people accused of committing crimes has had. I believed a client or two who did not tell me the truth when I began to practice law. But even then, if you are a thorough lawyer, you check out the facts soon enough, and soon enough you get the bad news. Of all the clients I've ever represented, James remains the only one about whom I can say I was certain of his innocence after my first interview with him. And I have checked out every allegation that he has made. I've never found that he even exaggerated or strained the truth an iota."

In a short period of time the defendant asked his lawyer to represent him at the trial. "Mr. Robinson, I trust you, and I need you. Will you stay with me?"

As the first interview was concluded, Robinson walked out of the Arcadia jail wondering what answer he would make when he saw his client next. "I knew it would wreck my practice and get me just the kind of notoriety in the South, as distinguished from fame, that I was not looking for. I had been teaching a course on constitutional law most recently. I believe in the adversary system, in cross-examination and due process. There was a man in that jail I had just left who was facing the electric chair for a crime I was convinced he knew nothing about. The cost of protecting my practice and my social standing would have been too high. I would have had to turn my back on all that I had taught my students. I called my partner from Arcadia and told him that I was going to represent Richardson."

"When Johnny called," Whitson told me, "I took a deep breath and said, 'Those rednecks have tried him already. They have taken full advantage of him.' Anyway, I told him that I would cover in the office for him and that I would give him all the help that I could. I never thought that he would have a chance, no matter what the evidence showed. I said, 'Johnny, you got a real tough one. You try if you want, and I'll help, but don't break your heart if you can't help the guy.'"

A WRIT OF HABEAS CORPUS

Immediately after entering the case, Robinson examined all of the available evidence against his client. "It didn't take very long" he said. "There was none.

"The case consisted of statements by Cline and Hayes. A flow of distorted, prejudiced, biased, and unwarranted statements based upon the assumption of guilt. The closest thing to evidence was the release of confidential and privileged information given to the news media regarding polygraph tests administered to Richardson. That wasn't too close, either. We weren't observing a judicial proceeding, but preelection maneuvering. I decided to bring the matter back into a courtroom where it belonged." Robinson then filed a petition for a writ of habeas corpus, returnable on November 16. Even as he did, the press reported a new development: "In the meantime, Sheriff Cline continued his inquiry into the case, seeking additional evidence. He flew to Tallahassee with State Representative James Tillman to seek fingerprint identification on several items in the case. He said he expected to continue questioning witnesses, including a former wife of the suspect, who now lives in Jacksonville and bore some of his children."

In the application for the writ, Robinson demanded that his client be released from the De Soto County jail. The petition charged that the county officials had evidence, "which, if presented to this court, would wholly exonerate" the defendant. The writ required that the State present sufficient evidence against Richardson to justify his continued imprisonment. If the State was unable to do so, the court would be obligated to release the defendant. Thus the stage was set for the first adversary aspect of the case since the arrest.

The parties assembled at one o'clock in the afternoon in the courthouse in Arcadia. Schaub and Treadwell were present for the State, Robinson and Whitson for the defense. An examination of the record reveals only that it was agreed that the parties would adjourn to the judge's chambers for a discussion and that they thereafter emerged with a stipulation, the nature of which was not at that time disclosed. The record does not divulge that November 16 was perhaps the most decisive day for Richardson, including those that preceded and those that would follow.

The prosecution was required to present its evidence, and it had none that could stand the test of cross-examination. Treadwell approached Robinson, "Look, why don't you just plead him guilty to something? Let's get rid of this case. Can't this be worked out?" Robinson replied that there was no basis for compromise, since he was convinced of his client's innocence. "What can we plead him to? Bigamy?"

Schaub asked Robinson if he would abandon the demand for a hearing on the writ if the State agreed to recommend that the court set bail for the defendant. Robinson was perplexed. Bail in a mass murder case was almost unheard of. Reasonable bail in such a case was without precedent. All of the participants were cognizant of the facts. Richardson was penniless; even bail set at a modest figure would be without meaning to him. Perhaps if the court set bond under ten thousand dollars, sufficient funds could be raised to effect the defendant's release pending the trial. Yet how could the court establish bail at the rate of little more than one thousand dollars per crime, when the crime charged was deliberate and premeditated murder?

Robinson and Whitson pondered the offer. The State, through its offer, had conceded that it was desperate to avoid the hearing and the consequent exposure of its case to public scrutiny and to that most effective engine for arriving at the truth, cross-examination. It seemed to the defense lawyers that the prosecution was indicating its willingness to abandon the charge against Richardson, albeit in slow and underpublicized steps. Today Robinson remembers the scene quite vividly. "If they wanted to ease out of the case, and it certainly appeared that way then, we weren't going to make it hard for them or even embarrassing. The man was innocent. The hearing would have proved it, in my opinion, but perhaps the judge, in light of the local hysteria, would have bound him over for trial anyway. Here they were talking about bail in a case which involved seven murders. I reasoned then that if they were going to set low bail, they had just given up on the case, and if that's the way they wanted to withdraw, I was not going to impede them. Not with my client in jail and facing, theoretically, the electric chair. I decided to see how low a bond they would set."

Schaub announced to the Court, at the bench and out of the hearing of the public and the press, that he had no objection to bail for Richardson and that it was his thought that "a discussion as to what constituted reasonable bail in the case should take place in the judge's chambers."

Whitson later remarked, "They sure didn't want any publicity when they backed down. This was quite a contrast with the State's approach when the wild charges had been circulating just a few days before. We couldn't have cared less about the publicity. We came there to get an innocent man out of jail, and if the State was too far out on the limb to cut it off, if they would rather have climbed back, that was fine with us. We went into chambers with the judge and the two prosecutors."

In chambers, Treadwell again asked Robinson if Richardson could not be persuaded to plead guilty to some lesser crime. Robinson was adamant. "The man says he didn't do it, and I believe him. How can I try to persuade him of something else, something that is false? Why don't you just drop the whole thing? You know he didn't do it. You've got no case at all. Nothing."

Schaub addressed himself to the question at hand. "Judge, we do not object to your setting bail in this case."

Judge Justice, however, was reluctant to take the responsibility for Richardson's release. He asked the prosecutors what bail they would stipulate to with defense counsel. Very neatly he passed the ball back into the State's Attorney's court. No doubt he reasoned that if the prosecutor's office was not prepared for a hearing and could not show good and legal cause to justify the continued detention of the defendant, he was unwilling to bear the sole public responsibility for releasing him. Treadwell, a resident of Arcadia, responded quickly and with some passion, "How am I going to face these people around here if we let the nigger out?" Whitson sought to reassure the prosecutor. "You won't be letting him out. The bail is set, and if he can make it he gets out." Treadwell responded that legal niceties were not reality on the streets of Arcadia. Schaub spoke. "We are talking about a bond. Now, we have no objection to bond. It is just a question of the amount. I do not oppose bond being set in the amount of one hundred thousand dollars." Robinson looked up and said, "Gentlemen, let's just go ahead with the hearing." Schaub asked what was wrong with his suggestion, and Robinson said that substantial bond, not to say high bond, was the same as no bond in the given circumstances. Schaub asked, "What do you want?" Robinson answered, "Five thousand dollars. He may not be able to make that. It's almost certain that he can't make much more." Schaub rubbed his chin and said, "Well, we'll come down to seventy-five thousand." Robinson again suggested that the hearing should proceed. Schaub asked, "What's the highest you can go?" Robinson repeated his original estimate, and Schaub reduced his demand to fifty thousand dollars.

In stages the State's figure withered away until it reached twenty thousand dollars. The judge remarked that Robinson was not really bargaining in good faith, since he had not moved from his original request. When Schaub finally agreed to stipulate to bond in the amount of ten thousand dollars, Robinson was persuaded to state that he would accept seventy-five hundred. Schaub replied that such bond would constitute probably the lowest bond ever set in the State of Florida in a murder case and very likely the lowest bail in the entire country for a man charged with multiple murder.

Robinson was of two minds. If the State did consent to such low bail and if Richardson did walk out of jail, the case would probably never be tried. In time, perhaps the prosecutor would agree to a motion to dismiss the charge, but if not, the defendant would very likely never be jeopardized by a trial. A hearing that afternoon could settle the matter more cleanly, but not without some risk. Robinson, not even certain as to which option he hoped the State would select, said, "Gentlemen, it's either seventy-five hundred dollars' bail, set right now, or we will insist upon the hearing now."

Schaub stuck his jaw out; Treadwell started to speak, but Schaub silenced him with a wave of the hand that was more an admonition. Schaub was the next person to speak. "It's seventy-five hundred."

The matter having been settled by the parties, it remained the responsibility of the court to perfect the record. The group returned to the crowded courtroom. Judge Justice spoke but a few words. "The hearing has been resolved by stipulation between counsel." Whitson and Robinson were amazed that the public and the press were not informed that bail had been set in the case.

In the back of the courtroom an old and wizened farmer sat, dressed in a wrinkled sweatshirt worn under spotted coveralls. His hair was long, and he appeared to have a six- or seven-day growth of whiskers. He spit tobacco onto the courtroom floor, there being no cuspidor in the spectator section. As Whitson and Robinson left the courtroom, the farmer announced, "Look at them two Daytona Beach hippies." Both of the lawyers wore dark suits, black shoes, white shirts, and conservatively hued ties. Later the elderly gentleman inquired of Whitson's son, who had traveled with his father to observe the processes of justice and who sat next to Annie Mae Richardson during the discussions, "Is that nigger lady your wife?"

Still later, one irate observer called "Nigger lover" at Robinson as he walked out of the courthouse. When he merely looked away, the observer spit at him.

Treadwell had accurately assessed the depth of the passion that had been aroused in Arcadia. Yet if those who run with the hounds were angered while the defendant was imprisoned, they surrendered themselves to white-hot fury when the hare was to be released. News of the bail agreement struck Arcadia deep in its pride. On the streets, and under the "tree of knowledge," the large elm where the old-timers gather to talk about the old days, one heard pre-lynch-mob mutterings. "That nigger ain't out yet. Frank will never let him walk out of the jail." After all, had not the County Judge previously said that Richardson would not be released even if he was able to make bail?

BAIL

Back in Daytona Beach, Robinson tried to make arrangements to secure his client's release. "Having bail set was the first step. The second was to find someone to put up the required sum." Seven hundred and fifty dollars in cash was the sum required to purchase the bail bond. Benjamin Brown, a Negro bondsman, agreed to waive his fee, thereby reducing the amount considerably. Robinson would have gladly paid the bonding company the amount that was needed but for the State law which prohibited such conduct by attorneys. Days passed, and the most diligent efforts among Richardson's poverty-stricken friends failed to raise the several hundred dollars. Robinson observed, "We thought it was all over then. We didn't know that the feelings in Arcadia were really boiling over. I just had to get that man out, especially if the State was never going to try the case."

Suddenly Robinson announced that the requisite money had been secured. Where it came from remains a rather closely guarded secret which this account will not betray. Immediately Robinson and Brown started out for Arcadia to post the bond. It was almost midnight when they arrived. One radio station reported that, "The night is dark, and perhaps Richardson will never make it to freedom." Hundreds of citizens were assembled on the courthouse steps waiting for Robinson and Brown to arrive. It was the South, at the turn of the century. Robinson was frightened, although not visibly so. Later, when one observer remarked that it had required some courage for him to have mounted those steps walking with a black man at his side, he responded, "Hell, I was sure glad he was there. Ben was a professional football player for the Pittsburgh Steelers. Needless to say, he can take care of himself, and then some."

Even *The Arcadian* reported the story under the headline, "Richardson's Release on Bond Last Week Had Aspects of a Perry Mason Thriller."

Cline refused to accept the bond offered by Brown on the grounds that he had not been certified as a bail bondsman in De Soto County. According to Duncan Groner of the St. Petersburg *Times*, "Robinson observed that short of being a native, it might take some doing to be certified as anything short of a criminal in the little county-seat town."

After midnight the clerk of the court completed various papers and Brown was duly certified. A reporter for *The Arcadian* asked Brown if some organization was behind him. When he responded in the negative, he was asked why he would take such a big risk. Brown said, "I think he's a good risk. I know personally something about him, and I know and respect his lawyer." The reporter then turned to Robinson. "You say you are taking this case without fee. Do you take many of these type cases, without fee, because you think an injustice may have been done?" Robinson said that he had taken a few cases without fee in the past five or six years. Then the reporter, who is also the publisher of *The Arcadian*, sprang his trap. "Would they be the cases of predominantly Negroes?" Robinson replied, "Yes, for the simple reason that Negroes often find themselves in this kind of position with no way to help themselves."

Television crews from outside the area began to arrive. Reporters from throughout the State were there. Finally James and Annie Mae Richardson came to the main door of the jail, almost blinded by the klieg lights and strobes, the nighttime tools of the television cameramen and news photographers. They carried brown paper bags into which their possessions, taken from them upon their arrest, had been placed. They were required to certify that all of their property had been returned and then to sign a release. James Richardson was solemnly asked if, "You got what you came in with? Let's see. You got a ten-dollar bill? You got a wallet with some papers? You got a crucifix?" They were free, and they embraced for the first time in four weeks. Richardson was asked for a comment by the reporters. "I thank God that I'm out and that I'm with my wife again and that we can start life together again." Robinson said to his client, "Well, you're out for good, James. You're not ever going to have to go back. We're going to see to that."

Groner, standing just a few feet away, summed it all up.

"In Arcadia, the Richardsons' chief claim to fame until a month before was as a couple so devoted to each other they went together to pay their weekly $7.50 rent. As the two emerged peering incredulously at each other and torn between tears and laughter, they clung to one another, kissing and muttering for several moments. But Cline could only glare."

4. The Trial

PRETRIAL

GRONER WAS NOT ENTIRELY CORRECT. While there was little that Cline could do at that moment, it soon became apparent that he, and the others who had been publicly associated with him in charging Richardson with the crime, had been badly hurt by the compromise which freed the defendant. Treadwell again asked Robinson to consider pleading Richardson to "some crime." Again Robinson declined.

"The reaction to the bonding of the defendant was sharp in Arcadia," Robinson said. "I was afraid that the grand jury there might indict him at once, so I moved for a change of venue." That action, almost unprecedented, gave Judge Justice the opportunity to send the case out of his jurisdiction. He acted quickly, and the matter was shifted to Hillsborough County. The prosecution announced that it would call thirty witnesses. However, Schaub issued subpoenas for eighteen, and some of the witnesses who had been subpoenaed were not called. The hearing was secret. Neither Robinson nor his client was present, and none of the witnesses was subjected to cross-examination. While the testimony is not available for inspection, Schaub told the press that his "principal witness before the grand jury was Sheriff Cline, who spent nearly three hours there." The grand jury listened to testimony for less than five more hours and then returned an indictment against Richardson for murder in the first degree in the death of his eight-year-old daughter, Betty Jean Bryant. In all jurisdictions the indictment is of no probative value; it is merely a charge.

A short time later Cline and Schaub informed the press that they had traveled to Daytona Beach and Jacksonville in pursuit of evidence against Richardson. Cline said that the trip had "proved profitable."

Once issue had been joined by the indictment, the defense lawyers moved into action on several fronts. They were concerned that a law-enforcement officer might testify that Richardson had made admissions while he was being questioned. Robinson said, "I do not believe that he said anything that might be inconsistent with innocence, but some officer might decide to innovate a little. This bothers me, because without the development of some kind of admission, there just is no sense in them trying this case. They will have to come up with something or just consent to a motion to dismiss."

To guard against the awful potential of such newly acquired evidence, the lawyers filed a motion to suppress defendant's statements. The defense lawyers then addressed themselves to the atmosphere that surrounded the case. They filed a petition for citation for contempt against Sheriff Cline, charging that he had denied the defendant the right to a fair trial by making repeated claims to the news media.

Robinson and Whitson authorized an investigation into the Arcadia climate. More than one hundred citizens were questioned. Relying primarily upon the survey, the attorneys charged that although "there was an oral expression that the defendant could not get a fair trial in De Soto County because of detrimental publicity and hostility toward the defendant," not one of the interviewees "would sign such an affidavit." In the motion for a change of venue, or in the alternative, to dismiss the charges, the defense stated that, "Persons contacted for this purpose stated that they would not sign such affidavits because they were afraid to do so because of the pressure and fear of reprisal from law-enforcement officials of De Soto County, Florida."

Next the attorneys filed a motion to dismiss the indictment. The basis for the motion was the alleged violation of various technical requirements, as well as the charge that "the defendant could not obtain a fair and impartial trial anywhere in the State of Florida because of wide, prejudicial publicity and pronounced hostility toward the defendant." In addition, the motion stated that Schaub and the De Soto officials had placed restrictions upon various investigators which prevented them from discussing the subject matter of the investigation with counsel for the defense.

In an additional motion to suppress, the lawyers asked that the evidence taken from Richardson's home be proscribed, since it was "seized without a search warrant having been issued, nor was the property seized incident to a lawful arrest of the defendant." In another motion, Robinson pointed out that the law had been flouted, since Richardson had never been arraigned as required by statute. The lawyers also filed for a list of prosecution witnesses and for the production of the physical evidence so that they might inspect it.

The last pretrial motion filed on that occasion was for a bill of particulars, calling upon the prosecution to provide some of the facts upon which the charge was based. Specifically the motion demanded that the State set forth the exact time and place of the murder alleged in the indictment, the method used to perpetrate the alleged murder, and the exact manner and means engaged and employed by the defendant in the perpetration of the alleged murder. Whitson explained, "We were entitled to that information under the law. It is very hard to try any lawsuit, to defend any man against a charge, without being in possession of the full particulars. We certainly expected answers to the relatively simple questions that we posed." Yet Whitson was being optimistic. Those simple questions were never answered by the prosecution through motions before the trial, or even through witnesses at the trial.

The State filed a series of replies to the applications that had been filed on behalf of the defendant. The replies, however, were often less than responsive. In certain cases the State filed, rather than mere replies, motions to strike the original application. This tended to emphasize the prosecutors' ire. Treadwell prepared and signed the answer to the motion that reflected upon the fairness of the area that he resided in. The motion for a change of venue was, he wrote, "biased, opinionated, and highly prejudicial." In addition, he demanded that the defense provide the names of those persons who claimed that they were afraid to give their names. Treadwell also signed the motion to strike the defendant's application calling for a citation of contempt against Cline. In essence the motion said that the petition was "improper." The State agreed to make the names of its witnesses known "upon receipt of defendant's witness list."

The reply to the motion to suppress alleged that all statements that were made by Richardson followed advice to him that he could remain silent. As to the physical evidence, primarily the pots and pans, "all physical evidence including the defendant's personal property were voluntarily surrendered unto Frank Cline, Sheriff of De Soto County, or his designated deputy and/or were obtained through a valid and legal search warrant properly obtained prior to the taking into custody of such items."

The demurrer to the motion to dismiss was quite technical and apparently sound until it made reference to the paragraph that held that a fair trial for the defendant was not possible due to community hostility. That paragraph, Treadwell wrote, contained "improper allegations."

On February 21 Treadwell filed a notice of hearing, by which he informed Robinson that all pending motions were to be heard before Judge Justice on Thursday, March 7, in the courthouse in Arcadia.

The Court listened to argument from both sides and some testimony from the prosecuting authorities. He denied the motions from the bench. He did grant a motion made that day by counsel for the defendant. Robinson demanded a preliminary hearing as provided by the statute. The judge set March 25 for the hearing and then addressed Schaub, "If you don't have enough evidence to show probable cause by that time, I am going to have to dismiss this case." That same afternoon Ernell Washington was released from jail as the result of the testimony of Frank Cline.

On March 25 the defense lawyers and their client arrived in Arcadia confident that the case would be dismissed. The prosecuting authorities, however, had evidently taken the judge's warning seriously. They were prepared with new and startling testimony. Prior to the hearing date, Robinson had written a letter to the court demanding that a court reporter or stenographer be present to record the testimony. Richardson had previously been declared an indigent person and was therefore entitled to a transcript of the proceeding without the payment that is usually required. The stenographer was present in the courtroom. Schaub, however, said that the State would not pay for the transcript. He said that it was "up to the State's Attorney, and I don't think that it's necessary" for the defendant to have a record of the testimony. At that point Judge Justice told the stenographer that she was dismissed, and she left the courtroom, over the strenuous objections of the defense lawyers.

Ernell Washington took the stand to state that Richardson had admitted to him that he had killed the children. The admissions took place while both men were incarcerated in the Arcadia jail, Washington said. James Weaver, another cellmate, testified that Richardson had made important admissions to him also.

Judge Justice revoked the bail, ordered Richardson jailed once again, and suddenly granted the motion for a change of venue. Robinson had asked that the case be tried in some sophisticated (read nonbigoted) city in Florida. He suggested Miami. The court ordered that the trial be held on May 27 in Fort Myers, just one county removed from Arcadia. It was still to be south-central Florida, in a city which had more than adequately publicized the case, and in an area where Klan activity is still recorded. In Arcadia many of the whites who had become incensed over the release of the defendant were somewhat mollified by his rearrest. Some were a little troubled also, for before October 25, Richardson was known, to those in the white community who had known of him at all, as a "good nigger." He supported his family, stayed out of trouble, was God-fearing, stepped aside for the white folks, averted his eyes when they passed, and was a hard-working citrus-fruit picker. A trial in Miami might well have been a relatively fair search for the truth. Although the defendant was not known there, an impartial examination of the facts seemed a likely result. A trial in Arcadia could hardly be considered adequate, even though the defendant's reputation there might have been of some assistance.

But a trial in Fort Myers promised no redeeming qualities. The relentless effort to convict James Richardson moved forward another step or two on March 25. Two new witnesses had appeared, no record of their testimony was made so that it might be properly evaluated at a later date, the defendant had been incarcerated again, and the case was set for trial in nearby Lee County.

The judge's ruling that Richardson must be placed in jail appears to have but one explanation. The testimony of Washington and Weaver no doubt convinced him for the first time that the State had some evidence. The remarkably low bail had been a response to the understanding that no case existed at that time.

It became clearer than ever that had the defense insisted upon going forward on its habeas corpus writ on November 16, rather than accepting low bail in lieu of the hearing, Richardson would have been discharged that day and the matter thereby terminated.

TRIAL

The trial began on Monday morning, May 27, 1968, at the Lee County Courthouse, in Fort Myers. While the press predicted that it would take "several days" or perhaps even "a week or more" to choose the jurors, before three that afternoon a jury of twelve and one alternate had been selected. All of the jurors were white. As is often the case in trials in relatively small towns, several of the jurors said that they knew other members of the jury. Defense lawyers generally try to guard against a homogeneous group and always are fearful of small cliques within the jury. Under Florida law in capital cases each side may make ten preemptory challenges, or challenges to jurors for which no reason need be offered. There is no limitation upon the number of challenges for cause that may be made. Such a challenge is related to the prospective juror's inability to judge the case fairly, but it is within the discretion of the judge to determine whether such a challenge is valid.

Within a short period of time Robinson had exhausted all of his preemptory challenges but one. He was concerned about utilizing his last challenge for fear that the subsequent prospective juror might be more biased than those already seated. A cursory examination had revealed that several former members of the KKK remained on the panel from which the last juror was to be chosen. The court had ruled that seventeen otherwise acceptable jurors could not sit in judgment upon Richardson, since fifteen of them had said that they opposed the death penalty and two others expressed doubt about convicting a man upon nothing more than circumstantial evidence. Just a few days later the United States Supreme Court was to rule in another case that those who oppose the death penalty may not be excluded from jury service in a capital case upon those grounds.

At three the court recessed the trial until nine the next morning, when Schaub was scheduled to make the opening statement for the State. Schaub and the other members of the State's prosecuting team expressed satisfaction with the jury. Robinson and Whitson were dismayed. "What does a challenge for cause mean in a case like this?" Robinson asked rhetorically. "Why, you ask some redneck if he is prejudiced, he answers, 'No, sir, I'd believe a nigger if he was telling the truth,' and the judge rules that he's impartial." The defense lawyer added, "Of course, if he opposes the death penalty he is automatically removed, thereby leaving only the bloodthirsty among the bigots to try the defendant."

Despite what both sides appeared to agree was an anti-Negro and pro-prosecution jury, the defense remained confident that there would be an acquittal, and Schaub could express hope only for "some type of conviction," with a conviction for murder in the first degree beyond his aspirations.

For regardless of the natural propensity of the jurors, there remained the troublesome question of the evidence, or more precisely, the lack of evidence. Treadwell again approached Robinson about a deal.

THE OPENING STATEMENT

In no uncertain terms, Schaub, his booming baritone voice echoing about the chamber, castigated Richardson as a murderer and a miser, in his opening statement. The defendant, said the prosecuting attorney, was motivated by a desire to "collect life-insurance policies upon the children's lives." In addition, Schaub said, "he was looking for a way out from under the children, and he had become disenchanted with Annie Mae."

Richardson, the jury was assured, had "a pathological adoration for money." This, combined with Richardson's "complete self-interest," worked out very badly for the children. They were ill-fed, having nothing but grits to eat three times each day, were poorly clothed, and were generally unhappy and rejected. Thus Richardson, Schaub explained, who had treated the children so poorly during their lives in order that all of the funds might be used to better his own life, finally killed them so that they would no longer be able to compete with him for money and so that he might benefit from the insurance policies that he had taken out the night before the murder.

The State would prove, said Schaub, that Richardson "was so satisfied" with the insurance upon the children's lives that he asked for "a double-indemnity policy for each one of them." Only four persons were present when the insurance was originally discussed, Mr. and Mrs. Richardson, the salesman, Purvis, and Bessie Reese. Since the State could not call either of the Richardsons as witnesses (a defendant may not be asked to testify by the prosecuting authority, and his wife may not testify against him without his permission), Schaub had promised in his opening statement to produce Purvis or Mrs. Reese, or both of them. Schaub told the jury that he would prove that Richardson placed the poison in the food and that he would prove it "beyond a reasonable doubt," as required by the law for conviction.

The bag containing the parathion was found "on Richardson's premises" said Schaub, "just where he had hidden it after killing the seven children." The State implied that it would present Charlie Smith, reported to have found the poison in the shack behind the apartment building occupied by the Richardson family. Within a few minutes Schaub had referred to the body of essential evidence that could be developed on the witness stand only through the sworn statements of Gerald Purvis, Bessie Reese, and Charlie Smith.

THE FIRST DAY

The evidentiary aspect of the case began when Assistant State Attorney Leroy Hill and Cline carried several boxes containing parathion, and articles said to contain parathion, into the courtroom. Cline had carried the boxes in his naked hands up to the courtroom steps, but before coming into the jury's view, both he and Hill donned bright-yellow rubber gloves. Hill explained that Cline had suffered nausea and headaches even with careful handling of the boxes.

To Robinson the entire drama was staged to create prejudice. His motion for a mistrial was summarily denied by the court.

The State called its first witness, Myrtice Jackson, who identified herself as a first-grade teacher at the Smith-Brown School in Arcadia. In her classroom, on October 25, 1967, was Alice Richardson, age seven. Under questioning by Hill, Miss

Jackson established that Alice appeared to be in good health during the morning.

Q. Now, directing your attention to the morning of October 25, do you remember what time she came to school that morning?

A. It was around eight-thirty.

Q. Prior to this, had her school attendance been regular?

A. Yes, sir.

Q. Did you notice anything unusual about her behavior that morning?

A. No.

Q. Was she in class the entire morning?

A. Yes.

Q. Did her health appear to be all right?

A. Yes.

Q. Did she appear alert and able to do her schoolwork?

A. Yes.

Q. What time did you dismiss the class for lunch?

A. Eleven o'clock.

Q. Did Alice leave for lunch?

A. Yes.

Q. At about what time?

A. About eleven.

After lunch, however, the situation was very different.

Q. What time did she return from lunch?

A. About a quarter of twelve.

Q. Did you notice any change in her behavior at this time when she returned?

A. Yes.

Q. At about what time did you notice the changes, and tell the jury what you noticed?

A. It was immediately as she came into the room when she

sat down. She began to perspire, grabbed ahold of her desk; her mouth came open. I asked what was wrong. She never said anything, so I sent for Mr. Anderson and Miss Fiason. Miss Fiason came immediately. We took her from the desk. She was just holding the desk.

Q. Give us an idea.

A. She was sitting in an individual desk. She grabbed ahold of the table part and she was retching and her head was going back and she was perspiring.

Q. Did you notice any muscle tremors?

A. She seemed to be trembling as she held to the desk.

Q. Did she say anything?

A. Never said a word.

Q. Was she standing or sitting?

A. Sitting.

Q. Did you notice anything wrong with the other first-grade people in the class?

A. No.

Q. Did you notice anything else about her physical appearance—first, let me ask you, did this behavior on her part alarm you, or how did you react?

A. When I saw her, I thought she was having an epileptic fit, and I sent for help, because it was the first time I had seen her in that condition. I didn't know what it was, so I sent for help.

Q. You say there was excessive saliva around the mouth. How would you describe that? Was it a little or lot?

A. Quite a bit, because it was about three minutes, I guess, or maybe four before we moved her from the desk, because I couldn't move her by myself.

Q. Could you describe it as foaming?

A. It hadn't gotten to that stage. It was saliva, clear.

Q. What did you do then?

A. I sent for help, and Miss Fiason and I took her from the desk and carried her to the principal's office.

Q. Did you have to carry her?
A. Yes.
Q. Did she appear in pain?
A. Yes, she was drawing up.
Q. Was she crying?
A. No, she never made any noise.

Miss Jackson also testified that moments later, in another classroom, she also saw Susie Richardson, who appeared to experience the same symptoms. She added that she also observed Betty Richardson a short time after that. "At that time her symptoms did not show like the others. I held her by the arm. She was able to walk. I didn't say anything to her."

On cross-examination Robinson made no effort to shake the teacher's testimony as to the reaction of the children to the poison after the luncheon recess. Instead he concentrated on destroying Schaub's picture of the children as rejected and miserable. Miss Jackson conceded that Alice drew pictures and that "she might have" taken the drawings home to her mother and father. Robinson then attempted to draw the somewhat reticent witness out on the question of the personalities of the two Richardson children she had an opportunity to observe.

Q. Basically there is nothing you could say about this child that would show that she had an unhappy family relationship based upon what you saw as a teacher; isn't that true?
A. Yes.
Q. Outside of what you have testified to, you don't know anything else about this case?
A. No, I don't.
Q. You just happened to be present on the day that the children became sick; isn't that true?

A. That is right.
Q. Isn't it true that Betty was a little more outgoing?
A. Yes.
Q. She wasn't as withdrawn as Alice?
A. No, not so because she helped Betty quite a bit.
Q. Isn't it also true that Betty was a normal, healthy, active child?
A. She was a little more active than Alice.
Q. There is nothing you know of which would make you think she was an unhappy child, is there?
A. No.

The State's second witness, Gustava Harvey, was Susie Richardson's teacher. She too testified to the child's apparent good health before lunch and to her unusual behavior after lunch at approximately 11:45 A.M.

A. She made a sudden jerk like this. I thought the boy next to her struck her. I called to him and asked if he hit her. He said no. I called to Susie. She didn't say anything. I said, "Can you say anything?" And she couldn't, so I got up and I went.
Q. Did you notice anything else that alarmed you?
A. Saliva began to flow from her mouth.
Q. How much?
A. It was a long stream that just hung there for a while until some of the children wiped her mouth.
Q. What did you do then?
A. The children—I had them to take off her shoes and wipe her mouth. In the meantime, I told someone to go next door to tell Mr. Floyd.

Miss Harvey explained that others took the children to the hospital and that she then went to the Richardson home. "I

heard there were more children at home, so I said that someone needed to be there."

Hill asked the witness to describe what she saw when she
arrived in the area of the Richardson apartment.

A.   I saw four children, two lying down, one standing up
     crying, and Bessie Reese was holding onto one.
Q.   You saw two children lying down. Where were they
     lying?
A.   On Bessie Reese's porch.
Q.   You say one was standing?
A.   Behind the broom of the door of this house.
Q.   Which one was crying?
A.   I didn't know them, I just knew it was one.
Q.   Where was the fourth one?
A.   Bessie had one.
Q.   She was holding one?
A.   One was standing, and she had it.
Q.   What did you do then?
A.   I grabbed two and put them in my car and rushed to the
     hospital.
Q.   Will you tell what their physical condition seemed to
     be to you?
A.   Saliva and mucus was running out of their nose and
     mouth. I was trying to get to the hospital.

Miss Harvey testified that two other teachers "came right
behind me," bringing the other two dying children with them
to the Arcadia General Hospital.

On cross-examination Robinson again tried to establish,
through the State's witness, the relationship between the children and the parents and the personality of the deceased. He
asked if the witness could state "normal, healthy child," and
Miss Harvey replied, "Yes."

Having established the positive, he felt safe enough to probe about in the area of a possible negative, always a risky undertaking with a witness presented by the other side.

Q. Do you know anything in her background or personality which caused her to be an unhappy child?
A. No.
Q. Isn't it a fact that she was a happy child before this incident occurred?
A. Yes, I would say so.
Q. Do you know of your own personal knowledge whether she loved her mother and father?
A. I think she did.

MR. SCHAUB: This is completely improper, not a competent question. What a deceased child might have felt of someone is impossible to answer.

THE COURT: The question was does she know. She can answer yes or no.

Schaub, having painted a dark picture of the family's home life, was evidently reluctant to have it modified, particularly by his own witness.

The next witness, Nathaniel Mayo, testified that he too taught at the Smith-Brown School and that he had assisted Miss Harvey in taking a stricken child, whose name he did not recall, from Miss Harvey's classroom to the Arcadia General Hospital.

Betty Luther testified that she had been Betty Jean Bryant's teacher. Schaub showed her a picture of the deceased child, asked her to identify it, and then offered it in evidence over the defense objection that it was being offered for purposes of prejudice only.

It is difficult to conjure up any other purpose for the ghastly picture of the child taken after her death. Such a photograph hardly constitutes a typical picture, and in any event, her identity was never in doubt. The court overruled the objection, and the photograph became Plaintiff's Exhibit Number One. Miss Luther said that Betty's health appeared to be "good" that morning but that after she returned from lunch, "she just put her head down." She testified that Miss Jackson then asked her if Betty was ill, since, "Well, they had already found the two children that were sick in the first grade."

Then Miss Jackson, according to the witness, "didn't explain anything to me. She just got her, Betty Bryant, and carried her down the hall."

On cross-examination Robinson again attempted to establish that Schaub's view of the Richardson family was entirely out of focus.

Q. We had some discussion on the other children—Alice, Betty, and Susie. Mrs. Jackson and Miss Harvey said the other children—Alice, Susie, and Betty—were also normal, average, healthy children. Would this be your observation, too?

A. I would say so.

Q. As a matter of fact, Mrs. Harvey said Susie loved her parents. Do you know—

MR. SCHAUB: Object to what other people said. I don't agree with his interpretation of what the other witnesses said.

THE COURT: Sustained.

Q. Did she seem to be a happy child?

A.   Well, I would say so. She didn't complain about anything. Anyway, she was a quiet child.

Q.   Do you know of anything personally in her background as her teacher which might have caused her to be upset in her home life?

A.   No, sir. See, I only had her a very short while.

Q.   Isn't it true that as a teacher that if there was a problem with the child, a teacher usually is the first person to recognize it?

A.   I would say so.

Q.   You have recognized them before, have you not, with other children?

A.   Yes.

Q.   Don't you think if there had been a problem in this particular child's life, you would recognize it, too?

A.   If I had more time, but since school had started only a short while, I don't know. She was quiet. Maybe if there had been enough time she would eventually have started talking more in class, so that is just it.

Q.   Did she appear to be a well-fed child, healthy?

A.   Satisfactory, I guess.

Q.   Average?

A.   Yes.

Lewis Anderson, principal of the school, appeared next for the State. He said that the records revealed that Betty Jean Bryant lived with James and Annie Mae Richardson. He then told of his experience with the Richardson children on the afternoon of the day on which they were poisoned.

A.   When I was called concerning the child who was ill, the first child, I walked outside the office door, and Miss Jackson and Miss Fiason had Alice Richardson in their arms. I immediately took the child, and thinking that the child was having epileptic seizures, I had Miss Fiason open the car door. I rushed her as hurriedly as I could to the Arcadia General Hospital.

Q. What symptoms did you observe that led you to this belief?

A. Some twitching.

Q. Whereabouts?

A. Just jerking.

Q. Did you notice any excessive saliva?

A. I didn't until I reached the hospital.

Q. What did you notice at that time?

A. I noticed that quite a bit of mucus was forming in the mouth, and it seemed to be congealing. The nurse attempted to get rid of this by using a tongue depressor.

Q. Were you the person that carried Betty Jean in the hospital, or was she able to walk?

A. I assisted carrying Betty Jean in.

Q. What other symptoms did you observe of her condition at this time? Did she seem to be in pain?

A. Betty Jean was the only one who said something to me, and she said, "I am all right, there is nothing wrong with me." I said, "Sure you are all right. Be cool."

Q. Did you then take her in the hospital?

A. She was in the hospital at this time.

Q. Then, did you see any of the other children while you were there?

A. I saw the other teachers bringing the children in, but they were carrying them in different rooms. The only other child that I saw was the boy, who was placed at the foot of the cot.

Q. A very small child?

A. I don't recall whether it was the first child that was brought from the house or not. This particular one was placed near the cot where Betty Jean was.

Q. Were these symptoms consistent with what Betty Jean had?

A. No, somewhat lifeless.

Q. What else did you observe about him?

A. The nurse attempted—I mean, used a stethoscope to check his pulse. She replied to me she felt a faint pulse. I checked the pulse and I said, "This one is gone."

On cross-examination Mr. Anderson said that he had purchased the grave sites and the simple granite headstones for the children. The funds had been sent to him by Robinson.

Q. Mr. Anderson, as the custodian of the records at the school, are you in a position to state at this time whether or not the three girls who were students there at the school—whether their attendance was good?

A. Yes, from our records.

Q. So basically what you have testified to this morning is all you know about this case?

A. This is all.

Q. Did you attend the funeral?

A. Yes, I attended the funeral.

Q. You saw Mr. and Mrs. Richardson at the funeral?

MR. SCHAUB: Object and ask that be stricken from the record. Certainly that is not a proper subject of the trial. It has nothing to do with the issues of the case.

In this instance Schaub was overruled and Anderson was permitted to say that the parents did attend the funeral.

Martha Bowers, a librarian, testified that she accompanied Mrs. Harvey to the vicinity of the Richardson residence between 11:30 A.M. and noon on October 25. Bessie Reese, she said, "had one of the kids in her arms" on the porch, while "two of the children were lying on the floor on the porch, and little Doreen and Diane was standing behind a broom." She testified that Mrs. Harvey put two children in her car.

A. Shortly after we arrived, Mrs. Fiason came up behind her. Mr. Anderson sent her from the school. Mrs. Fiason came up behind us. She put two of the kids in the car. She put one in them. I grabbed Doreen and put her in the car, in Miss Fiason's car.

On cross-examination Miss Bowers, as was the case with most of the other teachers, testified that she did not attend the children's funeral. The defense did demonstrate a decided interest in the October 25th activities of Mrs. Reese.

Q. You saw Bessie Reese at the residence when you got there?
A. Yes, she was tending the children. She was there with the kids.
Q. She looked like she was supervising?
A. She seemed to have been somewhat to me.

The most coherent presentation of the events at the school and at the Reese residence came from Ruby Fiason, the last teacher to testify.

A. At eleven forty-five I was going to the school library to get a film strip, and a little boy came running up the walk behind me and said, "Miss Fiason, Miss Jackson said to come to her room for a minute. Hurry." So I ran back up the walk and went to Jackson's room. When I got there I found her standing over Alice Richardson, and this child—when I looked I said, "I think she is having some kind of seizure." So the child was—the saliva was coming from her mouth. Her head was back, and she was grabbing the desk. We pried her hands from the desk.

Miss Jackson and I grabbed the child up and went to the office. We met Mr. Anderson coming out of the office. We put the child in Mr. Anderson's office. We opened the car of Mr. Anderson and put the child in the back seat and left.

When I went to Mrs. Harvey's room, she was holding one of them. I said, "It must be poison." The Mexico case had been published. I went to Luther's room. She was coming out of the room with Betty.

Q. What did you do with this child?

A. I took Betty Jean to the hospital. Mrs. Burris got in the car with me. She said, "You want me to go?" I said, "Yes." I asked this child, "What did you have for dinner?" She said, "We had rice, gravy, and beans." She began to break out in perspiration, and her breath was short. I said, "Don't say anything."

Q. Then what did you do?

A. I went to the hospital as fast as I could. When I got to the hospital, Mr. Anderson took the child out. He said, "Miss Fiason, go to the house and see about the children at the house."

Q. What did you see when you got there?

A. When I went to the house, Mrs. Harvey was there, and Mrs. Bowers and the neighbor, and this one child was standing up holding the broom and the other was lying on the floor of the porch. Mrs. Bowers was doing something. I said, "What are you doing?" She said, "I am trying to clean them up." I said, "Just put them in there, there is no time to clean them up"; so Mrs. Harvey took two and Bowers brought one to my car and Hattie James brought one. I drove to the hospital.

Q. Is that the Arcadia General?

A. Yes.

Q. Now, directing your attention to your observation of these children, the Richardson and Bryant children that you saw that afternoon, did you notice whether or not they were having any trouble breathing?

A. Well, from what I could see, they were suffering from the same type thing, the same foaming.

Q. What did you observe they were suffering from?

A. The saliva running from the mouth and this shortness of breath and twitching.

Q. Did you notice anything unusual about their eyes?

A. The eyes, when we looked at Alice, her eyes had already —they were tight or weren't focusing, and the one that I took was the same way.

Q. Did you notice whether or not they were having any problem controlling their bowels?

A. Yes, the one that I took in was having diarrhea.

Q. I believe you said that all of these children seemed to be suffering from the same symptoms, is that correct?

A. Yes.

On cross-examination Miss Fiason stated that she attended the funeral and that in fact she "planned that funeral."

The first of several medical witnesses to testify for the State was Dr. Elmer Schmierer. He stated that he arrived at the Arcadia General Hospital at "about ten after twelve." Under Schaub's questioning he told of his activities there.

Q. Did you see some colored children there?

A. Yes.

Q. What did you do upon your arrival?

A. I was directed into the cast room, where they were giving artificial respiration to one of the patients. I listened to her heart and found no heartbeat or breath at the time and pronounced her dead.

Q. Then what?
A. I was directed to two other children who were pro-
nounced dead on arrival, so I went to see if we needed
to do anything or not.
Q. What did you observe of their condition?
A. Those two children were dead, and there was an odor of
fecal material in the air.
Q. Was there any salivation?
A. Yes, there was foam on the lips and mouth.
Q. So you pronounced three dead?
A. Yes.
Q. Did you see any others ?
A. Yes, I was directed into another room, where there were
three children on stretchers, two on one stretcher and
one child alone. Dr. Martin was there at that time and
seeing one of them. I ordered atropine for the other two
children.
Q. What is atropine, doctor?
A. It is a chemical drug that we use for drying up secretions
in patients and also in parathion poisoning.
Q. What is the purpose in parathion-poisoning cases?
A. It is to counteract the parasympathetic actions that are
created of the access of acetylcholine in the patient.
Q. You went to another child?
A. Yes, I was directed to the other child in the X-ray room.
Q. What did you observe of the symptoms?
A. The child was rolling around on the X-ray table moaning
and groaning, and I again noticed that there was an odor
of fecal material in the air.
Q. Did the child appear to be in pain?
A. Yes.
Q. Any signs of pulmonary edema?
A. Yes.
Q. What is that?

A. Congestion of the lungs, a lot of fluid in the lungs, and it is noted by listening to the lungs and also bubbles in the mouth, a foamy sputum in the mouth.

Q. Were you the physician that pronounced the seven children dead that afternoon?

A. I pronounced four of them that noon.

Q. During the day you did have occasion to see all seven of them?

A. I saw them, yes.

Q. Did you execute the death certificates for these children?

A. Yes.

Through Dr. Schmierer, Schaub offered evidence that is probably unique in the history of American jurisprudence.

Q. I hand you what has been marked for identification purposes as State's Exhibits 3 through 9 and ask you if you will look at each one of these please and see if you executed them.

A. Yes, I did.

Q. What are they?

A. These are the death certificates on these seven children that we saw this day.

Q. These are the children that you are testifying about?

A. Yes.

Q. Were the symptoms you observed of these children consistent?

A. Of those that were alive, yes.

MR. SCHAUB: I would like to offer these in evidence.

MR. ROBINSON: We have no objection. Your Honor, please, the only objection we have, we will stipulate with this—we are dealing with one party, and he wants to introduce certificates to seven children. We would object to six, which are not responsive to the one involved under discussion.

THE COURT: It goes to the *res gestae*. They will be admitted.

Why the defense did not object to the offer of each certificate remains a mystery, for Dr. Schmierer had given as the official and medical cause of death "premeditated murder." On cross-examination Whitson tried to undo some of the damage, but very likely in the eyes of some jurors a major portion of the case had been established. Someone had, according to the odd documentary evidence, murdered the children. It was now up to them to decide who the culprit was. The State was, as Schaub later confided to me, "halfway home" due to what appeared to be a defense lapse. Often in a poison case the State considers that its greatest problem is to overcome the jury's suspicion that the poison may have been accidentally ingested. Plaintiff's Exhibits three through nine seemed to overcome that obstacle in this case.

Q. After first observing these children, what was your diagnosis?
A. First, because they were all of one family and all came in together, I thought of a poisoning. What type, at the moment, I had no idea.
Q. After you continued to observe these children and medicate for them, what opinion did you form then as to the nature of the poisoning?
A. We came to the conclusion that probably it was parathion poisoning.
Q. What are the antidotes for parathion poisoning?
A. Atropine and protopine.
Q. Were these administered to the children?

A. Atropine was given to three of them, and protopine was given to one of them.

Q. As you observed these children, how did their condition progress?

A. They were congested failure, and the one that later on died wasn't at the time, when I first saw it, but she progressed into congested failure. The hearts would slow down and stop. We would give them external cardiac massage and resuscitation and adrenalin. Their hearts would begin to beat again, and then they would start breathing again.

Q. You say one survived; how long did this child survive?

A. Until the next morning about five-thirty.

Q. You then pronounced her dead at that time?

A. Yes.

Q. What is the end result of parathion poisoning? I don't mean just death, but what is the physiological result?

A. The parathion poisoning causes a decrease in the choline esterase of the body. Therefore, the body cannot function as usual, and it causes an increase of muscle stimulation in the intestines, causing them to vomit and having diarrhea. It constricts the pupils, slows down down the heart, constricts the bronchials in the lungs in reducing the amount of air space that the air can pass through to the lungs and reduces the oxygen the patient can receive.

Q. And this effect on the respiratory system, is that really the ultimate cause of death, paralysis of the muscles?

A. Paralysis of the muscles and congestion of the lungs so there isn't room in the lungs for air, but the lung spaces are filled with fluid.

Dr. Schmierer told Schaub that he believed that the parathion was taken orally by the children. He said the effect of the poison was always "rapid," and even more rapid when taken orally as compared with absorption through the skin or by "breathing it in."

After Schaub tendered the witness to the defense, Whitson cautiously began to attack the portion of the death certificate related to the cause of death. He proceeded by indirection, careful to prevent the doctor from knowing what his ultimate objective might be.

Q. How many death certificates have you prepared during your practice?

A. I have no idea; I couldn't say.

Q. Has it been literally hundreds?

A. I wouldn't say literally hundreds.

Q. Two or three hundred?

A. No.

Q. A hundred or so?

A. Probably I would say a hundred at least.

Q. You are familiar with the method for preparation of a death certificate, are you not?

A. I don't know exactly what you mean.

Q. You know how to make one up, don't you?

A. Well, the usual practice is that someone types them up and it comes to me to fill in the portion of the cause of death.

Q. I show you again this death certificate that has been introduced into evidence on Betty Jean Bryant. Portions of the death certificate are typed in; portions of it are written; is that right?

A. Right.

Q. Did you do the writing?

A. Yes.

Q. All of it?

A. Yes.

Q. Did you do any investigation into this case itself before

you prepared this, other than seeing the children and
so forth?

A.   Other than seeing the children, no.

Q.   And talking with some other doctors about how it happened?

A.   Yes.

After Whitson had made it clear, through the doctor's own
testimony, that he possessed no knowledge to warrant a conclusion regarding the possibility of murder, he then asked the
question that he had been leading up to.

Q.   Can you tell me why you placed under "Describe how
the injury occurred," the words "Premeditated murder?"

A.   A conclusion. Someone put some poison into the food.

Q.   On the conclusion that someone put some poison in the
food?

A.   Yes.

Q.   On that basis—in this death certificate you charged that
premeditated murder had been committed; is that right?

A.   Yes.

Q.   Did you talk with Sheriff Cline?

A.   No, I didn't talk to him on this basis.

Q.   Who did you talk with on this basis, doctor?

A.   Judge Hayes.

Q.   Judge Gordon Hayes?

A.   Yes.

Q.   Who else?

A.   The only one I talked to on this basis.

Q.   On the basis of what he told you, you then made a charge
of premeditated murder in an official document?

A.   Yes.

When Whitson completed his examination of the witness,

Robinson, anxious to destroy the death certificates as viable evidence, began.

Q. In your lifetime you signed 100 certificates. Have you ever, in any case, ever placed down there in that box where we are talking about that the cause of death was by premeditated murder?
A. Other than this, no.
Q. There has been a whole lot of talk about this case in your city; isn't that right?
A. Yes.
Q. This was prior to the time James Richardson was charged that you put this in there, premeditated murder?
A. Yes.
Q. So you took it upon yourself how seven children died after talking to a county judge, that that was premeditated murder?
A. Yes.

Dr. Gordon McSwain was the next witness. He too treated some of the children at the Arcadia General Hospital. He testified that he arrived at the hospital at "about 12:30." He was, he said, "active in treating two of the children, and then I saw a third child who Dr. Martin and Dr. Schmierer were treating." The two children he treated, Doreen and Susie, were, he said, very near to death when he arrived.

Q. Did you observe any symptoms at this time?
A. The most marked symptom was pulmonary edema.
Q. What is this?
A. A lot of fluid in the lungs. The layman commonly says drowning in their own fluid.
Q. How is this manifested?
A. A lot of foam and making a lots of noise when they

breathe, as if there was a lot of moisture in the chest. You could hear it without using a stethoscope.

Q. What did you do, if anything, in the way of treatment?

A. Well, by the time I arrived, Dr. Schmierer and Martin had almost concluded that it was one of the organic phosphates that was the cause of the poisoning, and they had started all the children on atropine, so I just started treating those two, and we just started giving massive doses of atropine.

Q. Did you reach some conclusion as to what they should be treated for?

A. Yes.

Q. What was that?

A. We decided they had organic phosphate poisoning.

Q. Parathion?

A. We couldn't say which. There are several of that group. You just couldn't pinpoint it at all. You would say it was that type of poisoning.

Hill tried in several different ways to get the doctor to state that the children had been poisoned by parathion. Yet Dr. McSwain was unable to be that specific.

Q. Do you have an opinion as to the cause of death of the two children that we spoke about?

A. Yes, sir.

Q. What was that?

A. My opinion and diagnosis was organic phosphate poisoning.

Q. Parathion poisoning?

A. All I can do is put it in that group. I have no way of making a chemical diagnosis.

Robinson developed that possible discrepancy on cross-examination.

Q. Just one question, which I am not trying to get you in a bind in or something. You really can't say it was parathion based on what you just testified; isn't that true?

A. I can say this, that I think it was an organic phosphate.

Q. But that doesn't necessarily make it parathion within itself; isn't that correct?

A. No, that is just like saying a rabbit is an animal and all animals are rabbits.

Q. What I am asking you, really, you can't state under oath that it was actually parathion poisoning, can you?

A. No, I can say organic phosphate.

Q. But you can't say it was parathion?

A. No.

Robinson had clearly scored a point, but it was in a different game. Lawyers often tend to exploit weak points, sometimes even forgetting that the issue they are developing is irrelevant. Clearly the children had died of parathion poisoning. Although Dr. McSwain could not be certain, the State was ready to offer others who would testify more explicitly.

The third doctor to testify, Dr. Calvin Martin, had arrived at the hospital moments before Dr. McSwain did.

A. I was called to the hospital by the nurse. I immediately went to the hospital and found in one room three children, two on one stretcher and one on another stretcher. These were Betty Jean Bryant, lying on a stretcher by herself, and Doreen Richardson and Susie Bryant were on the other stretcher together. They were the smaller children.

I was told that there were three others—I guess three other children—already dead. I didn't see those. I looked at these three.

In observing the children, the outstanding things that

I saw were the muscle fasciculation, the twitching of the muscles.

Q. What is muscle fasciculation?

A. Twitching of the muscle like a bag of worms—contracting by themselves without any coherent action. Pulmonary edema and fecal incontinence.

Q. What is that?

A. Stool uncontrollably. Salivation and tearing—just the general moribund condition of the children, the three that we saw. Rapid, labored respirations.

Q. Did you administer treatment?

A. Yes, because of the pulmonary edema. That, of course, suggested trying to clear out the airways to remove the fluid. Because of the apparent pulmonary condition, we started aminophylline, a drug used for pulmonary edema, since it was not clear as to what was causing the difficulty in the children.

A very short time after that, we went ahead and gave atropine, first in a small dose, because we didn't know what it was. As it became clear to us what the problem was, we increased the dosage of atropine; and, of course, continued with supportive measures, such as suctioning the airways, artificial respiration, and later cardiac massage and adrenalin.

Q. How long did this treatment continue, to your best estimate?

A. Well, in the neighborhood of twenty-five or thirty or possibly forty-five minutes. It was pretty hectic there for a while.

Q. Did these children at some later time expire?

A. Yes, sir.

Q. Do you remember in what order or fashion?

A. They were so close together, it was hard to tell. I think Betty Jean Richardson went first, followed by Doreen and Susie—pretty close together.

Q. From your observation of the initial symptoms that you related, did you reach a conclusion as to what they should be treated for?

A. If you mean by initial symptoms when I first walked in, no, but as observation continued and we were able to observe these children, it became clear that this was a poisoning or at least intoxication by organic phosphates.

Q. Did you reach an opinion as to the manner in which the three children that you have named received this poison?

A. Yes, sir, we suspected, of course, ingestion. There was not any evidence of residue of powder on the skin. It just didn't seem possible or likely that a dose that would cause this magnitude of symptoms or the rapidity with which they occurred could have been gotten through the pulmonary system.

Q. Rapidity, to what do you associate that?

A. Intestinal absorption.

On cross-examination Dr. Martin told Robinson that he could not state that parathion was the cause of death.

The State next called Virginia Nash, who was working in the hospital as a nurse when the seven children were brought in. Her testimony was an indication of the care with which the State had constructed some elements of its case. Mrs. Nash testified for just a minute, long enough to state that James Richardson identified the children for her that day and that she subsequently placed identity bracelets on their wrists.

The next witness, Margie Provau, also had little to offer. She identified some seven sheets of hospital records regarding the brief confinement of the children at the hospital.

After a luncheon recess, the court convened at 1:30 P.M. to hear the testimony of Dr. Millard White, the Sarasota County Medical Examiner, who had performed the autopsy on the bodies of each of the seven children.

In response to Schaub's question, "What is a pathologist?" Dr. White said:

A.   A pathologist is a physician specialized in the application of basic science to the diagnosis and prognosis of disease and also assists in many instances in recommending treatment for disease.

The basic application of science is the entire field— bacteriology, toxicology, tissue examination, autopsy work, chemistry, and any related scientific fields that apply to the human and human disease.

Q.   Would it be accurate to say that a pathologist is a medical scientist?

A.   You could call it that, yes.

MR. WHITSON: Objection, he has already told us what a pathologist consists of. Medicine is an art, and the court is aware of that, and not a science.

THE COURT: Overruled.

Q.   Would that be an accurate definition?

A.   We are in no position to call it a science.

Dr. White, who had relinquished his scientific status for the role of artist on short notice, appeared prepared for a comeback when asked to explain what an autopsy is.

A.   An autopsy basically is the scientific investigation of the body to determine the cause of death and the nature of the disease or disease processes. It includes opening various body cavities and examining the organs and removing the organs and examining them in more detail.

In those tissues that appear to be involved in a change from normal, small specimens are taken which are sent to the Histology Department for the purpose of microscopic examination.

Q. Is the principal purpose of an autopsy to determine cause of death?

A. That is one of the purposes.

The pathologist then stated that he examined the body externally as well as the cavities of the body for the purpose of determining the cause of death or of any disease process or evidence of injury. He then removed the organs of the body and submitted them for toxicological examination. Some of the organs he delivered to Dr. Antonio Maceo in Miami and others to Dr. John Davis and two other men at the Arcadia Courthouse. Dr. White said that by using infrared spectographic analysis upon some brown powder furnished to him by Sheriff Cline, he "got a characteristic wave pattern, which is in our opinion excellent identity of the compound parathion."

Assistant State Attorney John Treadwell testified that he had retained a registered land surveyor. "I requested that he prepare me a diagram or a sketch of the area in Arcadia that is located on 131 Watson Avenue, which is commonly referred to as Barnes Hotel." Although Schaub never asked Treadwell if he knew who had resided in the building on October 25, Treadwell provided that information on two separate occasions. Once when asked if he could identify State's Exhibit Eleven as the surveyor's work, the witness answered in the affirmative and then added that "Mr. Richardson, the defendant, and a Bessie Reese" lived there. Later, when Schaub asked if there was more than one refrigerator in the Richardson apartment, Treadwell responded:

A. There was one other refrigerator that was on the south

side of the wall of the kitchen, which contained a refrigerator used for storage.

The apartment to the immediate east of the Richardson apartment, or the one that would front Watson Street, is the apartment of Bessie Reese. She lived there with her daughter at the time the poisoning occurred.

To the immediate west—this is a concrete stairway as it goes upstairs to the upstairs—to right under these stairways there is what we refer to as an outhouse. It contains one unusable commode right in this corner. That would be the northeast corner of the outhouse.

Q. What is this building?
A. This building right here would be what we refer to as an old storage building. It was not occupied.
Q. How far is that?
A. Approximately 50 feet from the north of the Richardson apartment.

Dr. Antonio Maceo testified that he had received some "toxicological specimens" from Dr. White and that he delivered them to "our Pesticide Laboratory in Miami." Ostensibly Dr. Maceo was called by the State to show the unbroken chain which connected the specimens from the time that they left the point of origin until the time they were subjected to analysis. However, since they were never identified by Dr. Maceo, his testimony added little to the trial record.

The next State witness, John Wilkey, was also presented as a link in the possession chain. He too delivered "physical objects" from Dr. White to the Pesticide Laboratory maintained by the Board of Health in Miami. His testimony was also flawed by Schaub's failure to elicit a positive identification of the objects from the witness.

The State then called Sheriff Frank Cline. Cline, who had

developed the evidence and who had shaped the entire case against Richardson, was clearly the most important witness of the first day of the trial. Yet he had surprisingly little to say on direct examination. He testified that as soon as he heard about the poisonings he reported to 131 Watson Avenue, the building where, he said, "James Richardson lives." Mrs. Reese lived there also, but Cline made no mention of that in his direct examination. He arrived at the premises "shortly after noon," he said. He was accompanied by "the Chief of Police and County Judge, Gordon Hayes."

Q. What was the purpose for your being in the house at this time?
A. We had the report that several children were bad sick and some dead at the hospital.
Q. Was anyone home?
A. No.
Q. The door locked or unlocked?
A. Unlocked.
Q. Did you examine the premises, looking for something, then?
A. Just briefly, because we didn't know what we were looking for.
Q. Did you find anything or take anything at this time?
A. No, sir.
Q. Approximately how long were you there, would you say?
A. Approximately ten minutes.

Cline said that he went from the Richardson apartment to the hospital and talked to Richardson there.

A. I asked if he had heard that his children were in bad shape and some died already, and we would like to look around the house, the premises, to find something. Did he know anything they could have gotten into, and if we

might have his permission to look. He told me that the
place was locked up and he said, "I have the keys." He
gave me the keys from around his neck.

Q. Did he say what the keys would gain access to?

A. The two refrigerators. He said the house keys and said
the keys there were two sets for the refrigerator.

Q. What did you do then?

A. Went back to the house, still not knowing what we were
looking for.

Q. Did the defendant go with you?

A. No.

Q. Who went with you?

A. The second trip Judge Hayes, one of my deputies, and—

Q. You recall which deputy sheriff?

A. No, sir, I don't, not that trip.

Q. About what time was this that you went back to the
premises?

A. Possibly around two o'clock.

Q. What did you do then.

A. We looked over the entire area, still not knowing what
we were looking for.

Q. Outside or inside?

A. Both, the outside buildings and in the house itself.

Q. Did you take anything from the premises?

A. I did not.

Q. How long were you there?

A. This time possibly an hour.

Cline said that he returned to the hospital and then at
"about four-thirty in the afternoon" he made his third visit
to the Richardson apartment. At that time he took, he said, a
pot lid, two pots, and a frying pan.

He gave the utensils to Jim Foy, who he identified as an
investigator for the State's Attorney's office. Cline testified
that during that visit he secured from the defendant, "an

insurance receipt from the Union National Life Insurance Company."

Q. Would you describe what it looked like and what it had on it?

A. It was a yellow card with the name of the children on the back with the amount of insurance and the advertisement on the front signed by Joe Fergus.

Q. Did he say in what capacity he signed it?

A. He is the agent for the insurance company.

Q. What insurance did it indicate for the children?

A. One thousand dollars each.

Cline said that the question of insurance had been discussed at the hospital by Judge Hayes and the defendant, but he could not remember or could not hear what had been said by the two men.

At approximately eight-thirty that evening Cline made his fourth visit that day to the premises, he testified. On that occasion, he said, he talked with Richardson.

A. We still did not know what had happened to the children, and we were still trying to determine the cause of death, their sicknesses. He [Richardson] advised we had his full cooperation to look anywhere, to take anything we desired, to help ascertain what happened.

Q. Do you remember his exact words, what he said, or was that the general tenor?

A. That was the general text, not the exact words.

Q. Did you take any items at this time?

A. Yes.

Q. Did the defendant assist you in gathering up any of these items?

A. Yes.

Q. What items were taken on this fourth visit?

A. Those were the items I mentioned previously: the blue sweater, windbreaker, brown work glove, right hand, white work glove for the left hand, and blue corduroy coat, a green and white pick sack, and a brown and white pick sack and a scarf.

Q. That was your fourth visit to the premises on October 25, 1967. Did you again visit the premises for a fifth visit on that same date?

A. That night close to midnight, not inside the house, but the outside area.

Q. You were confined to a search on the outside?

A. Yes.

Q. Around midnight?

A. Yes.

Q. Anyone with you?

A. Not that I recall at that time, no.

Cline searched the area again the next day. On that occasion he "found" the murder weapon, the bag of parathion. Yet neither he nor the State's Attorney appeared sufficiently interested in the discovery to permit the jury to hear the facts related to it.

Q. Now, Sheriff, were you back on the premises on October 26, which would have been Thursday following the date the children were taken to the hospital?

A. Yes, sir.

Q. Did you remove anything from the premises at that time?

A. Yes, sir.

Q. What did you remove?

A. A bag of parathion partially filled with parathion.

Q. I show you what has been marked for identification purposes as State's Exhibit 17 and ask if that is the bag containing the parathion that you found?

A. Yes, sir.

Q.   Where did you find this?
A.   Sitting in an outbuilding in the same area.

In a sense, Cline had testified truthfully, for anyone who saw the poison can be said to have "found" it. The judge could have testified that he "found" it when he looked down from his bench and saw it on the exhibit table, and visitors from abroad can claim, with equal accuracy, that they have, each of them, "discovered" America when landing on our shores. Nevertheless, for the State to leave the impression with the jury that Cline found the parathion was at best an example of recklessness, not consistent with the fashion in which the rest of the case had been constructed, and at worst a deliberate effort to mislead the jury and to obviate the necessity of calling otherwise essential witnesses, Mrs. Reese and Charlie Smith.

Three weeks later Cline again returned to the Richardson apartment, this time with a search warrant issued by his associate in the investigation, Judge Hayes.

Q.   Were you again on the premises on November 17, 1967?
A.   Yes.
Q.   For what purpose did you go to the premises on the 17th?
A.   Pursuant to a search warrant.
Q.   Issued by whom?
A.   Judge Hayes.

Surely the most extraordinary aspect of Cline's direct examination came during the last moments of his presentation. The prosecutor asked his witness:

Q.   When you first went into the apartment, the Richardson premises, did you smell any unusual odor?
A.   Yes, sir.
Q.   Could you describe the odor or what it resembled?

A. It left a metallic taste in your mouth. It was real strong that hung in the air.

Q. Did you associate this with anything you had experienced before?

A. I used to use parathion sprays around groves. It reminded me of that.

The State's Attorney inquired again:

Q. You say this was a strong odor?
A. Yes.
Q. When did you first notice it?
A. Upon walking in the house.
Q. Was that on your first visit?
A. Yes.

Long after the trial when I interviewed Cline, he described the smell that had greeted him that day in greater detail. I was interested in the subject and pursued it with him. He told me that he noticed the smell "almost like very strong poison gas, coming from the house" when he was "at least, say, twenty-five feet or more away from the building." He said "that smell was everywhere, and it was strong." "It was so strong," he said, "that you could taste it." He asked me, "Did you ever put a penny in your mouth? Well, that's what it smelled like, like the taste of a penny in your mouth. You could hardly breathe in there. We had to cover our faces with handkerchiefs," he said. The smell he said, "was coming from the stove, from the pans and pots on the stove. We had to open the windows and everything, it was so strong in there."

Cline had been informed that children had died and others were dying and that they had all been at 131 Watson Avenue. He rushed to the premises, ostensibly to find the cause of the illness. He testified, "From the information at the hospital, the children were sick, dying from some unknown reason."

He added, "I was looking around the premises to see if there was anything they might have gotten into to cause them to be sick."

Before entering the premises, he smelled the unmistakable odor of parathion, a poison that he had used himself in the fruit groves.

Yet on direct examination Cline informed the jury that he had stayed for just ten minutes, made no mention at that time of the overpowering odor which he recognized as a deadly gas, did not tell the jury that the odor emanated from the stove, and explained, in fact, that he examined the premises "just briefly," explaining that "we didn't know what we were looking for." Yet if the rest of his testimony is to be credited, he was looking for the cause of death, and he had found it.

Robinson's cross-examination of Cline failed to develop the important conflicts in his testimony and some of his departures from the known facts. Robinson was convinced that the State could not make out a serious case against his client, but cautiously laid the predicate for a new trial in the event that there was a conviction for some lesser crime than murder in the first degree. Question after question was put to Cline regarding the number of visits to the Richardson apartment, who accompanied him on each trip, how long he remained, and what he took with him. The defense lawyer established a record showing repeated illegal searches and seizures. He demonstrated as well that in certain areas Cline's memory was less than perfect.

Robinson then moved into Cline's work record.

Q. Before you went to work for the Arcadia Sheriff's office, where did you work prior to that time?
A. The city of South Bay.

Robinson asked Cline if he resigned voluntarily from that

job, and Cline first answered, "No," but later denied that he had been "fired for incompetence." Cline admitted that he had been employed for "a while" by the Highway Patrol but was not required to answer Robinson's question, "Who did you have a run-in with that time?" due to an objection by the State.

When Cline appeared a trifle rattled by the references to his previous employment, Robinson began to explore the story that Cline had found the parathion. Cline then appeared to reverse his earlier testimony.

Q. Where did you find this stuff, Sheriff?
A. It was not found by me.
Q. Who found it?
A. I was called by Police Officer Joe Minoughan at the city police department.
Q. Let me ask you about this bag of stuff. Where did you find that stuff in that big bag we were looking at a minute ago?
A. When I first saw it, it was in an outbuilding on the same property as the Richardson property.
Q. What time was that?
A. Early in the morning of the 26th, around six or six-thirty.
Q. Didn't you make a thorough search of that outbuilding on the 25th?
A. Yes.
Q. You just about tore that building apart, you and your deputies?
A. Yes.
Q. It wasn't there?
A. Not there.
Q. But it was found there the next day?
A. Yes.
Q. Where?

A. Sitting just inside the building, probably 18 inches from the door, in plain sight.

Q. Reckon you maybe accidentally missed it when you went in there?

A. We didn't miss it.

Q. Somebody put it in there?

A. Yes.

Robinson then began to trace the movements of the bag of parathion from the time it was "found" by Cline, and its presumed movements before then.

Q. Sheriff, after you found this stuff, what did you do with it?

A. It was taken to the county jail and locked up.

Q. Did it have a hole in the bag?

A. Yes, sir, in the bottom of it.

Q. How big was that hole?

A. Pinholes.

Q. How many did it have in it, two or three?

A. Not many, enough for you to see it drop out the bottom, just minute quantities of it.

Q. Did it run out pretty fast?

A. No.

Q. Wasn't the bottom of the bag rolled up a little bit to keep it from coming out?

A. No.

Q. I believe the bag was damp?

A. Yes, it was.

Q. What does that lead us to believe?

A. The bag was sitting outside somewhere. It was wet, as if it was wet from dew. Placed inside of this building sometime prior to the time it was found.

Q. So somebody must have put it in there?

A. Yes, sir, it was not in the building the day before.

Robinson knew that neither Cline nor Minoughan had found the parathion, and by that time, Cline knew that Robinson knew more about the discovery of the poison than had been revealed in court. Robinson was relentless.

Q. How did you find out it was put in there?
A. Officer Joe Minoughan from the city police department.
Q. Did he find it?
A. No, it was shown to him. He did not find it personally.
Q. Who found it?
A. It was shown to him by Charlie Smith and Bessie Reese.
Q. Charlie Smith and Bessie Reese King?
A. Yes.
Q. Where does Bessie live?
A. Next door to the Richardson apartment.
Q. Did you search her apartment on the 25th?
A. Not inside the house.

For the first time, the jury had some inkling of the odd circumstances in which the parathion had been discovered. Robinson now appeared to be on the verge of securing all of the facts about this crucial episode.

Q. You stated that Charlie Smith and Bessie Reese King found the bag?
A. That is what was told to me.
Q. You didn't see them find it?
A. No.
Q. Did you make any investigation as to them?
A. No.

Yet Charlie Smith had been jailed by Cline for months as "a material witness" in the case. Smith later told me that he had been questioned on numerous occasions by Cline. Bessie Reese, whose potential testimony might have been more relevant and more material than Smith's, told me that she had been thoroughly questioned by Cline. She had in fact been placed in Cline's jail one night when Robinson was in Arcadia looking for her. Just after Robinson left town, unable to see Mrs. Reese, Cline ordered her released.

Cline himself told me that he had literally "hundreds of hours of tapes of Charlie Smith and Bessie Reese." Yet he informed the jury that he had not conducted any investigation as to them.

Of course, Robinson knew that Cline had imprisoned both of the witnesses and accordingly he inquired:

Q. Were they ever in your jail?
A. Yes.
Q. What for?
A. An investigation of this case. Charlie Smith was there. Bessie Reese King was there, I think, by her parole officer.

Robinson was anxious for the jury to learn that Mrs. Reese was on parole for having murdered her husband. The State was just as concerned about suppressing that fact.

Q. What was she involved in parole with?

MR. SCHAUB: Objection, nothing responsive to the cross-examination. We will be here all day if we can go into history.

THE COURT: You say not responsive to—

MR. SCHAUB: Not responsive to the direct-examination testimony of this witness and completely immaterial and irrelevant at this time.

THE COURT: Not proper cross, sustain your objection.

For all the jury knew, Mrs. Reese had had a traffic problem. Even a juror who had followed the case closely in *The Arcadian* would have secured no additional information. For the editor was just as careful as the judge about this delicate matter. The local newspaper reported that "Bessie is on parole at this time from a previous brush with the law."

Efforts by the defense to impeach Cline's credibility were objected to by the prosecution, and the objections were sustained by the Court. Robinson had uncovered some allegedly questionable conduct on Cline's part that involved a young lady. He sought to explore the area directly. He asked Cline if he knew the woman. Cline hesitated, looked directly at Schaub for help, and then answered, "Yes." Cline stared at Schaub, and Schaub, realizing at last that something was amiss, asked, "What was the question?" Robinson repeated the question to Schaub and pointed out that when the question was asked, Cline "looked directly at you." Schaub responded with an objection.

MR. SCHAUB: Objection, first to the acting we are getting and ask that the jury be instructed to disregard it, and also we would like to object to the question. It has nothing to do with anything brought out on the direct examination of this witness.

Robinson replied that insofar as the record thus far had disclosed the facts, the woman in question "could be any person from the hospital." Schaub responded, "She is not. I know what he is referring to. It is completely improper."

Robinson tried again. This time he asked Cline about a joint press conference regarding the case, called by Cline and Judge Hayes.

Q. I believe you and the Judge had a press conference in this case, didn't you?

MR. SCHAUB: Objection, improper cross-examination. Nothing brought out on direct.

THE COURT: Which judge are you talking about?

MR. ROBINSON: I am talking about Judge Hayes.

MR. SCHAUB: Objection, nothing to do with anything brought out on direct.

THE COURT: Sustain the objection.

As Cline left the witness stand, the Court announced a recess. An investigator for the State's Attorney's office, James Foy, was the first witness after the afternoon recess. He said that he had arrived at the Arcadia hospital at "approximately two-thirty in the afternoon." This was the first indication that the State's Attorney was involved in the investigation just hours after the poisoning. Foy testified that he had spoken with Richardson at the hospital that afternoon.

Q. Did he say who he lived with?
A. With his wife, Annie Mae Richardson.
Q. Did he say they lived with any children there?
A. Yes.
Q. What children?
A. There were seven of them. I would have to refer to my notes if I may. Susie Bryant, Betty Bryant, Alice Richardson, Diane Richardson, Vanessa Richardson, Doreen Richardson, and James Richardson.
Q. Did he say who the parents of the five children were?
A. Yes, he did.
Q. Who did he say the father of those children were?
A. Leonard Bryant.

Q. Did he say where the children had been that day?
A. Yes, he did.
Q. Where did he say?
A. He said the three older ones had been at school and the other ones had been at home.
Q. Did he say if he had made any arrangements with the children that were at home?
A. Yes, he did.
Q. What did he say?
A. The girl next door was to baby-sit that day.
Q. Did he say what her name was?
A. Excuse me just a moment, Dorothy Bracey.

Foy then said that he had questioned Richardson two days later in the office of John Treadwell and that Richardson made the same answers then to similar questions.

On cross-examination Robinson established Miss Bracey's identity.

Q. Did Mr. Richardson say who his regular baby-sitter was? Did he ever tell you that? You mentioned Dorothy Bracey sat for him on the 25th?
A. My recollection was that she was his regular baby-sitter.
Q. Wasn't she the daughter of Bessie Reese King?

Foy appeared to give the very definite impression that the children were not cared for while at home on October 25.

Q. Did she baby-sit on the date of the 25th is what I want to know.
A. He said she was supposed to baby-sit for him that day.
Q. Do you know who did baby-sit?
A. I don't believe anyone did.
Q. Didn't her mother take over, Bessie Reese King? Didn't Dorothy have a doctor's appointment in Sarasota?

A. I understand that she went to Sarasota on that date.
Q. But you don't know who actually baby-sat, if anyone?
A. I don't believe anyone did.
Q. You don't know, though?
A. Well, it is my understanding that no one did.
Q. Why do you understand that to be the way it was?
A. I couldn't find anyone that did.

Robinson knew that Mrs. Reese had been with the children during the day and had participated in at least some aspect of preparing the poisoned food for them. He knew that Foy, who had just stated that he had looked into that area, was also familiar with some of the relevant circumstances.

Q. And in your investigation, didn't it show that Bessie Reese King was there next door and had actually cut the portions of food for the children?

MR. SCHAUB: I don't know what this has to do with the direct examination of this witness.
THE COURT: Overruled.
WITNESS: Yes, she was supposed to have gone over there and cut the grits. As far as saying she baby-sat all day, she did not.

It seems more than a trifle disconcerting that the State's investigator could speak at some length, both on direct examination and while being questioned by defense counsel, about who cared for the poisoned children on the day that they were poisoned, and never reveal, until asked directly by counsel for the defense, that he knew that Mrs. Reese had helped to portion out the food for the children. And it is more than alarming that Schaub, the State's Attorney, deliberately sought to suppress that information with an objection as to relevancy.

On both direct and cross-examination Cline had testified that he was certain that he was with James Foy on his most important third visit to the Richardson apartment and that Foy was with him when he took various pots and pans, later found to contain parathion, from the premises. Foy testified, however, that Cline was wrong.

Q. Sheriff Cline says that you and he went to the James Richardson house between four and four-thirty. Is this true or false?

A. On the 25th?

Q. On the 25th.

A. I would say that he was in error on that particular occasion, because we went over with Chief Barnard on the 25th. We didn't go to the house, and he may be thinking of another time.

Q. So he might be in error on that particular time?

A. Yes, I did go to the house with him, but not that particular time.

Q. On another day?

A. Yes.

Q. It wasn't on the 25th?

A. I didn't go with Sheriff Cline on the 25th.

Q. You didn't get the pots and pans out with Sheriff Cline on the 25th between four and four-thirty? You already answered you didn't.

A. Not from the house. I took some from Sheriff Cline from the jail.

Q. But that was at his office, is that correct?

A. That is correct.

Q. They weren't taken out of the house in Sheriff Cline's presence, and you and Sheriff Cline carried them out of the building, did you, Jim?

A.   No, sir.

Audrey Chedick testified that she had received some "exhibits" from Mr. Foy which she turned over to Dr. White. Carl Adams testified that he is a deputy sheriff and that he picked up some exhibits from Dr. White and delivered them to the Pesticide Laboratory. Emory Wutrich, the County Sanitation Director, said that he had posted a "condemned sign on the apartment" that the Richardsons had resided in, after the children had been poisoned. None of these three witnesses had relevant testimony to offer; the first two could not aid in the establishment of a chain of possession, since they apparently were unable to identify the exhibits they had handled, and while one may approve of the prompt action of the Sanitation Director, it had little to do with the issue before the jury—what had transpired at the apartment before the children were poisoned. As the courtroom day was drawing to an end, it became clear that the prosecution's plethora of inconsequential witnesses could only succeed in confusing the basic issues, and perhaps the jury as well.

Schaub called David Stebbins, who testified that he was employed by Sorrell Brothers and that on October 25 he saw James Richardson working in the Ryles County Line Grove, located some sixteen miles from Arcadia.

On cross-examination Stebbins said that he was the foreman of the crew that picks fruit and that both Mr. and Mrs. Richardson were in the grove with him when they were notified that there had been "an accident in their home." The notification reached them between twelve-thirty and one o'clock, Stebbins said.

The last witness called that day was Eugene Hudson, one of the owners of the Ryles grove. On direct he said that parathion had not been used in the grove. In an aside to the jury, Schaub, in the guise of engaging in colloquy with counsel, said, "He knows the grove doesn't use parathion.

Therefore, there would be no reason for this man (indicating Richardson) to have parathion." Whitson requested that the Court instruct the jury to disregard Schaub's remark. The Court said, "The last statement made by the State's Attorney is not evidence, and the jury will disregard that." Yet the jurors had heard Schaub. The court recessed for the day.

The long and tedious day was over. The jurors had heard twenty-three witnesses testify. Yet not one witness had even begun to relate the murder to James Joseph Richardson. Nevertheless, the prosecutors had scored two most telling points. Before the trial had begun, the jurors no doubt had been under the impression that Richardson had solicited insurance upon the lives of his children the very night before they were poisoned. References by Cline to the "insurance policies" in all probability gave further credence to the newspaper reports. Thus, while no evidence against the defendant had been adduced at the first day of the trial, the question of motive had been indirectly alluded to and perhaps even satisfied in the minds of some of the jurors, and the cause of death, "premeditated murder," had been presented to the jury in the official death certificates. No damaging admissible evidence had been offered, but telling points had been compiled by an overly zealous prosecution unchecked by lax judicial conduct.

THE SECOND DAY

If the defense had been under the illusion that the jury might somehow be prevented from discovering that parathion, not just some organic phosphate, was the cause of death, the testimony of Dr. John Edward Davis, Director of Community Pesticide Studies for the State Board of Health, shattered that hope. Dr. Davis had published several works on parathion poisoning and investigated, he testified, some twenty-five poisonings each year, seventy-five percent of them being parathion poisonings. The doctor said that the poison was "developed during the Second World War by the Germans, initially as a war gas. It was never used, and its potential as an insecticide was realized and developed closely after the end of the Second World War." When absorbed through the skin, inhaled, or ingested, the parathion, he said, "produces inhibition of an enzyme called cholinesterase. The result of that is to produce symptoms of sweating, convulsions, weakness, nausea, usually vomiting, diarrhea, passing on from convulsion to coma and death."

When asked to define cholinesterase he responded:

A. Cholinesterase is an enzyme in all tissues of the body whose function is to break up a chemical which is liberated at the muscle junction called acetylcholine.

So any of the organic phosphates combined with the cholinesters can leave acetylcholine unbroken down and producing all the effects. All of the effects are due to the acetylcholine.

Q. Does it cause pain in the victim?

A. The contractions of the small bowel would give violent cramps. The pain would come from abdominal cramps.

Schaub asked Dr. Davis how rapidly a lethal dose might cause a young child to die. While the question was poorly put, as the hypothetical query left undelineated far too many improbables—the amount of the poison; the age, height, and weight of the child; and the route of entry of the poison—it appeared that an answer could be helpful to the defendant only if the effect of the poison was rapid. The Richardsons were in the fields, some sixteen miles from the children, when the lethal meal was served. Yet Whitson objected, explaining, "It seems too great for this man's specialty." Robinson was immediately on his feet in an effort to mitigate the damage done by the objection. "It would be dependent on the health of the child, the size of the child—we have no objection to this line of questioning if properly asked."

The Court suggested that Schaub "might be more specific," and he was, although Dr. Davis' answer was not.

Q. On children of an age between two and eight years old, does it have a rapid or slow effect?

A. Parathion is more toxic to the child than it is to an adult; and the rapidity with which the symptoms come on does depend on the dosage, route of entry, and the physical weight of the patient.

The epidemiologist then described some of the standard tests to determine the presence of parathion.

A. The chemical can be detected by various analyses of tissues or excreta of the body.

Q. What type of tests are these?

A. There is a chromatography test for—first of all, parathion breaks down into paranitrophenol. We may use P & P for short. P & P is the breakdown of parathion, theoretically. The breakdown could be the breakdown of four other phosphates. First of all, we measure for P & P. This is called the Elliott method. This is conclusive evidence of one of the four.

Q. Is this what we call a—

A. Alveolar test. That stops with parathion and converts it to paranitrophenol. There is so much paranitrophenol around, there is no need to convert to paranitrophenol, because it is there. You measure it direct by the Elliott method.

There is another way for measuring for pure parathion, and that is by gas chromatography. It utilizes a microcoulometer as a detector, a sensitive chemical tool when handled properly. It is an electrical charge producing a deflection of it on the recorder. The conditions are so set that with the packing of columns that this is specific. The specificity is developed by good chemists by the utilization of one or two columns.

Q. What are the columns?

A. Columns are U-shaped instruments in the detector through which the gas is passed, and it is packed with mesh, and you can get different forms of packing, each of which gives you a different retention time. If you get another column and another column, this is proof of the nature of the chemical, especially if you use a completely different detector.

Q. What reaction are you looking for applying the gas chromatography?

A. Well, it presents itself as a depiction in point of time after the ingestion of the material.

The small-town, almost rural jurors probably were long lost by this time, but they were no doubt at least equally impressed as well.

Dr. Davis said that his staff "had a box of materials of various organs" taken from the bodies of the children. The organs had been delivered by Dr. Maceo, Dr. White, and Mr. Wilkey, he said. "We had blood from some and stomach contents from others. What we did on the first day, we had a conglomeration of tissues from several of the children, and first we ran bloods for cholinesterase testing. We found those runs showed marked inhibition, proving there was organic poisoning. Secondly, we ran tests on the gastric contents for those we had."

The tests were conducted by three members of his staff, Joseph Freal, Anna Barquat, and Mildred Parker. The staff also tested various pots and pans, lids, and other kitchen utensils, Dr. Davis testified, using the same procedures that had been utilized in testing the organs. In addition, infra-spectophotometry, an electric method that is of value only when used upon large quantities of pure material, was employed with reference to the powder.

Schaub was then ready to establish that parathion had caused the death of the children.

Q. Do you have any opinion whether or not parathion poison was present in the bodies of these seven children?
A. In my opinion, parathion was present.

Schaub then sought to establish that more parathion had been used than was really needed.

Q. As to these doses that you determined or the amounts that you determined in these bodies, how did this compare with the amounts of parathion you had found in many other cases you are acquainted with where it was determined that it was a cause of death?
A. Values in all these children were some of the highest we have encountered.
Q. Was it a massive dose?
A. It was a lot of parathion.
Q. What significance, if any, do you attach to the fact that out of the seven children from the same household, each received such large doses?
A. Yes.
Q. Why is that?
A. Because of all the people that risk death or die, which means, as a rule, ingestion of a large amount of material.

   If I may digress for a moment to give an analogy from an accidental epidemic such as Tijuana. There they had a number of deaths and 300 nonfatals. Here we have all seven die.

Again the prosecution tried to show the rapidity with which the poison operates. "Based upon the findings that were made at your lab and under your direction, assuming that children of the age that these children were showed symptoms consistent with parathion poisoning about eleven forty-five A.M. on a certain morning, could this have resulted in an oral ingestion of this parathion much earlier than eleven A.M. that same morning?"

And again Whitson objected to the question. "Object to the question, improper predicate. It doesn't have the proper dedication from this witness. He is calling for an absolute conclusion without laying sufficient facts from which this witness can draw such a conclusion.

"He hasn't asked whether this position is from a reasonable medical specialty. He is asking for speculative opinion that this witness is not capable of answering."

Schaub explained what it was he was after. "Whether it could have been obtained earlier. I am trying to get the rapidity."

The Court overruled the objection, and Dr. Davis responded, "The magnitude of the amount found in Betty Bryant, coupled with the knowledge that we obtained that they were all in perfect health at the school, almost certainly suggests that the poison was ingested after leaving school going home to lunch."

The beginning of the defendant's alibi had been established by a prosecution witness, despite the objections of defense counsel.

As to the cause of death, the doctor could not have been more specific.

A. This evidence of large amounts of parathion in the stomach, together with the presence of metabolite in other areas of the tissue, together with the clinical history that we received, are classic of organic poisoning and in my mind leave no doubt that the cause of death was parathion poisoning.

Q. Can you state with reasonable medical probability the cause of the death of Betty Jean Bryant?

A. Parathion poisoning.

Q. Do you have a medical opinion as to the route of entry of this parathion poisoning?

A. The route, in my opinion, was predominantly gastric. I have no other way of telling that.

Q. How would it have gotten there?

A. Be eaten, ingested.

On direct examination Schaub tried to have the doctor state that the large amount of parathion present in the organs was an indication that premeditation, not accident, was the proximate cause. Since the doctor was understandably reluctant to join Dr. Schmierer as a criminologist and the presiding judge realized that Schaub was flirting with cause for a mistrial, the prosecution's aspirations were frustrated. Whitson was more successful in securing favorable information about parathion vis-à-vis death, in general, during his cross-examination of Dr. Schmierer.

A. Adult poisons have all the characteristics of accident— industrial poisoning and so forth; whereas the children are accidental or ingested. The entry of nearly all is ingested.

Q. Nearly always accident?

A. In the majority of them it would be accident.

Q. Have you had any that weren't accidental, forgetting this case?

A. No, forgetting this case, we have not encountered children poisonings of pesticides that were not anything but accident.

But more favorable though it was, it was still far removed from the issues before the court.

Whitson asked Dr. Davis to estimate the amount of parathion that the children had ingested. The doctor said that it was not possible to answer that question, since he had data only in regard to two organs. On redirect Schaub had Dr. Davis tell the jury that the parathion had traveled to other parts of the body as well and that some of it might have dissipated in urine. On cross-examination Robinson was able to establish that a very small quantity of parathion, considerably less than a teaspoon, was sufficient to constitute a lethal dose.

The prosecution had evidently sought to show that a large quantity of the poison had been placed in the food, thereby hoping to have provided assurance that no accident was involved in the children's deaths. Robinson's examination of the witness, however, appeared to rebut the premise.

Two members of the staff referred to by Dr. Davis testified next. Joseph Freal said that the laboratory had received stomach contents, body tissues, and clotted blood to analyze as well as some pots, lids, dishes, and a frying pan. On direct examination he told the prosecutor that parathion had been detected on the eight-inch pot and lid. The defense objected to the State's offer of the pot, lid, frying pan, and spoon into evidence. The objection was overruled.

On cross-examination Robinson demonstrated interest in the analysis of the contents of the frying pan.

Q. How much of what you just testified to did you find in that frying pan?

A. In the frying pan I did two tests: No. 1 test, I took a piece of meat and I found a trace by the chemical technique I just told you about. The other portion of the pan, I took out. You can see a section of the combination of fat and meat. I thought it wouldn't be representative if

I just took meat. I took meat and fat. I analyzed half a gram. In that I found approximately two-tenths of a microgram.

Q. Did you determine what had been in that skillet?

A. It looked to me like some meat and some sort of grease.

The children had not been fed from the frying pan. James and Annie Mae Richardson had secured their lunch from the frying pan. Robinson and Freal had planted a seed that might take root in the mind of an alert juror. If the pots and pans on the stove had been poisoned by the defendant in the morning, before Mrs. Richardson made sandwiches for her husband and herself as the State contended, why were the parents not poisoned as well? Or, to approach the matter from another view, had someone poisoned all of the food on the stove after the sandwiches had been prepared and after the Richardsons had left the apartment?

Miss Barquat said that she had examined portions of the liver and kidneys of Betty Bryant and determined the presence of parathion. On cross-examination she told Robinson that parathion has a "strong" and "very peculiar" smell.

Dr. White returned to state that in his opinion, "all of these children died of parathion poisoning, and the route was by ingestion."

Schaub stated to the Court that he hoped and expected to complete the State's case that day. There was time for just one more witness to testify before the noon recess. Schaub's estimate regarding the time that it would take to complete his case was almost precise; he required but five minutes for a rather inconsequential witness the next morning. The State had presented most of its witnesses; twenty-six persons had already testified. Yet not one of them had even begun to relate the crime to the defendant. Nevertheless, if the defense sighed with relief at that moment, it was premature. Before the day was over the prosecution would present the testimony of three men who had allegedly shared a cell with Richardson in the jail maintained by Cline. Each would be heard to say that Richardson had made very damaging admissions.

James Cunningham was the first to offer testimony regarding Richardson's alleged admissions. In response to questions by Hill, he said that he lived in Arcadia, was married, and had two children. The fact that the witness was married was not material to the issues before the Court, except as it might characterize Cunningham as a settled and mature citizen. The prosecutor, having established previously that the witness was married, dwelt for a while upon those circumstances.

Q. Do you have any children?
A. Right.
Q. How many?
A. Two.
Q. How long have you been married?
A. Eighteen years.
Q. To the same woman?
A. Yes.
Q. How old are the children?
A. One 15 and one 16.

Cunningham's status may have slipped a bit in the view of the jury when he was required to state that he had met the defendant in the De Soto County jail. The witness was there, he said, for thirty days for being "drunk." He said that he could not remember the day that he saw the defendant but that he was certain that he did see him when he was arrested. Cunningham stated that he occupied the lower bunk in the cell and that Richardson had been assigned the upper bunk. He said that he had had "a good many" conversations with Richardson, so many in fact that "I can't count all of them."

Hill then asked the witness about the incarceration of Mrs. Richardson.

Q. Do you know if the defendant's wife was in jail also?
A. Yes, sir, she was up over us.
Q. She was staying above you?
A. Above us.
Q. That would be in a different cell on another floor?
A. Another floor.
Q. Would that be directly above where you and Richardson were?
A. That is right.

Then Hill moved directly to the matter at hand.

Q. While you were in jail, did you ever have any conversation with this defendant, Richardson, relative to how his children died?
A. He said—this is what he told me—he said, "They are going to kill me." I said, "Kill you for what?" He said, "I killed my children."
Q. He said, "They are going to kill me"?
A. He said, "They are going to kill me." I said, "For what?" He said, "I killed my children."
Q. Did he say anything else at this time?
A. He said, "I didn't cook, though." I said, "Who cooked, though?" He said, "My wife cooked."
Q. What did he say about cooking?
A. He said, "I didn't cook." I asked him who cooked.
Q. What did he say?
A. He said, "My wife cooked."
Q. Do you remember whether his wife entered into this conversation, or do you recall?
A. She wasn't in it.

Cunningham said that another prisoner, Ernell Washington, had a conversation with the defendant in his presence.

Q. Did you hear conversation between Ernell Washington and the defendant?
A. Yes, sir.
Q. Will you tell us what was said?
A. Ernell asked him, "James, you can tell us. Did you kill them? You can tell us."
Q. What did the defendant say?
A. He said, "Yes."
Q. Now, who was there when Ernell asked him that, if you recall?
A. I think Blue was there, I know.
Q. Do you know his last name, this man you referred to as Blue?
A. No.
Q. Do you know who else was there?
A. I don't know all the fellows' names who was in jail at the time.

Cunningham said that he had also overheard remarks made by Mrs. Richardson to her husband, although how such testimony could be considered admissible in any American court is beyond comprehension.

Q. You say the defendant's wife was just above you?
A. Yes, sir.
Q. Later on again, while you were in jail, did you hear any conversation between the defendant and his wife?
A. Yes, sir.
Q. Will you tell us what was said?
A. She hollered downstairs once and said, "Why did you kill my children?"

Q. That was Annie Mae?
A. Yes.
Q. She said, "Why did you kill my children?"
A. That is right.
Q. What did he say?
A. He didn't say nothing.
Q. What was he doing?
A. He just looked up.
Q. Where was he at?
A. In the cell.
Q. Standing, sitting, or what, do you recall?
A. He was sitting, I think, on his bed.
Q. You say he just looked. Where did he look?
A. Up.
Q. He didn't answer?
A. No, sir.
Q. Do you remember what her actions were at this time, whether she was happy or sad?
A. She was happy.
Q. Did he appear to be?
A. He was sad.
Q. Again, did you hear after this, after this conversation between the defendant and his wife—did you hear any other conversation between the defendant and his wife?
A. Yes, sir.
Q. What did that consist of?
A. She told him to pray and read the Bible.
Q. She told him this?
A. Yes.
Q. What did he say?
A. He said okay, he was going to pray.
Q. All right, now, do you recall any other conversations between the defendant and his wife relative to the death of the children?
A. No, sir.

In this exchange related by the witness, the defendant is not alleged to have made any admissions. His wife was not charged as a co-conspirator in the crime; therefore, any statements that she, or anyone else, might have made about a belief in the guilt of the defendant would be without relevance and clearly beyond the boundaries of the rules of evidence. Since the statements were allegedly made by the defendant's wife, the prejudice that they might have caused is difficult to calculate with any degree of precision, but in all probability considerable harm was done.

Cunningham also said that Richardson had "said he started telling his wife when he got to the orange grove that he had a feeling that something was going to happen. He started to tell her."

Q. Did he say whether he did tell her or not?
A. He didn't say he told her or not. He didn't say.

On cross-examination Robinson discovered that one of Cline's deputies had been driving Cunningham and James Weaver (another prisoner, who was soon to testify about Richardson's alleged admissions) from Arcadia to the courthouse each morning and back to Arcadia each night. Intrigued by that development, Robinson probed further.

Q. Are they going to take you back today when you get through?
A. I guess so.
Q. And bring you back again tomorrow?
A. I don't know.
Q. Do they come by your house and pick you up in the morning? Did the Sheriff come by this morning?
A. Picked me up this morning.
Q. At home?
A. At the jail.

Q. You met him at the jail?
A. I was in jail last night. They kept me there last night to come over here.
Q. Where did you stay the night before last?
A. I stayed in Arcadia. I have forgotten the name of the street.
Q. Did you stay at home?
A. I mean—it was a room.
Q. Who lives there?
A. I forgot the lady's name, but I stayed there—another boy has a room, and I stayed there.
Q. You rented the room?
A. He rents the room.
Q. You stayed with him?
A. That is right.
Q. Where is your wife?
A. In North Carolina.
Q. I was under the impression that you and your wife and family were living in Arcadia.
A. My wife is living in North Carolina.

When Robinson asked the witness when he last saw his wife, the State objected. Robinson commented that "the impression was cast that he had a family," to which Hill replied, "He said he was married." Both sides were correct, of course. The prosecution had presented Cunningham as a family man, and the disturbing thought that the facts had been artfully elicited by the State's attorney was hardly overcome by Hill's precise response. Robinson pursued the matter.

Q. When was the last time you saw your wife? Has it been a year or two or six months?
A. It has been over six months.
Q. A year?
A. Over a year.

Q. More than two years?
A. Yeah.
Q. Three years?
A. About ten years.

On re-cross-examination Cunningham told Richardson that he had been in jail for fifteen days recently and added that he had just been released from jail the day that the trial started. Robinson inquired why the witness was back in jail again.

Q. And then you went back to jail last night?
A. That is right.
Q. Now you making another 15 days, or did they just let you stay there?
A. They picked me up last night.
Q. What for?
A. It wasn't nothing I done.
Q. They just said they wanted to look after you?
A. They wanted me to come over here today.
Q. So they gave you a place to stay at the jail?
A. Didn't give me a place to stay, just locked me up until today.
Q. Didn't charge you with anything?
A. No.
Q. Did you complain about being put in jail and you weren't charged?
A. I told them, "I ain't going anywhere, why do you lock me up?" He said, "We are locking you up for the night."
Q. You mean the Sheriff locked you up last night and didn't charge you with anything?
A. The Sheriff didn't lock me up, another man.
Q. The Deputy Sheriff; is that right?
A. The deputies, that is right.
Q. Do you realize you could sue that sheriff for false imprisonment?

MR. HILL: Objection, there were only two questions on redirect.

THE COURT: Sustained. We will recess until one-thirty.

During the afternoon session Robinson concentrated upon the jailhouse scene at the time that the defendant allegedly made the admissions referred to by the witness. He asked if there were a number of other prisoners about when the statements were made. Cunningham agreed that others were present. He asked if the others could have heard the admissions. Cunningham agreed that that was likely. The witness could not recall who was present in the jail at the time, however. "I don't know everybody's name that was in the jail when I was in there," Cunningham replied when asked to give the names of those he remembered as being present when the admissions were made. The defense lawyer asked Cunningham how long he had known Richardson before he made the admissions to him. Cunningham answered, "About an hour, I guess." When Robinson ridiculed the assertion that his client had bared his soul to a man he had not known, the witness reacted by saying, "He said it loud enough for everyone to hear it." He added, "He wasn't telling me personally." As the lawyer probed more deeply into the circumstances of the alleged conversation, the witness agreed that Richardson had never talked to him about the case. "I overheard it," he said. He explained why he listened, "The reason I listened to him talk, because they said they were going to kill him, so I stood up to him."

Q.   Yes, did you ever ask him any questions about it, or did you just overhear him talking to other people.

A.   I ain't never asked him.

Q.   You ain't never asked him nothing, did you, yes or no?

A.   You said I asked him.

Q.   Did you ever ask him anything about it, or did you just overhear him telling others about this?

A.   I never asked him.

Q.   You never asked him nothing, did you? That is just what you told me. You said, "I never asked him." Did you ask him or didn't you, yes or no?

A.   I didn't ask him.

On direct examination Cunningham had remembered the short conversation quite differently. He had told Hill, an hour before, that he had asked Richardson why they were going to kill him. He had also told Hill that he had asked the defendant who cooked the food. When reminded by Robinson of his earlier testimony, Cunningham reverted to it. However, when Robinson asked him to state the admissions exactly as he heard them, Cunningham paused, thought, and gave his best recollection. "He said, 'They are going to kill me.' I said, 'For what?' He said, 'For killing my children.'"

They are going to kill me "for killing my children" is a statement that is inconsistent with a belief that one will be vindicated in a court of law but is not clearly inconsistent with the belief that one is innocent. In fact, it is something less than an admission. If Richardson said anything, did he say that, or was the jury to believe Cunningham's direct testimony—"He said 'I killed my children'"?

Robinson asked when Cunningham first revealed his damaging assertions to the police. Cunningham could not recall but thought that he had told a Negro officer known as Bad Boy about the alleged admissions sometime in November. To whom was Richardson referring, Robinson asked, when he said "they are going to kill me"? The witness answered, "I don't know who he was talking about, the Sheriff or what or the State." The defense lawyer asked the witness if he had ever seen him talking to Ernell Washington.

Q. Did you ever see me talk to Ernell during my visits?
A. One time.
Q. You saw me and Ernell talking?
A. Yes, sir.
Q. If Ernell said I never talked to him, would he be telling the truth or lying?

Mr. Hill: Objection.
The Court: Sustain the objection.

Why was the witness testifying, he was asked. "He, the Sheriff, said they wanted me to come over here, so I had to come."

Ernell Washington had allegedly heard the defendant make admissions. He had testified at a preliminary hearing which took place some two months before the trial, but in the interim he had been shot to death in a barroom. Although this was a capital case and the protection of the rights of the accused and of all of the evidence was of importance, no record had been made of Washington's testimony. Schaub explained to me, when I asked him about that apparent dereliction, that preliminary hearings generally tend to assist the defendant and that he, therefore, did not want anything at that hearing to be perpetuated by an official record. Clearly if a court reporter had been present the introduction of a certified copy of the transcript would have been proper. Since that was no longer possible, it seemed that the prosecution had lost one of its witnesses through death, not an uncommon experience for either the defense or the prosecution in any case which encompasses the passage of time. For in most states where the rules of evidence prevail, the death of a witness, in the absence of an accurate transcript, ends the matter. One of the strangest exceptions to the hearsay rule, an odd procedure that evidently still remains viable in some Florida courts, was utilized by the prosecution to selectively perpetuate a portion of the preliminary hearing. Five witnesses were called by the State to tell the jury what they remembered about Washington's assertions. From all accounts, Washington was a brute. Not long before his death he had been charged with assault with intent to commit murder. Prisoners in Cline's jail agreed that Washington, a huge and powerful man, terrorized the other inmates. His presence on the witness stand might have been somewhat embarrassing for the prosecution, but his death spared the prosecution the necessity of presenting him. Instead the State was able to place five respected citizens on the witness stand to relate portions of Washington's earlier assertions. They were respectable, but not all were free from prejudice.

The first witness was Assistant State's Attorney Treadwell, who said that he heard Washington testify on March 25, 1968.

Q.   Please tell us what he had to say in his testimony that day?

MR. ROBINSON: At this time the defense will enter an objection based upon the fact that this is hearsay evidence and inadmissible.
THE COURT: Overruled.

The hearsay rule having been thus disposed of with one word, the prosecution was invited to continue.

Treadwell said that he recalled that Washington said that Richardson told him that Mrs. Richardson's first husband told the defendant that he, the first husband, wanted "to take his children back to Jacksonville with him." Treadwell then related what he remembered of the Washington testimony. "Ernell also testified and questioned him as to how he—did he kill the kids, and he said yes, that the defendant said he had. He asked how he did it, and he said Annie Mae, the wife, was cooking grits that morning before they went to work at approximately seven o'clock that morning and that he put the poison—that was the exact words that Ernell used—that he put the poison in the grits while they were cooking. Upon further questioning of Ernell, it was tried to determine as to the type of poison that the defendant has used. Did he make any admission to the type of poison? Ernell said that he did not, that he did not know the type of poison; that it was merely poison, and that he, Richardson, had admitted that he put it in the grits while Annie Mae was cooking the grits."

Treadwell recalled that Washington had also placed Lee McDonald and a man identified only as McQueen at some of the conversations. Then Treadwell said for the third time in his very brief appearance, "Ernell testified that Richardson told him that he had taken poison and put it in the grits that were cooked that morning, that Annie Mae had cooked that morning."

Treadwell's testimony was concluded a moment later.

Q. Do you recall anything else that Ernell testified to at that preliminary hearing?
A. No, sir.
Q. Where is Ernell Washington at this time?
A. Ernell Washington is deceased.

On cross-examination Treadwell said that he had "a real good memory." Treadwell had not made any reference to the fact that Robinson had cross-examined Washington in his presence.

Q. Do you recall the cross-examination?
A. I recall the cross-examination.
Q. Tell the jury.
A. As I recall, you tried to cross up Ernell. You got him pretty rattled, as I remember, all to no effect that I could see.

Other prosecution witnesses were to confirm the fact that Washington had on cross-examination vehemently denied ever talking to Robinson and specifically denied ever signing a statement for Robinson. In fact, Washington had told Robinson that if he ever said that such a statement had been signed by Washington, it was clear that Robinson would be a liar. For many in the courtroom that was strong talk by a black man, charged with assault with intent to commit murder, to address to a distinguished white lawyer in south-central Florida.

For many in the courtroom it was an unforgettable moment. The next moment was equally striking, for when Robinson showed the signed statement to Washington, the witness admitted that he had signed it and that he had in fact talked to Robinson.

Yet Treadwell remembered the cross-examination as having been ineffectual. Robinson pursued the subject.

Q. Let's talk about that a minute. Do you recall when I asked Ernell Washington if he had ever seen me before?
A. No, I don't recall.
Q. You don't remember that? You do recall this other stuff, but you don't remember me saying, "Do you remember seeing me before, Ernell?"
A. I am testifying from what I recall.
Q. Let's get that testimony. Do you recall me asking Ernell Washington if he ever talked to me?
A. No.

Q. You don't remember that either?

A. I don't recall it.

Q. Do you recall me asking Ernell Washington if he signed a statement for me under oath?

A. I do.

Q. What did he say?

A. At first he denied it.

Q. He denied it pretty strongly, didn't he?

A. Yes.

Q. In fact, he said if I said he signed the statement, I was a liar?

A. I don't remember it.

Q. He called me a liar?

A. I recall it.

Q. What did he do when I gave him the statement?

A. He read it.

Q. And then what did he say?

A. I don't recall.

Q. You recall me asking Ernell Washington if he ever signed this statement, which stated in essence that Bessie Reese and Charlie Smith had been seen together in a local bar —do you remember me asking him that?

A. No.

Q. Do you recall that I went right down this affidavit in almost reading it into the record, had there been a record, trying to refresh his signature at the bottom?

A. I remember you showing it to him.

Q. Do you remember ever seeing this before?

A. No.

Q. So you recall quite a bit of what he said on direct examination?

A. Just from my own recollection.

Q. But you don't recall too much what was said on cross?

A. Naturally, as an assistant state's attorney, my primary

responsibility is to pay more attention to the direct, because it is my case.

If the Florida Legislature should consider eliminating the anachronistic statute which permits this exception to the hearsay rule and encourages clearly tainted testimony, it would do well to examine the testimony of the Assistant State's Attorney, who may have helped his case along but who did little to assist the cause of justice.

The next witness provided even a better, that is, a more extreme, example of blindness induced by prejudice.

Thelma Ted Bryant identified herself as a "news correspondent" for the Fort Myers *News Press* and the Tampa *Tribune*. She later admitted that she was just a stringer for the two newspapers and she never did tell the jury that she had been a reporter for *The Arcadian*. Miss Bryant and that newspaper played an important role in developing such community hostility toward the defendant that Judge Justice felt constrained to rule that he could not fairly be tried in Arcadia. The most relevant example of *The Arcadian*'s objectivity, not to say its perception and accuracy, was its coverage of the death of Ernell Washington. Not much than a month before Miss Bryant testified for the prosecution about the testimony of the deceased, the weekly publication featured a front-page, major-headline story—"State's Case Hurt Badly by Slaying of Key Witness in Richardson Case"—lamenting the harm done to the State's case by Washington's death. The first mention of the defense attorney in the news article, written by the paper's editor and publisher, referred to "publicity-conscious John Robinson of Daytona Beach." The Washington testimony, said the newspaper, "had been the most damaging yet brought to light against Richardson." But, wept the editor-publisher, "now the voice of Washington has been stilled." Not precisely. It had been amplified more than five times over.

The newspaper was more than a little suspicious about who would want the star witness for the State done in. The article stated that the woman who killed Washington "was not a native" of Arcadia, a crime to be equated with murder in any event, and that "according to one report garnered by *The Arcadian*, she may have arrived here not more than a week or two before the shooting." It was at this point in the story that the editor pointed out that Washington had just testified "less than three weeks before his death," "coincidentally" just before the out-of-town hired gun presumably rode into town packing a .22-caliber handgun in search of the star witness. *The Arcadian*, sniffing about for a conspiracy, perhaps related to the defense, added, "The case has its mystifying aspects, since no close relationship between the dead man and the Cosey woman could be immediately established." The newspaper quoted Cline as saying, "We are looking into it further." As to the prosecutors, the newspaper reported that their "chins were down here over the slaying of a key state witness in Arcadia."

When it finally became clear, even to *The Arcadian* personnel, that the death of Washington was a windfall for the State's case, the mystifying aspects of the case were evidently sufficiently clarified for them; no further reference to the possible conspiracy to murder Washington was made.

Under questioning by Schaub, Miss Bryant said that she remembered "Ernell saying that he had had several conversations with Richardson, the defendant, in the course of their being locked in the same cellblock; that Richardson had said that he wanted to get up from under it all. That was in reference to his wife's former husband. I guess you call it husband." She continued, "There had been a discussion by Ernell of Annie Mae's former husband. I guess it is husband, I don't know—the Bryant children's father, and that he had either come or was going to come to Arcadia to visit the children; and under protest, Ernell said that Richardson said he wanted to get out from under it all. This was prior to the death of the children. He said not only one but several conversations he had had with Richardson in the cellblock; and at that time the defense counsel and he were having a hassle over some testimony; and I think they ended up by calling each other liars. The acoustics were rather bad."

The acoustics, evidently adequate during Washington's direct examination, presumably worsened on cross-examination. The reporter had been sitting in the jury box and said that she had been covering the proceedings. She did manage to hear the deceased state that "Richardson had said that he had killed the children, in effect." Some peculiarly southern mannerisms generally associated with the turn of the century were evolving in Miss Bryant's testimony. All Negroes were referred to by the first name only, except the bad nigger, who was just plain "Richardson," and colored folks may have children, therefore, we may speak of father, mother, and child with certainty, but when it comes to legal, not biological relationships, the best we can do is "guess you call it husband."

Her direct testimony concluded with one more answer.

Q. Do you remember anything else that Ernell testified to?
A. No, I can't recall.

Whitson asked the witness if she recalled that Washington had first denied ever having seen Robinson before. She answered, "He denied it at first." When asked what Washington's response was to Robinson's question, "Mr. Washington, if I said that I had seen you and I secured a statement from you and you signed it, would I be lying or telling the truth?" Miss Bryant agreed that Washington denied signing any statement for Robinson.

Q. Then do you recall Mr. Robinson came back over to him and handed him this statement and saying, "Ernell

Washington, is that your signature," and what did Ernell say?

A. He laughed and said, "I reckon it is."

Richard Oppel, an Associated Press reporter, was the next witness called by the State to present the testimony of Ernell Washington. He said that the only quotations attributed to Washington in the A.P. story that he had filed that day were, "This is a direct quote of Ernell's: 'He said he had a problem and wanted to get rid of it. He said he did it. He was aggravated. He said he had a problem and wanted to get rid of it.' These were the only quotes I used in the story."

When questioned by Whitson about the cross-examination to which Washington had been subjected by Robinson, the witness recalled quite clearly that Washington had first denied that he had ever signed a document for Robinson or had ever seen the defense lawyer before. Whitson asked the witness if he recalled Robinson having asked Washington, "Weren't you allowed out of jail as a result of coming up here to testify?" He answered, "Yes, I do. I believe there was—Mr. Robinson asked Washington if he received some kind of gratis from Sheriff Cline in trade for his testimony on behalf of the State."

Whitson then tried to question Oppel about a hearing at which Sheriff Frank Cline appeared as a witness for Washington so that Washington, charged with assault with intent to commit murder, might be given a suspended sentence. Schaub was on his feet before Whitson could go beyond reference to a "hearing [that] was held in Arcadia, Florida." "Objection, nothing to do with the cross-examination of this witness as to what he heard that day, and this is certainly no way of just testing his recollection—to talk about something else that is not before the court."

The Court sustained the objection and it appeared that the jury might never learn of Cline's kindness toward the convicted felon. However, Robinson had asked Washington about the alleged deal, and Oppel recalled the exchange. The reporter testified, "I think Mr. Robinson asked Washington if Sheriff Cline did not testify at his own court hearing, I believe it was, on a charge of aggravated assault or assault with intent to commit murder—if the Sheriff did not testify for him to get the charge reduced perhaps or get the sentence suspended. I can't remember exactly what the situation was there. I believe Washington acknowledged that Sheriff Cline did testify in his behalf but—denied that this was a result of any deal made between the parties."

Two more witnesses testified for the State about what they remembered Washington's having said. Each testified for approximately two minutes; each remembered only Washington had said that Richardson had said that he put poison in the food. Neither could recall what was said by the deceased on cross-examination. Neither was questioned by the defense.

Schaub presented and questioned Dorothy Lee Bracey. It remains unclear why. She was on the witness stand for less than one minute. She said that the Richardsons had said to her, "Keep an eye on the children," but that she informed them that she "had to go to Sarasota." The conversation took place, she testified, several hours before the children were poisoned.

When questioned by Robinson she said that her mother was Bessie Reese. Since the witness had planned to be out of town that day, her mother agreed to watch the Richardson children, "She [her mother] say she will keep an eye out for them." Yet the State's investigator, Foy, had testified that his investigation revealed that no one was in charge of the children that day. Foy flatly stated that "as far as saying she [Mrs. Reese] baby-sat all day, she did not." Foy never did share with the court and jury the basis for his conclusion. It appeared more essential than ever that Bessie Reese be called by the State to resolve, if possible, this possible conflict.

The next witness was Mary Frances Rector, the court re-

porter who had transcribed the testimony of Judge Gordon
Hayes on March 25. She identified State's Exhibit twenty-six
as the document which she had transcribed and certified.
Schaub indicated that he would read the Hayes testimony to
the jury at a later point in the trial.

James Weaver was the last of the three ex-convicts to refer
to Richardson's alleged jailhouse admissions. He too lived in
Arcadia. He had originally been jailed for petty larceny. The
essence of his direct testimony came in the form of four
answers to four questions.

Q. Did he ever make any statement to you relative to the
death of the children?
A. Once he did.
Q. Do you know when this was?
A. I don't recall.
Q. Was anyone else present with you and Richardson that
you remember?
A. I can't actually say.
Q. What did he say?
A. He just said, "I killed my children." That is all he said.

Although there was testimony that Washington had said
that Weaver had overheard Richardson's alleged admissions
to him as to how the defendant had committed the crime,
Weaver indicated that that was untrue.

Q. Did you have any subsequent conversations with him
relating to the death of the children?
A. No.
Q. Did he say he had killed them?
A. No, he didn't.
Q. Did he say how he had killed them, by what manner or
means?
A. No.

Although Cunningham had indicated that Weaver had overheard Mrs. Richardson's conversation with her husband, Weaver said that that was also untrue.

Q. Did you ever hear any conversation between the defendant and his wife relative to the death of the children?
A. No, I didn't.

With Weaver fast becoming less than a solid corroborative witness, the prosecutor decided to ask no more questions. Weaver, who had been referred to by the prosecuting staff as one of the State's most important witnesses, had been on the stand a scant five minutes.

Nowhere in the court record was there a more classic example of southern informality and almost charm than in Robinson's cross-examination of this important hostile witness.

Q. Mr. Weaver, nice to see you again.
A. Nice to see you again.
Q. What is your occupation?
A. Laborer.
Q. Have you changed occupations since the last hearing?
A. I have.
Q. What were you then?
A. I am a working man.
Q. What were you at the last time we had a talk?
A. I told you I gamble.
Q. Where do you gamble?
A. Everywhere.
Q. Specifically, where were you gambling at the time of the last hearing?
A. In Polk County.
Q. I believe you testified you were running a gambling house?
A. Right.

Q. What type of gambling?
A. Cards and dice.

According to a number of observers, Weaver had made a startling disclosure at the preliminary hearing. He had told Robinson that only one person knew that he was running the gambling house. When Robinson asked who the person was, Weaver retorted, "Sheriff Cline." Since that time Weaver had been jailed in Cline's jail as a material witness. At the trial Weaver said that he didn't remember making the statement that only one person knew that he was running a gambling parlor. He also denied having said that Cline was that person.

Weaver said that he had roomed with Richardson from the time of Richardson's arrest. He said that he had occupied the bottom bunk.

Q. You were on the bottom bunk. James Cunningham said he had the top bunk, so where did Richardson sleep?
A. I don't know about Cunningham when he was in the cell with Richardson. The only thing I can say is when I was in the cell with him.
Q. Cunningham said he moved in with him.
A. I don't have nothing to do with that.
Q. Mr. Cunningham this morning pointed out this was his cell along with Richardson when he moved. Did you make a mistake?
A. No I couldn't make no mistake.
Q. But you were the one that roomed with Richardson from the time he walked in there right on that second floor? That is what you said.
A. I say that again.

Weaver could not remember anyone else who had been in

the jail when Richardson arrived. On one occasion he said that he was present when Richardson was brought in. A moment later he said that he was out working when Richardson arrived. Within seconds he reverted to his original story that he was present when Richardson made his first appearance at the jail. He could not recall who was present then or at any subsequent occasion.

A. The onlyest that I can recall definitely is me. The other guys I don't know who. I don't even know the guys that come in, to be frank.
Q. Was there just the two of you?
A. Listen, attorney, the only thing I can verify is myself. The guys come in and out of the jail. I don't keep up on who comes and who goes out of jail.

Later he did recall one person who was present when Richardson was brought to the jail, Lee Andrew McDonald.

If Weaver failed to offer corroboration to Washington and Cunningham on peripheral questions, he was a disaster from the prosecution view on the basic issue. Unlike Cunningham, who had Richardson confessing to all who would listen upon his arrival in the first hour of his confinement, Weaver said that Richardson had made no reference to that subject at first.

Q. He didn't say anything that day about killing the children?
A. No, he didn't say anything about it.
Q. Didn't mention it?
A. No talk immediately when he come in the jail. He don't do anything about him.

Robinson asked the witness how long Richardson had been confined before he made his original confession. Weaver replied, "I couldn't say it was a week or two weeks or three weeks.

I can't say because I wasn't keeping time." Robinson sought
to secure a more definite answer, but the witness insisted that
he could not be more precise. If Weaver meant by his answer that Richardson did not make his admissions until at
least a week after he arrived, then the accuracy of Cunningham's tale was in question. As was the case with the only
other witness to appear at the trial who linked Richardson
in any way to the crime, Weaver came to court fresh from
Cline's jail. He too had been driven to court by a deputy
sheriff.

Q. Where have you been staying the last few days?
A. In Arcadia.
Q. Where in Arcadia?
A. I have been locked up.
Q. Why have you been locked up?
A. I don't know.
Q. Were you charged with anything?
A. No.
Q. You don't have charges pending against you at the pres-
   ent time?
A. Sure don't.
Q. You like to be locked up?
A. No, but what am I going to do with it?

Weaver showed signs of a recent assault. Robinson had been
informed that he had been beaten in the jail in Arcadia by a
deputy.

Q. Do you recall being beaten the other night, Thursday
   night, in Arcadia?
A. I wasn't beaten.
Q. By one of the deputies there? Do you deny that?
A. No deputy beat me. They had no reason.
Q. You are going to deny it at this time?

A. Yes, I am going to deny it.

Q. If somebody saw it happen, could you say they were not telling the truth?

A. Why would I be beat Thursday night?

Q. In the Arcadia jail.

A. No, I got cut. I flew town.

Q. What happened on that? You got cut up over there pretty bad a few nights ago?

A. I ain't been to a doctor or hospital.

Q. Where were you at the time?

A. Arcadia.

Q. Where?

A. Where I live.

Q. Did the Sheriff ask you how you got cut up?

> MR. HILL: Objection, completely immaterial.
> THE COURT: Sustained.

Weaver's denial and the restrictive ruling by the Court (lawyers are generally given very wide latitude when engaged in cross-examination) effectively prevented any further exploration of the subject.

In answer to specific questions, the witness said he had been convicted of felonies three times. The defense lawyer then turned to a question raised by Cunningham.

Q. While you were up in jail, did you ever hear Annie Mae yell down and say, "James, why did you kill the children?"

A. No, I have never heard them talking anything about that.

Q. Never heard anything about it?

A. I have never heard them talking anything about that.

Schaub was anxious to inform the jury that Weaver was not

presently confined as a defendant in a criminal case. Accordingly, the Judge read an order that had been directed to the Sheriff. "You are directed to take James Weaver, a material witness, to be held in custody until such time as he has posted bond in the amount of $1,000 with the Sheriff of De Soto County, conditioned upon the said James Weaver testifying at the trial May 27, Fort Myers, Florida, or at such later time as the cause may be held. Signed this 26th day of May."

Schaub took his seat, apparently satisfied once the jury had been informed that the witness had been jailed by the State "conditioned" upon his testifying for the State.

Richard Nellius, a reporter for the St. Petersburg *Times*, testified that he had interviewed the defendant the day after the children had died. He said he had asked Richardson if he had sufficient funds to bury the children. He said that Richardson replied that "he thought he had." "I asked the circumstances. He said that he had had $500 in insurance on each of the seven children, but the policies had lapsed, and then he told me that the insurance man came around and spoke to him about renewing them."

On direct examination Schaub refrained from asking the witness if Richardson told him that he had paid the premium. The jury was told only that the defendant "applied for insurance the night before. I think he said Tuesday night, which was the night before the children had died."

On cross-examination the reporter said, "I asked him if he had paid it. He said at the time he hadn't." Nellius also said that he thought that the insurance man said that "he would carry him for a couple of days." No effort to clarify that assertion was made by either side. Robinson assumed that the matter would be resolved through the testimony of the insurance salesman, Purvis.

The next witness to testify was a De Soto County deputy sheriff, Bill Trawick. He said that he opened refrigerators at the Richardson apartment on October 26, the day after the children were poisoned. He said the jail records revealed that Richardson was arrested on October 31, 1967, and released on November 30, 1967.

Mrs. Richardson was jailed for the same period of time, he testified. Weaver was committed on October 23, 1967, and released on December 14, 1967. Cunningham was committed on October 28, 1967, and released on November 13, 1967, and again committed on November 18, 1967, and released on December 14, 1967. Washington was arrested on November 4, 1967, and released on March 7, 1968. Robinson moved directly into the question of Washington's release.

Q. Do your records also indicate on the release of Ernell Washington—what do your records show, if you will pull them back out?
A. We only have the release date on this.
Q. It doesn't show why he was released?
A. I didn't bring the records showing why he was released. I only show the time that he was in jail and what time he was released.

Robert Jones testified that he accompanied Trawick, removed some articles from the refrigerator, and delivered them to Robert Adams. Schaub failed again to ask a chain-of-possession witness to identify the items that he removed and delivered.

Robert Adams stated that he was employed as a chemist with the Florida Department of Agriculture. He said that he tested various items that had been delivered to him. He found parathion, he said, in self-rising flour that had been in a two-pound bag, in a jar containing used lard, in a metal can of talcum powder, in cornmeal that was in a plastic bag, in meal that had been in a two-pound bag, in Nestlé's Quik, in baking powder, in lima beans, in salt, in rice, in soap powder, on a blue sweater, on a windbreaker, on a brown glove, on a white glove, on a pink washrag, and on a hard hat.

It was late afternoon. Schaub had but one more witness to call, but before presenting him he decided to read the transcript of the testimony given by Judge Hayes on March 25. Standing in front of the jury, transcript in hand, Schaub began to read. Hayes had identified himself as the county judge of De Soto County and also as the coroner of De Soto County. He said that he had been summoned to the hospital and that by the time he arrived two of the children were already dead, the others were dying. Hayes testified, "The nurses were a little upset about the great expense that was going to be had in handling these children. They asked about the insurance angle. Most of the colored people carry hospitalization."

According to Hayes, Richardson had said that he had insurance and that it was "double indemnity." He said that he went to the Richardson apartment that afternoon. He could not remember the address, so he described the location. "It is located there down here about two blocks right west of the Negro school."

A decade after the Supreme Court decision a county judge still spoke of reality in Arcadia—the Negro school. Hayes answered in the affirmative when asked if he "observed any unusual odors" when he entered the apartment. He said that Richardson had made no admissions to him regarding the crime and that when asked about parathion, Richardson said that he did not know what it was.

Robinson's questioning was related almost exclusively to the law.

Q. Judge Hayes, just a couple of questions, please. Did you at any time issue a search warrant in this cause to search the premises of Mr. Richardson's home?

A. Yes, sir.

Q. You did issue a search warrant?

A. Yes, sir.

Q. What was the date of issuance of the search warrant?

A. I don't remember, it was about a couple of months ago.

Q. It was after the pots and pans and other things were taken from the house; is that true?

A. After some of the pots and pans were taken.

Q. Let me ask you, isn't it customary as county judge when an incident arises where you want to go into a house for a specific reason—isn't it customary you yourself issue a search warrant?

A. I wasn't looking for anything in particular. I was trying to find out. I was trying to find out for the doctors if and what kind of poison the children got into.

Q. Answer the question.

A. I don't know, no, sir.

Q. Anytime an officer goes into a home in De Soto County, you don't issue a search warrant prior to the time you go into the home?

A. If he wants to make a search, yes, sir.

Q. The question I asked you, isn't it customary for you as county judge to normally issue a warrant when someone wants to go into someone's premises?

A. I went in myself. The door was wide open.

Q. Answer my question yes or no.

A. Yes, that is the practice, if you are searching for something.

Q. That is the law?

A. Sure, that is the law. I don't argue with that.

Q. But it wasn't done in this case, was it?

A. Not at the present time. We weren't searching for anything.

Q. It wasn't done that day or the next, was it?

A. No, sir.

Sheriff Frank Cline posing with his award from *Official Detective Magazine*—at the courthouse in Arcadia.

Frank Schaub, the prosecuting
attorney, at his office in Bradenton,
Florida.

Bessie Reese—in Nocatee, Florida
—a silent witness.

Mark Lane questions
Charlie Smith in Arcadia.

John Robinson talks with James
Richardson on death row, Raiford,
Florida.

Lane and Robinson confer in Daytona Beach, Florida.

White Arcadia—a home in the white community.

Black Arcadia—a shack in the black community.

The sign on the wall of the café in the Trailways bus terminal, the closest thing to a public café in town.

The sand graves of the seven children in the segregated cemetery. The white cemetery, for what it is worth to the departed, is lushly landscaped with palms and cypress trees.

Mark Lane standing between the shack where the poison was found (in the foreground) and the Richardsons' house (in the background).

Q. As a matter of fact, it wasn't done until a period of more than a week had expired; isn't that true?
A. I believe that is true.

After the jury was excused by the judge, Whitson argued at some length for the exclusion of all of the testimony regarding the witness Ernell Washington. The judge listened to both sides politely and then ruled. "I will have to deny your motion. I don't feel, as a matter of law, that their testimony presented is incompetent. I think that is a question for the jury to determine."

THE LAST DAY

The next morning James Griffin appeared for the prosecution. He said that he was employed by the Pesticides Regulation Division of the United States Department of Agriculture and that he had visited the Richardson apartment. He took various items from the kitchen and delivered them, he said, to Robert Jones. The defense lawyers had no questions for the witness.

With a stunning suddenness Schaub stated, "The State rests."

The State had failed to call the three essential witnesses upon whom it was presumed the case would be based. The case described by Schaub in his opening statement appeared to require the testimony of Bessie Reese, Charlie Smith, and Gerald Purvis. Their names appeared among the first twenty witnesses to be called when the State was required to list its witnesses under the Florida rules for procedure. Yet the State had called twice that many witnesses in a massive show trial, never once offering evidence of the mysterious appearance of the bag of parathion, never calling the person who helped to serve the poisoned food to the children while the defendant was miles from the scene, and never presenting to the jury the insurance salesman who was to have provided the only possible motive for the defendant's alleged actions.

Whitson rose and addressed a motion to the Court. "May it please the Court, at this time the defense moves for a directed verdict of acquittal and as grounds for such motion shows unto the Court that there has been no evidence whatsoever showing that these children actually ate any of the items in which parathion allegedly was found—no evidence whatsoever, circumstantial or otherwise, actually linking James Richardson with any parathion at any time. In fact, the contrary is found in Judge Hayes's testimony, in which it is stated that Richardson didn't even know what parathion was and had no knowledge of any of this.

"It has been conclusive from the State's case that Mr. Richardson left home fifteen minutes to seven; that the children ingested—if they ingested poison—was around eleven-thirty. Mr. Richardson was called from the groves at twelve-thirty. It has been shown by the State's case, the circumstantial case which they attempted to build, in no way points to the guilt of this defendant."

The Court: "It will be denied."

The defense called Carl Weston as its first witness. He was an investigator for the Florida Parole Commission and stated that he was based in Arcadia. In the regular course of his employment he had been called upon to supervise and participate in presentence investigations after persons had pleaded guilty in Arcadia. Weston testified that he was familiar with the charge against Ernell Washington and of the disposition of the case.

Robinson and Whitson had evaluated the evidence that had been offered against Richardson and had concluded that only the testimony of the three ex-convicts regarding the alleged jailhouse admissions was of any relevance. The first witness was called in an effort to place the testimony of Washington in a context, before it had become set in the minds of the jurors.

Weston recalled that Washington had been charged with "assault with intent to murder," a crime less serious than murder, but less serious than no other crime.

Q. Please tell, if you will, what was the final determination of the sentence of Ernell Washington?
A. He was placed on probation by the court for aggravated assault.
Q. Was this on March 7, 1968?
A. Yes.
Q. Do you recall any particular person who spoke in his behalf?
A. The Sheriff spoke in his behalf in open court.
Q. Sheriff who?
A. Sheriff Cline.
Q. Of De Soto County?
A. Yes, sir.

The penalty for assault with intent to murder in Florida is several years' imprisonment. Yet Washington walked out of the courtroom a free man.

According to Weston, Cline had vouched for Washington's character to the extent of stating that he "didn't have a serious criminal record."

Schaub only made matters worse for the prosecution when he questioned the witness. He evidently sought to show that Cline's testimony in his appearance for Washington was accurate, even if it was not possible to demonstrate that the appearance was proper or above suspicion.

Q. Had he had any prior felony convictions before this charge?

A. Let me put it this way, I don't believe I had any prior felony convictions and was in the process of finding out more—no local prior felony convictions—and we were in the process of finding out whether he had a record in South Carolina, but he was killed during the period of investigation.

Washington had been arrested on November 4, 1967. In March, 1968, it was decided that he be released. Cline arranged for the release within twenty-four hours. Washington then testified against Richardson that month. The forces of Justice in Arcadia were so pressed to release Washington during March, 1968, that the Florida Parole Commission was unable to act quickly enough to find out what Washington's criminal record was. He was nevertheless released, in the absence of such a report. He was only twenty-three years old when he was killed and had been in Arcadia for a short period of time. The fact that he had "no local felony convictions" (the definite impression being left that he had been convicted of one or more misdemeanors while in Florida) hardly can be sufficient for a reasonable man to conclude that he was a man of good character or even that he had not previously been convicted of a felony elsewhere.

Washington had lived in Arcadia less than ten months at the time of his death; four months of that time he was in jail. In jail he assaulted and abused numerous prisoners. All that the Florida Parole Commission was able to determine before Washington was rushed out of jail was that he had not been convicted of a felony for the six months that he resided in Arcadia and out of jail. There was not time for the report to encompass any of his activities for the previous twenty-two years. Parole officers generally require approximately three weeks to conduct an investigation; often an extra week or two is required for an out-of-state check. Washington had been in

jail since November. If Cline sought to reward him for cooperation with law enforcement by testifying against Richardson,
why was the probation department not notified in November
when the authorities were allegedly informed of Washington's
effort to assist the prosecution? Weston's testimony made it
appear possible that the jailhouse admissions were conjured
up in March, 1968, not made in October, 1967. For in March
the prosecution was called upon to present its evidence at the
crucial preliminary hearing. Without the alleged admissions,
it had none.

The next witness was Richard Whitson. He testified that he
resided in Daytona Beach and that he was an attorney-at-law.
At that point Schaub states, "If it please the Court, it is
rather unusual. Mr. Whitson has been participating in this
trial."

Immediately the Judge responded, "We are going to take
a few minutes' recess. Again, do not discuss the case or form
any opinion as to the guilt or innocence of the defendant."

Whitson had planned to testify regarding his conversation
with Ernell Washington. After the preliminary hearing, Whitson and Robinson spoke with Washington. Washington told
them that Richardson had never made any admissions to
him, that he had never said that he poisoned the children,
and that he personally had "nothing against James." Washington said, "Look, you know how long they can send me
away for this charge. I don't want to spend my life in jail, so
I got to do what they tell me. If you can get me out of this
assault case, I'll say anything you want. I'll tell the truth about
James and how he didn't say anything except that he was
innocent and that he loved the kids. I don't want to hurt him.
But with this case against me, I got to think of myself.
Anyway, they won't find him guilty, so I'm not doing him no
harm." When the Court was made aware of Whitson's proposed testimony, he warned him that he might very well be

disciplined for testifying in a case where he was appearing as counsel. Whitson was being advised that he faced possible suspension of his license or even disbarment for testifying about his interview with Washington. Robinson argued that the matter was entirely discretionary with the Court. He said to Judge Justice, "If you rule that Mr. Whitson's testimony is relevant and important, and so advise him, he can testify without any fear of action being taken against him. It's really up to you." The Judge responded, "I am advising him, very strongly, not to testify. I want to assure you that if it is suggested that the transcript be sent to a disciplinary board, I will not object." With the threat of disciplinary action, which might result in the denial of his right to practice law, Whitson decided to withdraw as a witness. At that time both defense lawyers were confident that Richardson would be acquitted in any event.

Had Washington lived and testified at the trial, he would have been confronted with the statements that he had made to Whitson after the preliminary hearing.

It might be noted here that John Treadwell, III, appeared with Schaub and Hill as one of the three prosecuting attorneys for the State. He sat at the prosecution table throughout the trial and participated with his two colleagues. Treadwell was also the only witness in the case to testify three times, once exclusively about Ernell Washington. He was not admonished by the Court not to testify. No proceedings were instituted against him for having testified.

Annie Mae Richardson testified on behalf of her husband. Her attorney might have addressed those in the audience in Antony's words—"If you have tears, prepare to shed them now." As this simple, attractive black woman described her relationship with James Richardson, sobs were heard from various sections of the courtroom. Quietly, and with a dignity and a directness that had not previously been present that week, Mrs. Richardson told of her life with her children and her husband.

Their life's routine was set. She and her husband arose before dawn, walked through the streets of Arcadia to a corner where they waited for a farm-labor truck to take them and at least twenty others to the fields. Together they harvested fruit, ate lunch in the fields under the orange trees, resumed work, and were driven by truck back to Arcadia. They were paid by the bushel of fruit, and so they worked as quickly as they could. Once home, James rushed to the children, played with them, ran outdoors with them, and sang with them. At night she read *True* magazine, and then her Bible. James, almost illiterate, watched television. Robinson asked about the relationship between the children and their father.

A. The relationship between all the children—he was a father to all of them. He loved every last one of them and treated all of them equal right. He didn't have no pick among all them.

We had talked it over and started putting up the children's clothes and toys because we had so many that we couldn't buy. We had to put up things in lay-a-way until we get them out.

Q. What event was this for?

A. For the Christmas things.

Q. What had you and James decided to purchase for those seven children for Christmas?

A. Betty Jean wanted a colored doll that walked, and a wheel. Susie said she wanted a tea set. She wanted one of those—you know, another doll. Doreen, she always say all of them wanted the same thing because we dressed all of them the same for all, all except the boy. We were going to get the boy a little tricycle and get him one of those wagons to be pulled in it.

Q. What kind of doll was that that you were going to get Doreen?

A. Betty Jean wanted one of the big old dolls where you pull a string and it talks.

Q. What type of doll?

A. It was colored. She is about this big.

Q. A colored doll?

A. Yes.

Q. What was the reason for that?

A. Well, she had seen the children next door had one, so she wanted one.

Q. How much time, approximately, in the evenings after work or on holidays when you had one—how much time did James spend with those children?

A. He devoted all his time with the children when he was home and we got off of work. He would sit up and play with them and sometimes go outdoors and run around and all like that.

Q. During this period of time can you state at this time whether or not you feel as a mother and as a wife that your husband loved those children?

A. Yes, he loved those children.

Q. Why do you say that?

A. Because he done everything in the world that any poor man could do for his family, and he was a man to them.

Robinson asked the witness about the allegation that she had accused her husband of killing the children when they both were confined to the Arcadia jail.

Q. Do you recall when Sheriff Cline put you and James in jail?

A. Yes.

Q. Where were you in relation to James in jail?

A.   I was on the third floor upstairs.

Q.   Where was James?

A.   He was on the second floor down.

Q.   Did you ever accuse your husband of killing the children?

A.   No, sir.

Q.   Why?

A.   Well, the reason why I have never accused him is because I know for myself that he done everything that he
could possibly do for the children.

Q.   Did you ever yell down in the De Soto jail and say,
"Why did you kill my children?"

A.   No, I did not.

Q.   If someone said you yelled down "Why did you kill my
children?" would that be a truth or falsehood?

A.   That would be false.

Mrs. Richardson said that she had talked to her husband
while they were in jail.

Q.   As a matter of fact, did you ever talk to your husband
down through the jail?

A.   Yes.

Q.   What did you talk about?

A.   How we missed one another and how we wanted to be
free and things like that.

Q.   Do you love your husband?

A.   Yes, sir, I do.

Q.   Do you think your husband loves you?

A.   He should have if he don't.

Robinson knew that the jurors had been informed that
Richardson was suspected of having killed three other children
or possibly even five, depending upon the edition of the newspaper or if the source for the article had been Cline, Schaub,
or Hayes.

Q. By the way, there has been a lot of talk about other children in the past that died under mysterious circumstances. Could you shed a little light on that, please? Do
you know anything about how many children there may
have been?

A. I had one child that was stillborn.

Schaub objected to the vagueness, and the witness was again
asked the question.

A. Well, it never did live, you know, in the world, so they
called it stillborn. It was born dead.

Q. Where was your husband at the time the child was born?

A. He was at work during the time. Then they called him
from the job and he come out to the hospital.

Q. Did your husband visit you during the time you were in
the hospital?

A. Yes, every day.

In an effort to resolve the question that had been repeatedly
raised in the press, through the concerted efforts of the prosecution, Robinson asked:

Q. Now, were there any other children that James Richardson had, perhaps by someone else, not yourself, that you
know of personally that died?

A. I know personally was two.

Q. Would you tell the jury what you know about those two
children dying?

MR. SCHAUB: Objection unless we find out she was
present and has the information.

Schaub did not object to the first question and answer, but
once the jury had been informed that two other children

had died, he was more than anxious to choke off further testimony, to prevent clarification of the issue. The Court sustained the objection. Schaub, quite cleverly, had prevailed.

Mrs. Richardson described her actions on the morning of October 25 with some degree of precision.

A. That morning on the 25th I got up that morning around five o'clock and I cooked breakfast. I cooked a pot of grits and then I went into the refrigerator and got out some beans and cooked them together. I took the rice from out of a rice box and put it into the beans. Then I washed out the pot and put on the grits. Then I went back into the refrigerator and got one-third of the chicken. By the time I got through cooking, it was around six-thirty.

I went in the bedroom and woke up my husband, and then he got up and went into the restroom. Then he got ready to go to work.

We be together at all times. We never separated. I did get him up. We got out there on the field. We had to wait until the trees get dry.

Q. You said you got up that morning and you fixed breakfast?

A. Yes.

Q. And I think you said you also fried chicken?

A. Yes, I did.

Q. What did you fry that chicken in?

A. In some leftover grease.

Q. Describe the grease.

A. The grease was some I had cooked other meat in before, but I used the other grease to cook it in it.

Q. What had you used the grease for before?

A. Hamburger, chicken, and pork chops.

Q. So this would be used grease that you are talking about?

A. Yes.

Q. Did you cook the chicken for your children, or what was the purpose of frying the chicken?

A. I fried the chicken for me and my husband to carry to work that morning. We carry our lunch every morning.

Q. What did you take to lunch on this day?

A. Fried chicken and a pack of corn cheese and two boxes of brown cookies. I think they call them Jack cookies. We stopped to the store and got them.

Q. Did you in fact make a sandwich with the chicken?

A. Yes.

Q. How many sandwiches did you make?

A. Four.

Q. Who was to eat these sandwiches?

A. Me and my husband.

Q. I hand you what purports to be a skillet and ask you if you have ever seen this before?

A. Yes, I have.

Q. Have you ever used this skillet before?

A. Yes.

Q. When was the last time you used this skillet?

A. That Wednesday morning.

Q. What for?

A. To fry chicken in.

Q. You fried chicken in this skillet?

A. Yes, I did.

Q. After you and your husband ate that chicken sandwich that you have testified to that you fixed that morning, or the sandwiches, did you receive any ill effects or did your husband have any physical illness?

A. No.

Q. I would like to direct you back again to the morning you fixed breakfast. What did you cook?

A. I cooked a pot of grits.

Q. Let's stop right there. What kind of container were they in?

A. It was a box of Jim Dandy Grits.

Q. How many times have you eaten those grits before out of that box?

A. It was a new box.

Q. Those grits were in a new box?

A. Yes, they was.

Q. When did you first open that box of grits?

A. That morning.

Q. What time?

A. About five or five-fifteen, because I woke up at five and started cooking.

Q. Let me ask you this question: After you opened this box of grits, did your husband leave you at any time?

A. No, because he was asleep.

Q. All right, after he got up out of bed, how much time expired before you and your husband went to work?

A. I woke him up at six-thirty and we had to leave there at quarter to seven. He didn't have none.

Q. You have testified that your husband was in bed during the time that you fixed the grits; is that correct?

A. That is right.

Q. How much time approximately expired from the time that he got out of bed and the two of you left to catch the work truck?

A. He didn't have because he wasn't in the kitchen at all that morning.

Mrs. Richardson stated that the night before the children died, an unsolicited insurance salesman "came to the door and knocked." He talked to her husband for some time, but the family had no money for the payment of the premium.

Mrs. Richardson said that she signed for the insurance for

herself, her husband, their seven children, and three others "down in Jacksonville." She said no money was paid to the salesman. Mrs. Richardson was not interested in the policy, she said. When asked if the salesman talked to her about the insurance, she said:

A. No, because I wasn't interested, because I know we couldn't afford it.
Q. Did he interest your husband in the insurance, in discussing the insurance program?
A. I wouldn't know.
Q. As a matter of fact, did you have any funds with which to buy any insurance on this particular evening?
A. No, none whatsoever.

She also testified that Bessie Reese was present during the discussion about the insurance. "She left three minutes after the insurance man left."

Schaub appeared unmoved, perhaps even slightly irritated, by Mrs. Richardson's testimony. In a workmanlike approach, he attempted to pick the essential aspects of it apart, section by section.

He began with what was clearly her most important contribution to the defense—the statement that the defendant did not have access to the food from the time that it was prepared, until the time that it was consumed. The most telling blow for the prosecution had been struck by the words of Ernell Washington quoting Richardson as having admitted that he placed the poison in the grits while they were cooking. Mrs. Richardson's testimony appeared to preclude the possibility that her husband was able to accomplish that. Schaub never did raise that subject while cross-questioning the defendant's wife. He concentrated instead upon the other food, which had been prepared the night before.

Q. Actually, you fixed this food the night before, didn't you, the food that the children were to eat? You prepared it the night before, didn't you?

A. Yes, the beans and rice.

Schaub tried to show that Mrs. Richardson had been sleeping while her husband poisoned the food, but she insisted that she had been awake the entire time.

Q. You didn't know what time he went to bed?

A. Yes, I do.

Q. How did you know what time he went to bed?

A. Because I was woke.

Q. How were you woke?

A. Because I know I was woke until he came in the bed.

Schaub insisted that the witness had been sleeping when her husband passed from the living room, where he had been watching television, to the kitchen, where he poisoned the food. The witness insisted that she was aware of her husband's movements at all times until they went to sleep together early that morning. Schaub was confident that he could prove that Mrs. Richardson had earlier admitted that she slept while her husband was awake. He had been informed that there was a tape-recorder interview of Mrs. Richardson conducted by an investigator from his own office. The witness remained adamant. She was asked, for example, if she had previously said that she "never woke up when he [her husband] got in bed." She replied that she had not made that statement. Schaub appeared confident that he could destroy the credibility of the witness by playing the much-heralded tape recording during the rebuttal. Schaub continued for some time in that vein. He compared statements allegedly taken from the recording with the more recent statements made by Mrs. Richardson during the trial. In most instances, and in all essential instances, Mrs.

Richardson denied making the earlier statements. Schaub then moved into the arrangements that had been made for the children's supervision that day.

Q. Where did you leave the children's food when you went to work that day?
A. Like I first say, on the stove.
Q. And you knew that day that Dorothy Bracey was going to Sarasota, didn't you?
A. No, I did not.
Q. You did not know that that morning?
A. No, her mother was supposed to have gone to Sarasota.
Q. I didn't ask you that. Did you know Dorothy Bracey went to Sarasota?

When the witness answered the last question, Schaub responded angrily, his voice almost quivering when he scolded, "I didn't ask you that." For the first time the jury learned that Bessie Reese decided at the last minute not to go into Sarasota, her daughter was to be sent instead, while the mother remained home, in the apartment next to the Richardsons' apartment.

Schaub retaliated with questions about Mrs. Richardson's previous husband, Leonard Bryant. She admitted that she was legally married to him, stated that she had not seen him in a long time and that she later married James Richardson, whom she loved and who loved her, and who cared for and supported all of the children. "How can I get a divorce [from Bryant] when I don't know where he is at?"

The prosecutor questioned her about a complaint that she had made some years before when she had been separated from Richardson. He supported the children, she said, but at that time he was not providing enough money for her to spend.

The next area explored by Schaub related to the accessibility of the contents of the two refrigerators. One functioned; the other did not and was used as a cupboard. Both had locks. There was some confusion about how many sets of keys were made, for how many locks, but through it all Mrs. Richardson insisted that one set of keys was always maintained, "on the Frigidaire in the house." This arrangement made the contents of the both refrigerators available to any adult charged with the responsibility for caring for or feeding the children.

When Mrs. Richardson was excused that morning, many observers agreed that she had been a most impressive witness. Most also agreed that if the tape recording to be played for the jury when the prosecution had its say again proved that she was wrong in any of several essential areas, her credibility would be severely diminished or perhaps destroyed.

Six of the next seven persons to testify were character witnesses. The public generally regards such witnesses as less than an integral part of the case, more in the fashion of nonessential appendages, whose role can hardly be decisive. The public's impression of what takes place in a courtroom is often fixed by close study of Perry Mason television programs and other similarly inauthentic reproductions presented to America in the cinema or at home. It would hardly serve the purpose of a dramatic writer to permit the fictional jury to carefully evaluate the exceedingly nonspectacular testimony of a character witness and decide that the defendant's past was so out of keeping with the current actions charged against him that it was unlikely that he would have attempted the crime. Yet, in the real world, in most jurisdictions, the judge is obligated to charge the jury that a single character witness, if believed, may create sufficient doubt in the minds of the jurors to constrain the jurors to return a verdict of not guilty. And that, of course, is as it should be, particularly in a case based primarily upon circumstantial evidence. To relate this abstract concept to the instant case—if it can be demonstrated that Richardson loved his family, that his children were most of the world to him, one would be hard-pressed to understand why he might kill them. Translate "hard-pressed" into a legal equation, and one may have—"reasonable doubt." One may have, as well, an acquittal.

Paul Howard, who had known the defendant more than fourteen years, was the first character witness to testify. He said that he had visited the Richardsons at home quite often. Although Howard was on the stand less than five minutes, Schaub interrupted his direct testimony on seven different occasions. In most cases the court overruled Schaub's efforts to prevent the jury from hearing the witness, and Howard was permitted to tell what he knew about the family.

A. Mr. Richardson was concerned about his children and family, very much. He devoted his time trying to keep working to keep the children and pretty well taken care of; and this is the truth, and he has done all he could, I mean from the time almost every week.

Q. How were the children dressed during your visit to the home?

A. Well, the children were dressed fair. Quite naturally, sometimes you work and the children couldn't get the best things in life, but he did the very best he could.

Q. How did James and his wife, based upon your observation, get along?

A. They seemed to get along. As a matter of fact, I was jealous they got along so good.

Q. Is there anything to lead you to believe that James did not love his wife?

A. I never seen no evidence of that.

Q. Is there anything to lead you to believe that he loved his wife?

A. I did.

Q. Is there anything to lead you to believe that his wife loved James?

A. I am quite sure of that.

Q. Is there anything to lead you to believe that James and his wife loved those children?

A. I am sure of that from the evidence I always seen.

Bernice Hartley testified next. She said that she had known the parents "ever since 1950." As to the children:

A. I probably took care of them and raised them cooking and feeding them.

Q. Did you have an opportunity to visit with them in their home?

A. Well, I slept in the house mostly every night and they slept in mine. We were just like family.

James and Annie and me worked together, always did. They were working for Ralph Butt at the garbage truck. James was driving one of the big trucks, and he had to leave at six o'clock every morning to drive the big trucks. Annie Mae had to get out and pick old papers and stuff out of the old trash and stuff. She had to leave at six, and I stayed right there with them children. I cooked and fed them.

Q. Why did Annie Mae pick up garbage?

A. That was her job. He had women doing this. They pick the old pasteboard. I got six children, and I wouldn't do it. She worked hard, and I do know that, and I was there.

Q. After James got off work at night and his wife got off work, did you see them?

A. I was there, I did the cooking.

Q. How did James treat the children?

A. The children met him at the fence. They run like rats running to meet their daddy. They would be on his legs and shoulders dragging him in the house.

He would be tired. He come in, take a bath, sit down, and look at TV. Then I fixed a hot meal. We eat. Then, he had his car. Sometimes he would get in the car and ride around.

Q. Did he like to take his children?

A. Yes, we all packed in there like sardines.

Q. What was the relationship between James and his wife?

A. Got along fine.

Q. Do you think James and his wife got along?

A. Yes, they never did no fussing or raising sand.

Q. Do you think Annie Mae loved James?

A. Sure, she loved him. Those two loved each other. They never had no fussing, cussing, or raising sand. I would be right there with them.

Q. Tell the court, if you will, did James ever buy anything for his children?

A. We would go to the store and buy stacks of potato chips and then we get grapefruit juices and icy in the big cans and we have them drinks for the knickknacks in the night besides our dinner, and then we also looked at TV. We get tired looking at TV and we get in the car. That boy loved the children. I have six children. I wouldn't work in that garbage.

Martha Tinsley, the defendant's sister, was the next witness. Her testimony about the Richardson family home life was similar to that offered by Mrs. Hartley. She said that her brother played with the children by "running around the room."

A. They would be all over him. When they got tired of doing that, they went to singing.

Q. Do you remember what they sang?

A. Mostly Christian songs.

Q. Christian songs?

A. Yes, one song was "Let God Abide."

Q. Based upon what you observed between James Richardson and his wife, do you feel that James loved his wife?

A. Yes, sir.

Q. Do you think his wife loved him?

A. Yes, sir.

Q. Do you think that they loved the children?

A. I know they loved them.

Jane Bonner, the defendant's sister-in-law, said that the family was unusually close and warm.

A. Well, what I think was love because James mostly, you know, acted, you know, like a father who loved his kids.

Q. What did he do to show that he loved his kids?

A. He took up as much time with them as possible, and he corrected them. By being a fruit picker he couldn't do all the things that he wanted to do for them.

Q. Do you feel that he loved his children?

A. Yes, I really does.

Robinson interrupted the flow of character witnesses for his client to call to the witness stand the Chief of Police for the city of Arcadia. Chief Richard Barnard was a well-respected law officer who had conducted an investigation into the seven deaths. He was at the hospital before the children died and that same day he talked to the defendant and his wife and examined the premises. After a thorough examination he stated that there was no case against Richardson. After the charges were filed against Richardson, Chief Barnard stated that the State did not have a case and that the case should be dropped.

With alacrity Robinson went to the point.

Q. Chief Barnard, referring back to October 25, did you have occasion to investigate some poisonings in that particular city of Arcadia?

A. Yes, sir.

Q. Who did you investigate those poisonings with?
A. The Sheriff of De Soto County.
Q. Following that investigation, did you at any time ever state, after your investigation, that the case did—that the State did not have a case and it should be dropped?

    Mr. Schaub: This is completely incompetent. The jury is going to decide that.
    The Court: Sustained.

The fact that the defense lawyer asked the Chief of Police whether he had stated that the case should be dropped, together with the objection by the State's attorney, certainly did appear to confirm the fact that both Robinson and Schaub agreed that the remark had been made.

Robinson then proved himself to be a most inventive attorney. Prevented from questioning the Chief of Police about his investigation of the crime and the conclusions that he had reached, Robinson attempted to turn Chief Barnard into a character witness. Not a positive witness for James Richardson, who he did not really know, but a witness to testify about Sheriff Cline's reputation for truthfulness. Quite likely never before in the annals of American jurisprudence had a defense lawyer called upon the chief of police to vouch for the poor reputation of the county sheriff in the area of truthfulness.

Q. Police Chief Barnard, I am going to ask you a question which may be a difficult question for you to answer, but I want to ask you, do you know Frank Cline?
A. Yes.
Q. What is his occupation in De Soto County?
A. Sheriff of De Soto County.
Q. What is your occupation?

A. Chief of police.

Q. How long have you known Frank Cline?

A. I guess I have known him 12 or 14 years.

Q. Do you know his general reputation in the community for telling the truth?

A. Yes, sir.

Q. Is that reputation good or bad?

A. Do I have to answer? Well, you mean for telling the truth?

Q. Right, is it good or bad?

A. Well, different people have different opinions.

Q. What is your opinion?

A. I would rather not say.

MR. SCHAUB: His opinion is of no materiality.

THE COURT: Sustained.

Q. Based upon your opinion, would you believe Frank Cline under oath?

MR. SCHAUB: Objection.

THE COURT: Sustained.

Schaub's comment as to the lack of materiality of the Chief's opinion of the Sheriff's devotion to the truth and his two objections to the questions again made it appear that both he and Robinson suspected what the answer, if permitted, might have been.

The importance of Robinson's efforts, Schaub's objections, and Barnard's testimony, brief though it was, should not be undervalued. Cline had constructed the case against Richardson. The Chief of Police for the area where the deaths occurred had conducted a thorough investigation, did not believe there was a case against the defendant, and quite obviously had some reservations about Cline's methods, his commitment to the facts, and his conclusions.

The defendant's brother, Allan, testified to the same conditions at home that the previous character witnesses had referred to. He said that James and the children sang "church songs" and that James and Annie Mae appeared to love each other, and the children.

The last character witness was Sarah Jones, the minister of the Sunshine Spiritual Church Center in Jacksonville.

Q. What has been your relationship with Annie Mae and James Richardson?
A. Their pastor, and they are more like my children than they are members. I might get emotional, but I can't help it when I am truthful.

   The children were wonderful. A white or colored man couldn't be any better to that family than he was to them.

   MR. SCHAUB: Object to the conclusion and ask that it be stricken.
   THE COURT: It is a conclusion on the part of the witness, and the jury is instructed to disregard the answer.

Q. How were the children clothed, do you recall?
A. Very lovely. He didn't only do for the children, he did for his brother and his sister's children.
Q. Did you ever see James and the children play together?
A. Yes, and also sing. He is a lover of quartet. He used to try to teach his children quartet.

Q. Do you remember any of the songs?
A. One, "Let God Abide." The other was "Precious Lord Take My Hand and Lead Me On."
Q. Have you heard him sing those songs?
A. Yes, because he sings in the church also.
Q. Do you think they loved their children?
A. Yes, I know they did.
Q. Did their children love them?
A. Yes.

Schaub had no questions for the Reverend Sarah Jones. The court was recessed for lunch. The testimony of the six character witnesses might ordinarily have caused reasonable doubt as to the defendant's alleged guilt. Yet that body of testimony was no doubt flawed in the minds of the jurors in two respects. Some of the witnesses were related to the defendant. And they were, all of them, black.

When the court reconvened in the afternoon, John Robinson said, "We call James Joseph Richardson."

Even sophisticated men of the world have difficulty on occasion in leaving the real world of communication behind and adapting to the restrictive rules of evidence. To juristic scholars and to practicing attorneys the rules are meaningful; without them a degree of order, often necessary for the difficult task of unraveling complicated and conflicting stories, would be entirely absent. Richardson, a former garbage collector, a day laborer in the fruit groves, a man who had never been adequately taught to read or write, a man on trial for his life, and a man who suffered from a pronounced hearing defect, was ill-prepared by his life's experiences to cope with the rules of evidence. Accordingly, Robinson sought to have his client tell what he knew about the relevant facts in a narrative form. This technique was not discovered by Robinson; it had been employed with varying degrees of success in thousands of cases in every jurisdiction in the country.

The defendant began to speak of late morning, October 25.

A. We was notified in the grove. Mr. Fred Steven come down the field and told us that one of our children was sick. Then he said, "If you come, hurry up." I asked my wife while we were coming down the ladder: "What do you think happened?" She said that she didn't know, and then I came on down the ladder. Mr. Fred Steven said to me, "James, can you stay and one of you go?" I asked my wife then did she want me to go with her. She said yes. I folded my sacks, with the other sandwich that we had, into a bag and picked up the rest of my tickets, put them on the box, and then we started to walk to the truck.

My wife got up in the front of the cab because the back of the truck was too high for her to get up there. I jumped and throwed my sack into the back of the truck and I got in, and Fred Steven cranked up and pulled off and rushed us to the hospital.

When we got to the hospital I jumped off the back of the truck, I was so excited. What did happen to my little kid? Then we went on in the hospital, and Miss Bessie King was standing on the outside. I asked her, "Miss Bessie, what happened?" She stated she didn't know.

MR. SCHAUB: Object to what somebody else told him.

Q. Don't testify to what somebody said to you, only what you said, okay?
A. Yes, we walked into the hospital very carefully with my wife. At that time I didn't see anyone but Bessie King.

Then Bessie King didn't seem to be worried. We went on it. We stood up about three minutes. Then some people came in, and then we stood there. I wondered to myself what did happen. Then the pastor of the church said to me—

Q. Don't testify as to what they said, just testify to what you did.

A. I asked what did happen. No one said a word. They led us on into the chapel. When we got into the chapel, I asked what we were here for. Then he said, "Just sit down."

We sit down about 15 minutes. The doctor came in. He looked at me and my wife, and then they walked out, and then the Sheriff came in, but I didn't know him as he was the Sheriff. Then he walked back out. Then the police came. They asked us—

MR. SCHAUB: I am going to object to the narrative form.

A. We prayed very hard.

Q. Who was present at the time?

A. I was so excited, wondering what happened, I don't know which ones. They asked us a lot of questions. People come from—just come from nowhere and started asking questions.

Q. Getting now to the identity of the children, when you went into the room to identify the children, tell me how this happened, if you will.

A. We learnt after that quite a while I found out what I was praying for. He said, "All your children are dead." They took us out. My wife fell out. I say, "What do you mean about all my children dead?" He said, "They are dead." We stayed there for a while. Then he walked out to give my wife a shot to bring her back through. I remember that we were going out the door. I asked my wife to identify children. She wasn't able at the present time. They asked me would I identify my children. I didn't want to, because they didn't get that kind of heart to know all my children were dead. They took us up—so I went on in. I identified them. They wanted me to call them name by name. Then they could identify them themselves. They was under a sheet. They said, "Who is this?" I said, "Betty Jean." Then they say, "Who is this one?" I said, "Susie." Then they asked me about the rest of them. I said, "It couldn't happen to me, we live too happy." We heard the people says we were living too happy and independent. They said—

MR. SCHAUB: I don't think this is in response to any question. I object to it as being improper.

THE COURT: I think I will call a halt to it. Ask him another question.

Later Richardson began to discuss the events of October 24.

A.   We bought a few more items. We left the store. We came on back home. Bessie King and her daughter said, "The children—"

MR. SCHAUB: Object to what she said.

THE COURT: Sustained.

The defense lawyer asked another question, but again Schaub, armed with the rules of evidence, broke into the testimony.

Q. Just tell us what happened, what you did.
A. We went into the house. The children weren't there to throw their arms around me. Her children throwed their arms around me. My children, they come to me. They say, "Daddy, Daddy, what have you all bought us from the store?"

MR. SCHAUB: Object again. Might counsel be asked to ask questions?

Cline had previously stated that the Richardson apartment was filthy when he entered it. Robinson inquired, and Richardson responded.

A. My wife, Annie Mae. We were cleaning up on the 24th. We cleaned that house upside down. I picked up the settee, picked up around the television. My wife washed the dishes. She cleaned up the kitchen. I scrubbed the bathroom and in the living room. My wife scrubbed the kitchen. We straightened up the settee, and we started to clean up the house, and I don't believe a fifth of what they said, because we had bought a brand new gas range and everything. I really loved my children, and I don't think nobody in the whole world can give his love to their children more than me.

After cleaning the house, Richardson said that he and his wife visited a Mr. Jackson, a sick friend at the hospital.

A. We went in the hospital. Me and my wife got in the hospital as a cousin. That is the only way we could have got in because he was sick and I felt that he needed help, and I give him that much care.

We went back to the hospital. We carried him cigarettes. I give him fifty cents. Then we left and came back home. The children were still in good health. That evening kind of early an insurance man came around seven-thirty.

Richardson said that he did have insurance previously for the whole family but through nonpayment it had "relaxed."

Richardson then discussed the appearance of the salesman on the evening of the 24th.

A. He knocked on the door lightly. I was looking at television. I didn't hear him at the first beginning. He knocked again, knock, knock. I thought somebody was out there, and I turned. I seen a shadow from the light. I got up from the seat by the door and said, "Yes?" He said, "I am an insurance agent. I come to sell you some insurance. If you would like for me to help you give you some life insurance, it is pretty good insurance."

I said I already had insurance but was collapsed because we stayed away from home so long. He said, "It is better you get some." I said, "I don't have no money." He said, "Well, I could talk to you about it. Will it be all right, because the insurance is very cheap?" I said, "Yes."

I heard my wife from the kitchen saying, "Who is that?" I said, "It is an insurance man." I opened the screen door to let him in. We didn't have no light in the front in the top of the wall, but we did have a light in the back. We had a settee in the back. We had a bed in the back, the settee was right beside the bed. We started to talk about the insurance.

He said, "Now, I can put you in insurance. How many children do you have?" I said, "We have ten children." He spoke and said, "I will put all of them in the insurance if you want it. It wouldn't be necessary for me to write it up, so I won't have to come back." I said, "You can write it up, but I don't have any money." He said, "When will you have it?" I said, "If you come Friday, I will give you your money." He said, "Well, I will think about it."

Then he sit down. He said, "What is the oldest child's name?" I said, "Betty Jean Bryant." He writ it up. He said, "What is your name?" I said, "My name is James Joseph Richardson," and he started to writing and figuring. He said, "I will make this statement, but it would not be in benefit until you give me some money."

I said, "Well, okay," so he writ us up, me and all the ten children and my wife. Then we started to talking about different things of TV. He said, "Good picture on television." I say, "Yes." He said, "Well, can I get you to sign these?" I said, "Yes."

At the present time, I wasn't no further from the kitchen and Bessie King. They were in the kitchen laughing and talking; so he asked me, "Can I get your wife to sign these, too?" I said, "Yes." I called my wife. She walked out of the kitchen. He asked me, "Well, James, that wouldn't be enough insurance. What about me putting a little extra on there?" I said, "How much would it cost, because I don't make too much money." He said, "I will figure it up and say."

He figured it up and it runs up to $3. He say, "You are sure of your money Friday?" I said, "Yes, because we get paid off on Friday." He asked me, "What kind of work do you do?" I said, "We do fruit work." He said, "How much do you make?" I said, "My check would be from $110 to $160 a week."

Q. That is the two of you?

A. Yes, that is why I know I give my children all the love I could. Then they never wanted for nothing.

Q. James, after the insurance man left that night, what did you do?

A. I remember walking back out to the front with him. He said, "Well, I tell you what I do, I won't be back by Friday because I have another route to go to. How about me coming next Tuesday to pick up the money?" I said that would be just fine, that would help me out a whole lot, because I have a lot of bills to pay and I would like to go along with that. He said, okay.

He walked out the door, and I returned and locked the screen door and went back in the back with Bessie King, and Miss Bessie King and my wife and I sat down, but I remember telling Miss Bessie King to lend me some money. She said, "I don't have a penny, James. You know I don't get paid off until Friday."

I remember the insurance man asked me was there anywhere that I could borrow some money. I told him no. Well, I could, but I didn't know it, and he left.

About three or four minutes after, Bessie King walked out the screen door and left it unlocked. I locked it back. She said, "Don't lock it, because I will be back." I said, "Okay." I told my wife I was going to continue looking at my picture. She was cooking fish. I continued on sitting down.

Robinson asked the defendant to relate his experiences in the Arcadia jail. He began by asking where he was placed by Cline's deputy just after he was arrested.

A. I was taken to the third floor when taken to jail, yes. They put me where they call a place where they get ready to send you to the gas chamber.

Q. Do you recall the day they took you down to the second floor and you went there?

A. Yes.

Q. Who was there; who was in jail that you recall?

A. Mr. Ernell Washington come in shortly after. Mr. Leon McDonald, Mr. James Weaver, Mr. James Cunningham—four or five others came in.

I stood up and McDonald said, "Here comes my buddy. What they got you for?" I said, "I don't know." He said, "Well, is this the first time you have been in this Arcadia jail?" I said, "Yes."

MR. SCHAUB: Object to what he said.

Robinson asked his client if he told any of the inmates that he had killed his children.

A. No, I didn't.

Q. You heard the testimony from this chair of three witnesses—James Weaver, James Cunningham, and the testimony of other witnesses to what Ernell Washington said. Was that testimony they gave true or false?

A. It was false.

Q. Did you ever discuss with the inmates in that jail anything about what happened to your children and about you may be liable for it?

A. I hollered to my wife. We were explaining about love and care, about what we were to do to start another family to try to lead a better life.

Q. Do you recall any time during the period of time that you and Annie Mae were in the jail that she ever yelled down at you and said, "You killed my children"?

A. No, sir, no, sir, no, sir.

Q. She never made that statement to you?
A. No, sir.

Robinson asked Richardson about his interrogation by Cline.

A. It was a deputy I think came up, got me, carried me downstairs, and started to talk. Mr. Frank Cline started to talk. He said he went to Jacksonville and got proof and evidence, and he had a suitcase in his hands. He said, "I don't want you tell me that I am a damn liar."

MR. SCHAUB: If it please the Court. I object to this as being hearsay.

As Richardson spoke of Cline's questions and statements, Schaub became more insistent in his efforts to silence the witness. Although the Court had just ruled that Richardson could testify about the session with Cline, Schaub objected again and again. "I don't want to object in contradiction to the Court's ruling. I don't know whether the Court ruled on whether or not this is hearsay. I am objecting it is hearsay. Sheriff Cline is on trial, and I don't believe he testified to any of these matters."

Richardson, who does not use profanity in his daily life, said that Cline started "talking all kinds of language." It is not proper to characterize one's remarks, although one may repeat them. This rule is designed to permit the jury to reach its own conclusions based upon the facts, rather than be required to accept the concept of the witness. Accordingly, Richardson was told to repeat Cline's actual words. Richardson was reluctant. He said that Cline used "just all the inflamed language." Finally, Richardson said that Cline had told him, "You need to be held by a goddamn rope." He went on. "He told me, 'You ain't nothing but a lover boy, ain't you? I hate some of you people to tell me a lie.' He called me a nigger. He told one of the deputies, 'Take his goddamn ass back up the steps.' I got ready to go back up the steps. He opened the door and told me, 'Get your goddamn ass in there. You ought to be hung by a rope, you goddamn son-of-a-bitch you,' and he shoved me before I could get inside this cell good and slammed the door that time. If I hadn't been fast enough, it probably would have broken my leg, but I staggered on in there, and everybody in there said—" Mr. Schaub objected.

The defense lawyer tried to have his client present a word picture to the jury of the home before the children died. Richardson tried, but the rules of evidence bemused and thwarted him.

Q. James, I want to go back to the time that we were just speaking of, say about six months prior to the death of the children in October of 1967. I want you to tell me in your own words what type of relationship did you have with children after you came home at night? What did you and the children do—

    MR. SCHAUB: Object to the type of relationship as asking for a conclusion. He is not a psychiatrist.
    THE COURT: Overruled.

A. I played with them; I sung Christian songs, and I know I believe in God and I am supposed to be a deacon.

    MR. SCHAUB: Object and ask that the answer be stricken as not responsive to anything that was asked.
    THE COURT: I am going to agree.

Q. Just tell me what you and the children enjoyed doing.
A. We enjoyed popcorn, potato chips—I give them much love and care.
Q. Did you spend very much time with them?
A. Very much.
Q. How much time would you spend at the end of a day?
A. With my wife and children I spent all the time with them. I never let my wife get out of my sight. My wife never let me get out of her sight. My children—we laughed and played on the beds. Sometimes we tear up the bed, and my wife would get at me about letting the children jump all over the bed. She said, "Do you love the children, James," a heap of times.

MR. SCHAUB: Object again.

Q. Did you love those kids?
A. Sure, anything any father treat their family more independent than any human beings in the whole world. Yes, I loved both my wife and children, and there is nothing in the world that I think any other children had that I went and got it for my children. That is why people said me living too independent.

MR. SCHAUB: I ask that the last be stricken as not responsive to the question.
THE COURT: I didn't get it.
MR. SCHAUB: Something about what other people said about him.
THE COURT: That portion of the answer is stricken, and the jury is instructed to disregard it.

Robinson asked the defendant if he loved his wife.

A.   Yes, I do. I love my wife and children very much.

Q.   Does your wife love you?

A.   Yes, sir, if I could take their place at the present time I would rather take their place and let them live.

MR. SCHAUB: I ask that that be stricken as completely unresponsive.

THE COURT: The jury is instructed to disregard that series of sentences just uttered by the witness.

Richardson was on trial for the murder of his children. He was unable to understand why he was not permitted to express to the jury of his peers how deeply he loved them and missed them.

Schaub, ever alert for any trespass upon the rules of evidence, sat on the edge of his chair, ready to spring up at the sign of the slightest infringement. Most of those present reacted differently. Many were crying openly. One juror wiped a tear from his eye. Another blew his nose.

Robinson had one more question to ask.

Q.   James, I am going to ask you one question: did you kill those kids?

A.   No, sir, I loved them children. I worked day and night.

MR. SCHAUB: Object, your Honor, as not responsive. He was asked if he killed the children. He said he didn't. I would ask the court to disregard the rest of the speech.

THE COURT: I am not going to strike it. Is that your last question?

MR. ROBINSON: Yes.

THE COURT: I will not strike it, then.

While Richardson testified on direct, Schaub's demeanor was severely circumscribed. He could do no more than utilize the rules of evidence for the purpose of preventing Richardson from saying too much, and he could time his rapid-fire objections to interrupt the witness's narrative and thus interfere with the flow. These techniques did not originate with Schaub; they are an unfortunate adjunct of the adversary system, and many effective prosecutors and defense lawyers count such skills as an essential part of their arsenal. But it was on cross-examination that Schaub, relentless, tough, and dextrous, could display his proficiency. Richardson was hardly a match for the accomplished prosecutor.

He began by asking about the children.

Q. I am going to direct your attention to the seven children that died October 25. Were any of these children Annie Mae's children?

A. I considered all of them were hers.

Q. Do you know whether they were—how many of them were her children?

A. Now, I don't know. She had them.

Q. You don't know? You weren't the real father of any of these children, were you?

A. Yes, I was.

Q. How many?

A. By my wife and myself there were three.

Q. You were the father of three of these children. The question was how many of these children were you the father of?

A. By Annie Mae?

Q. By anybody?

Richardson was plainly confused before the first half-dozen questions had been asked. A more educated witness or one with greater experience with debate tactics might have caused the prosecutor to look a bit foolish. Schaub knew there was little danger of a sharp response from the witness. Everyone knew that Annie Mae was the mother of the children. She had told Schaub that not long before. Schaub knew that Richardson was the father of three of the children, and the prosecutor's statement to the contrary was inexplicable by simple logic. It seemed clear that Schaub was inquiring just about the seven children "How many of *these* children were you the father of?" but when Richardson asked for clarification, he quickly changed the subject, "By anybody?" Before the cross-examination was two minutes old, Richardson was befuddled.

Richardson admitted that Annie Mae was his third wife and that he had not been divorced from the other two. Schaub then charged, "By marrying each of these women, you were able to gain more in the way of welfare, were you not? Do you understand the question?" Richardson answered, "No, sir."

There appeared to be no substance to Schaub's charge. Richardson was living with only one woman. He could not possibly benefit from any welfare check which might be sent to the other two women, and it was never established that the other two did receive any such check. Yet it is possible that the jury was more impressed with the foundationless charge than it was with the denial by the witness. The judge ruled that the question was proper. Schaub asked Richardson if three children that he had fathered, not including the seven who had been poisoned, had died. Richardson said that that was true. Schaub then charged that, "Each of those three children that have died, died from malnutrition and dehydration, didn't they?" The question was clearly improper, the judge so ruled, and the defendant was not permitted to answer it. Yet the jury had heard the question. The answer may have been almost irrelevant in any event, for it had been widely reported before the trial that Schaub himself had traveled to

Jacksonville to investigate the deaths of the other Richardson children. Schaub issued his findings to the jury in the guise of a question. When Robinson objected to the line of questioning, Schaub interrupted him to state, "He had bragged about what a wonderful father he was." Schaub was not above distorting the testimony just slightly in an effort to discomfort the nervous witness. Richardson had testified that he did not have life insurance on October 24 or October 25, since he was unable to pay for it. Nevertheless, Schaub asked:

Q. Other than this instance that you testified about, did you have any life insurance on Annie Mae or the children?
A. I always kept insurance on the children, myself, and my wife.
Q. You always have kept insurance, you say?
A. At the present time I wasn't making enough money to keep up insurance.
Q. So you had let the insurance lapse?
A. Yes, because my children had to eat.

The prosecutor tried to establish that the Richardson family had previously been insured for some weeks even though Richardson paid no premium at all.

Q. James, isn't it true that the last insurance policy you had that you let lapse you never paid ten cents for, that you ordered on credit and let it lapse from the first payment when it was essential that you make the first payment?
A. Beg 'o pardon?
Q. Isn't it true that the last life insurance you had on these children, that you had ordered this from Independent Life Insurance; isn't that right?
A. I imagine so.
Q. And you hadn't paid the man any money. He carried you

for about a month, and when you paid him no more, he let it lapse?

A.   More than a month?

Q.   Six weeks?

A.   You are wrong.

Q.   But you never paid him anything in premiums, did you?

A.   I have proof that I did.

Q.   I am talking about Independent Life. You say you paid him premiums for that last policy?

A.   Yes.

Q.   How much did you pay, and when did you pay?

A.   That insurance for $5.00.

Schaub insisted that Richardson had told Foy that he had not paid any premiums for the policy. Of course the proper way to try to impeach Richardson's testimony in that regard would be to offer the records of the insurance company, or failing that, to call Foy and have him recount Richardson's original statement to him on that subject. Schaub did not offer the insurance records, and although Foy testified as a rebuttal witness, Schaub did not ask him any questions about the subject. Schaub may have reasoned that Richardson's testimony had already been impeached just by the manner in which the questions were put to him.

Schaub then reverted to the question of bigamy. He showed Richardson the marriage application for the license to marry Annie Mae, and asked him to read it. Schaub said, "I am particularly interested in the second page of it." The defendant responded, "I can't read."

Schaub continued on with another question, and Richardson said, "Please to the jury, I wish him to speak louder. I am hard of hearing."

Schaub asked Richardson what he did in the evening after the children had died, but again he was confounded by the rules of evidence.

A.   Miss Bessie Reese came and told me—

Q.   Don't tell me what somebody told you, tell me when you next left the house. You said you were home about six that evening. I want to know the next place you went.

A.   I didn't go anywhere.

Q.   When did you leave the house? When was the next time you left your home?

A.   I had to go get some pills for Annie Mae.

Q.   When was this?

A.   And I wouldn't go but—

Q.   I am simply asking you—

> MR. WHITSON: If you would let him alone.
> MR. SCHAUB: He is evading me.
> MR. ROBINSON: He isn't evading, he just doesn't understand.
> THE COURT: Overruled.

Exactly what it is that the Court overruled is not clear from the record.

Richardson said that he stayed most of the night at his neighbor's apartment, since he was not allowed to return to his own.

Q.   About when did you leave?

A.   When my wife was able to walk.

Q.   When was that?

A.   About five o'clock in the morning.

Q.   Where did you go then?

A.   Me and my wife returned to Mr. Isaac Jackson's apartment.

Q.   How long did you stay there?

A.   We stayed there until around about quarter to seven or seven o'clock.

Q. Then where did you go?
A. There was some noise on the outside. My wife woke me up. I got up and looked out the door. I saw Bessie Reese King and Charlie Smith—
Q. The question was, where did you go then?

Schaub asked the defendant about the shack where it is said the bag of poison was discovered.

Q. And that is where the parathion was found the next morning; isn't that correct?
A. Well, I explained to you over and over. I don't know where the parathion was found there or not, but when I got out the door I seen Bessie King and Charlie Smith with a bag.
Q. Where was this, at the little house?
A. I run them out of there with a bag.
Q. That is when the police came?
A. Yes.
Q. So it was found in this building, wasn't it?

Richardson had said several times before that he did not know where the bag of parathion was found.

Q. Then there was some excitement out in the yard that morning and you came out; is that correct?
A. Yes, I went out the door.
Q. Then where did you go?
A. I stopped still. I walked out the door, and I saw Bessie King—
Q. Never mind what you saw. My question is, where did you go after you came out there?
A. I didn't go anywhere.
Q. After the police came, where did you go?
A. Then Bessie King—

Q. Don't tell me what other people did, tell me what you did.

The most flagrant incursions on the rights of a defendant came about through Schaub's questions and comments during the last minutes of his cross-examination of Richardson. It began this way:

Q. Have you ever been convicted of a crime?
A. No, sir.
Q. Never?
A. No, sir.
Q. I direct your attention to April 17 of 1964. Were you convicted of a crime in Volusia County at that time?
A. No, sir.
Q. Willful and malicious destruction to personal property. Complaint sworn out by Oreen Jackson. Do you remember that?

THE COURT: Mr. Schaub, Mr. Robinson wants to see what you are looking at.
MR. ROBINSON: Where was the conviction?
MR. SCHAUB: Right here. He was found guilty.

In colloquy with counsel Schaub announced for the entire courtroom to hear, "Found guilty," while he referred to a document before him which he had neither marked for purposes of identification nor offered into evidence. Schaub continued:

Q. But you were arrested on this complaint of Oreen Jackson's and convicted.
A. No, sir.

Q. You were not?
A. No, sir.
Q. You were never arrested on a warrant by the Justice of the Peace Court District Eight in Volusia County in 1964?
A. Arrested?
Q. Yes.
A. For what?
Q. Malicious destruction of personal property.
A. No, sir.

Many first-year law students know that the *most* improper question that a lawyer may put to a witness, particularly to a defendant in a criminal case, is "Were you arrested?" The only proper question regarding the possible criminal record of the witness is related to a conviction, never to an arrest. If the witness denies that he has been convicted, proof that he was in fact convicted may be offered by the inquisitor. No other approach is permissible; any other approach is improper, and a departure from that approach by a prosecuting attorney affords an opportunity for a motion for a mistrial.

Having been so successful once, Schaub tried the same manuever again.

Q. I ask you whether or not you were convicted for encouraging and contributing to the delinquency of minor children March 29 of 1966 in Daytona Beach?
A. I don't understand the word.
Q. Do you understand about contributing to the delinquency of a minor?
A. No, sir.
Q. You don't understand that?
A. No, sir.
Q. You have been arrested for it, haven't you?
A. No, sir.

Q. Have you ever been arrested for contributing to the dependency of a minor?

A. I wasn't arrested, but I was asked to come down to the office.

Q. You were arrested by a warrant?

A. They never did take me to jail.

Q. But that was contributing to the dependency, wasn't it? So you understand what it means, don't you?

A. I have never been arrested.

Schaub persisted, despite the denials by the witness.

Q. Let's go back to this one here. That was a different matter. This was the Williams girl. This was a complaint sworn out by Annie Mae. Did you want to look it over? Were you arrested on that charge?

A. What charge?

Q. Charge of encouraging and contributing to the dependency of minors.

Finally the Judge could permit the travesty to continue no longer. He said, "Mr. Schaub, come here, please." After an animated conference at the bench, the Judge decided that Schaub's questions and comments were improper. Then the Court addressed the jury. "I am going to make this ruling, that the line of questioning, wherein the affidavits and the warrants were exhibited to the witness and he was asked if he was convicted of these two offenses which were indicated in the affidavits—all that testimony is stricken, and the jury is instructed to disregard the questions and answers in arriving at your verdict."

The ruling was proper, but tardy. Despite the legal fiction, it would not be possible for the jurors, although so instructed, to disregard what they had heard. The jury had seen the prosecutor appear to read from documents, which even the learned Judge had referred to as "affidavits and warrants" in his instruction to the jury, and had heard him insist that Richardson was lying, that he had been convicted. Those facts had registered upon the brain cells of twelve men and one woman. A Court's admonition, however it may be considered by appellate courts, just does not operate as an all-cleansing vacuum cleaner that sucks up brain waves and restores the mind to its virginal state. In reality the jurors were left to ponder one question. Had the State's Attorney lied, or had the field hand?

Ruby Fiason, the fifth-grade schoolteacher who had been called as a witness for the prosecution, became the only witness to be called by both sides. The prosecution had stated that James Richardson was unmoved by and seemed unconcerned about the death of his children. Miss Fiason was asked if she saw him cry at the hospital. "Yes, shortly after the doctor announced that six of the children were dead, Reverend Fay said, 'Let us pray.' When we prayed, he got on his knees. When he got up, I noticed he was wiping his eyes."

She said that she saw Richardson a little later that day also. "Mrs. Draper gave Mrs. Richardson some kind of injection. I remember her saying that somebody had to identify the children. She asked him to come in and identify them. When he did, he came back to the car and said, 'All five of them are laid in one place, and little Diane is just breathing.' He was wiping his eyes again."

Prison inmates, whose lives are by definition completely under the control of law-enforcement personnel, including guards and sheriffs and their deputies, may be subject to various kinds of pressure or inducements to testify regarding the conduct of another inmate. Ernell Washington's statement to Whitson was but one example. It is rare indeed when a prisoner volunteers to testify on behalf of a fellow inmate, for by doing so he incurs the displeasure of his keepers and may suffer not inconsiderable harm. The plight of

James Richardson so moved some of his fellow prisoners that despite their peculiarly vulnerable situation, they came forward to tell what they knew about the case.

The first convict to speak for him was Lee McDonald, who had known Richardson before the children died. McDonald was brought to the court from the state penitentiary at Raiford, Florida. Of course, once he had been subpoenaed, the State was aware of his possible testimony. This gave the State an opportunity to talk with him about what he might say if he testified. The inmate was hardly in a position to refuse to talk to his keepers. Nevertheless, McDonald did appear at the trial. He said that he had been convicted of breaking and entering in Arcadia and sentenced to one year's imprisonment. The prosecution had access to McDonald's criminal record. The fact that he was not asked on cross-examination if he had ever been convicted of any other crime indicates that he had not been. Yet for the comparatively minor crime of breaking and entering in Arcadia, he was sent to the state penitentiary for one year, while Washington, for the much more serious crime of assault with intent to murder in Arcadia, was set free.

McDonald said that in three months he would be eligible for parole. He was aware of the fact that his presence in the courtroom as a defense witness would not be a factor to be favorably considered by the parole board.

Q. Were you, at the time James Richardson entered the second-story cell of the De Soto County jailhouse—were you an inmate at that time?

A. Yes, sir.

Q. Referring back to around the first of November, when he was brought down from upstairs, did you see him enter that cell?

A. Yes, sir.

Q. Could you tell the court approximately how many people were in the cell at that time?

A. About nine, I say.

Q. When James Richardson entered the cell on the second story, would you please tell what he did upon entering?

A. When they let him in, he just came right in and went straight to the back.

Q. Did he ever at any time sit down on the floor?

A. No, sir.

Q. Did he ever talk about the fact that his children had been murdered and that he was primarily responsible?

A. No, sir.

Q. Mr. McDonald, who did he room with when he was moved into that particular area?

A. Me.

Q. How long did he continue to be your roommate?

A. Until November 27.

Q. You mean when you were taken to Raiford?

A. November 27.

Q. When did you enter the De Soto County jail?

A. I don't know exactly what date it was.

Q. What month was it in?

A. It was in September.

Q. During the time that James Richardson was in the De Soto County jail, did you ever at any time hear him make any statements as to murdering his children?

A. No, sir, I didn't.

Q. There has been testimony before this Court by an inmate in the De Soto County jail, or who said he was an inmate, namely, Ernell Washington, James Weaver, and James Cunningham, that Richardson said he murdered his children. Do you know whether or not these are true statements?

A. It couldn't have been when I was there, no, sir.

Q. Why?

A. Because Richardson never had a conversation with them boys at all. He was supposed to be around me and some other boys. Nobody would fool with Washington or Cunningham.

Q. Did he fool around with these fellows?

A. No, sir.

Q. Did he discuss whether his children had died?

A. He come in and asked me, "Do I look like a man that would kill my children?" That is all. I told him no. The way he loved his children, I know he wouldn't do anything like that.

Robinson asked McDonald about Richardson's behavior while he was incarcerated at the Arcadia jailhouse. The witness said that the defendant "cried most of the time. I tried to calm his nerves down by talking to him, you know—worrying all the time, crying."

The lawyer then asked McDonald if Mrs. Richardson had "yelled down to her husband, 'Why did you kill my children?'" McDonald said that she had never made such a statement and that he would have heard it if it was said. McDonald also said that if Richardson had discussed the case with any other inmate, he would have heard it, since he was kept in the same small cell with Richardson during the entire time of his incarceration. McDonald then said that the previous Thursday evening, when he was temporarily transferred to the Arcadia jail from Raiford, he saw James Weaver.

A. Well, when we walked in, Weaver was just standing up at the bars, so I went to the back and he called James McQueen and David Johnson to the cell, to the first cell on the right, and then there was talking. That is about all.

Q. Did you see anything which had to do with he and a deputy sheriff?

A. Yes, sir.

    MR. HILL: Objection, this is absolutely immaterial, irrelevant, and incompetent. No connection with the case under discussion.

    THE COURT: I have no idea.

    MR. WHITSON: That same witness testified from this stand that a deputy sheriff did not touch him.

Q. Tell us what you saw between this deputy sheriff and the man you spoke of, James Weaver.

A. They took James Weaver down the street and made him drunk. When he come back he was slapping James—upstairs. When he went upstairs, he broke the windows out and they throwed him into another cell. He was up there just cussing everything.

Hill's cross-examination of McDonald bore very little upon the issues. He asked, "How do you know what Richardson said if he was still there when you left?"

The question was hardly logical or consistent with McDonald's testimony, since he had never stated that he knew what Richardson said after he was transferred to Raiford. He answered, "I was explaining what he said when I was there. I don't know what he said after I left." Hill became angry. A "prison nigger" was talking back to a respected state's attorney. He shouted:

Q. Are you going to sit there under oath and tell us that you heard everything that everyone said in that jail from the time you came in there? Are you going to tell us that?

Mr. Whitson: He is attempting to bully and badger.

Mr. Robinson: That has never been established that he heard everything in jail. He stated he heard everything that Richardson said and not everything in the jail.

The Court: Sustained.

Hill, unable to make the slightest headway with McDonald regarding the question before the court, then asked him if he had talked with Norman Dezlight of the Florida Bureau of Identification and Lee Hayes, a deputy sheriff. He said that both men had talked to him. Hill never asked the witness the nature of the conversations. It appeared that he was preparing to follow the classic pattern for impeachment of a prison witness; the production of law-enforcement personnel on rebuttal.

James McQueen came from Raiford to testify for Richardson. He too was serving a one-year sentence; he was scheduled for release in six months. He said that he had been placed in the Arcadia jail on November 13.

Q. When you entered the jailhouse there in De Soto County, did you see James Richardson?

A. Yes, I did.

Q. Had he already been admitted to the jail?

A. Yes, sir.

Q. Did you know him prior to going to the jail?

A. No, sir.

Q. Were you a friend of his?

A. No, sir.

Q. Did you get to know him while you were at the jail?

A. Yes.

Q. What type of relationship did you and James Richardson experience?

A. Well, I read the Bible to him a few times.

Q. Do you know how to read and write?

A. Yes, sir.

Q. What else did you do?

A. Well, that was about all, just read the Bible to him.

Q. Were you the only one that read the Bible to him?

A. Yes, sir, during the time I was there.

Q. Did you ever at any time hear James Richardson make any statements as to his guilt of killing his children?

A. No, sir.

Q. As a matter of fact, did he discuss this thing very much at all?

A. No, sir, he was, you know, mostly sat on his bunk with his head down thinking.

Q. Did he talk to very many people in the jail?

A. No, sir.

Q. Did you ever see him talk to James Weaver there?

A. Yes, sir. Weaver read a paper to him, you know.

Q. Were you usually around during this period of time?

A. He always come out and—when Weaver got the paper, he come out.

Q. Did James Richardson have any personal conversations with Weaver with no one else around?

A. No, sir, not that I recall, because Weaver was working with the city. In the daytime he was out, and the night it would be mostly, you know.

McQueen said that Washington had told him that he had "made a deal with the Sheriff." The jury was never to be allowed to hear McQueen testify about the nature of "the deal" made between Cline and Washington. McQueen said that he was present at a conversation between another inmate, Jim Jones, and Ernell Washington.

Q. Would you please tell the Court and jury what the nature of that conversation was?

A. It was about the deal that Ernell had made, but whenever they come back up, him and Jim were talking. Jimmy called me. He said, "James, this fool went down and made a—"

MR. HILL: Object to what the other man told him. As I understand, he is relating a conversation that one party had with Washington about the defendant, what this party says that Washington did.

MR. ROBINSON: He was present during that time and overheard the conversation.

(Counsel approached the bench, after which the jury was removed from the courtroom and the following proceedings were had:)

The next few minutes were among the most dramatic and important in the trial. The jury, however, was not present to benefit from the information. Judge Justice evidently thought that the magic words, "The jury is instructed to disregard the questions and answers," might not be sufficient in this instance if some inadmissible comment was made. In the absence of the jury, the ensuing colloquy took place:

THE COURT: It appears that the purpose of this conversation from a third party would be for establishing the truth of the statement made, which would make it hearsay and, therefore, objectionable, and the objection is sustained. The question asked the witness was concerning a conversation between one Ernell Washington and one James Dean, and this is the testimony of the witness on the stand, to the effect that Ernell Washington said to Dean, "I sure got myself in a mess, I am going to have to go down there and testify." That is the nature of it, and the answer which counsel for the defendant wishes to elicit from the witness on the stand is to the effect that James Dean then told Ernell Washington, "You sure got yourself in a mess."

MR. ROBINSON: Jimmy Jones told him he would get in bad trouble if he told the Sheriff this lie.

WITNESS: Jimmy Jones told him he would get in trouble if he told the Sheriff this lie, and Jones scared Ernell Washington and Ernell told us he was going to back out of his lie to Frank Cline about James Richardson; and Ernell beat on the bars and went down to see Frank Cline again. When he came back up, he was quiet about the whole affair.

THE COURT: Is this the testimony of this witness now, all of this from this witness?

MR. ROBINSON: He was present at the time, yes, sir.

THE COURT: Some of that seems to be from some other source.

MR. ROBINSON: What we are trying to get in, the only difference in this case is what Jim Jones told him while he was observing. Then he went down and told Cline. He beat on the bars and then when he came back up he was calmed down.

THE COURT: The part that I find objectionable is that conversation from this Jim Dean—

MR. HILL: Jim Jones.

THE COURT: Okay, that Jim Jones to the effect that the statement—he was branding Ernell Washington's statement as to being a lie, and that is hearsay. That is what I find objectionable, attempting to establish from this third party's statement that Ernell Washington's report, that he had overheard the defendant acknowledge that he had killed his own children, as a damn lie. That is hearsay. That is the part I find objectionable.

After the Court's ruling the jury was returned to the court-room and McQueen was permitted to say that Washington "rushed to the bars and called out for the High Sheriff. Then he went back down."

Q. Did he go downstairs again?
A. Yes, sir.
Q. When he came back up, what occurred? What did he say when he returned to the cell?
A. He said everything was all right, he went down and got it straightened out.

McQueen was permitted to testify that this took place after a conversation between Washington and Jones, but he could not tell the jury what the conversation was about. Yet had Washington lived he could have been asked about the discussion with Jones, and if he denied it, McQueen would have been permitted to testify about the nature of the con-versation. Since Washington's preliminary-hearing testimony was presented at the trial as if he were a living witness, and since Robinson had asked Washington at the hearing if he had received anything from Cline in exchange for his testi-mony against Richardson, McQueen, I believe, should have been permitted to testify regarding the subject of the con-versation. Testimony regarding a prior conflicting statement is regarded as an exception to the hearsay rule and is ad-missible.

In this questionable decision, or at the very least a close decision on the admissibility of the testimony, the judge cleared the courtroom of the jurors. Yet when the obvious violation of Richardson's rights took place during the final moments of Schaub's cross-examination of him, the Court considered that an *ex post facto* ruling was adequate.

One additional question is raised by McQueen's undisputed assertions. Why was he brought to the De Soto County jail in Arcadia a week before he testified? The trial took place in Lee County, and the Lee County jail is situated in Fort Myers, precisely where McQueen was eventually brought to testify.

Hill's cross-examination of McQueen was rather ineffectual. He questioned the witness about his ability to observe the other inmates.

Q. You feel you kept a pretty close watch?
A. We were all so close you could hardly do anything without one knows it.

He tried to raise doubts about Washington's statements before he came back from seeing Cline, evidently having forgotten that the jury was not privy to that testimony.

Q. How long had you known Ernell?
A. I never know him before I got in jail.
Q. Did you get to be pretty good friends with him?
A. Yes, sir. As a matter of fact, we slept in the same, you know, cellblock.
Q. Were you pretty good friends with everybody in there?
A. Yes, sir, I tried to get along with everybody.
Q. Any reason Ernell singled you out to tell you about the deal he made?
A. I think he had, you know, confidence.
Q. Confidence in you?
A. He mostly brought his problems, you know.
Q. Most of his problems he brought to you?
A. Really, he didn't have no problems. You know, just things he liked to talk about, somebody to talk to.
Q. Do you remember when Ernell brought this problem to you about his deal?
A. Yes, sir.
Q. Did all the prisoners bring all their problems to you, or just Ernell?

A. The rest of them didn't have a problem like he did.

Q. I wondered if all the rest of the prisoners brought their problems to you?

A. The other guys was only in for drunk. Ernell was in for assault.

Q. Ernell had a real problem?

A. I think so.

Q. Did he come to you to ask what he ought to do or what he had already done?

A. No, he didn't tell me he was going before he went down.

Q. You don't know why he did that without talking to you first?

A. I don't know why he went down.

Q. He had discussed this problem with you?

A. Not exactly. See, he was under the impression there was a lawyer downstairs. That is what he told us. He had been down once.

There is an unwritten rule about cross-examination that had been violated by each of the lawyers throughout the trial. The rule—do not ask a hostile witness a question to which you do not know the answer. Hill violated the adage once too often.

Q. Now you say he told "us." How many people did he tell about this deal?

A. Myself and Jimmy [David] Johnson. He was talking out loud but talking to us.

For some reason Hill decided to secure further details about the setting in which the confrontation had taken place, although the jury was not aware of the substance of the confrontation.

Q. What time of day do you think this was?

A. It was in the morning around ten-thirty, right before dinner this particular day it was.

Q. Any reason you remember the time?

A. No, but I know the city guys came in shortly after.

Q. Do you remember what day it was?

A. No, sir, I don't.

The defense lawyers had not asked McQueen to establish the month when the "deal" was made between Cline and Washington. Had Hill not inquired about the circumstances surrounding the deal, more particularly about the time, the hour and day, the jury would never have heard McQueen testify about the month on redirect examination. The defense is limited on redirect to questions raised by the prosecution during cross-examination. Hill had opened the door, and Whitson walked right in.

Q. He has gone into some times with you when this thing happened, that Ernell Washington told you that he had a problem and that he had made a deal with Sheriff, and you advised him to get out of it. Was this after James Richardson had left the Arcadia jail on December 1 or November 30, whenever it was?

A. Yes, it was.

Q. But this was after?

A. Yes, sir.

Q. Was it a good while after?

A. Yes, sir. As a matter of fact, it was in March.

Q. The early part of March, wasn't it?

A. Yes.

Q. The real early part of March?

A. Yes.

Q. Shortly after that you never saw Ernell Washington, did you?

A. No, sir.

Q. Do you recall when you left the De Soto County jail?
A. Right after March 18.
Q. That was prior to the preliminary hearing we had for James Richardson, was it not?
A. Yes, sir.

The circumstantial evidence, particularly the facts surrounding Washington's hurried departure from the Arcadia jail, had indicated what McQueen had confirmed with eyewitness testimony. The arrangement entered into between Cline and Washington was consummated in March, not in November.

David Johnson, who had been introduced to the trial record through the cross-questioning of Hill, was the next witness. He said that he was awaiting a decision of the parole commission regarding an alleged violation of parole. Despite his acute vulnerability, he was present.

Q. Do you recall a man by the name of Ernell Washington?
A. I do.
Q. From where?
A. Arcadia.
Q. Were you confined in the same jail with him at the same time?
A. I was.
Q. Could you tell me the approximate date?
A. From December 25 until January 7 or 8 of '67, and then again from January 28 until he was released on April 13.
Q. Wasn't it March 13?
A. That is right, March 13.
Q. Do you recall what he had been charged with?
A. Yes, I do.
Q. What was it?
A. Assault with intent to commit murder.
Q. Do you recall that he was released on March 13?

A. Yes, sir.

Q. Did you ever, during the period of time that you were in jail with one Ernell Washington, have any conversations with him in reference to James Richardson and Sheriff Cline?

A. No, sir, he didn't have any—he didn't make any direct statements about James Richardson. The only statements that he made was concerning himself being released from jail.

Johnson, who had not overheard a conversation between Washington and another inmate, but who had participated in a discussion with Washington, could not be prevented from repeating the substance to the jury. Without interruption he told of his conversations with Washington.

A. From the beginning he made a statement that he wanted to get out of jail. He said that is the onlyest thing he was interested in, getting out of jail. Approximately three weeks later he came to me and told me that he stood a chance of getting out. He didn't say how. He was going to get out.

He was called downstairs, and he made some kind of statement to the Sheriff's Department there, which in turn he came back upstairs and told James McQueen and myself that he was going to be released on probation. We said good, but he still hadn't told us on what grounds he was going to be released on, the reasons for his release.

So that began on Monday. He was called down and interrogated from Monday until Thursday morning; so from Monday up until Thursday he would come back and tell us just what was going on, which he made a statement that he was supposed to be released if he made a certain statement, which he didn't tell us what the statement was.

He told us this much, that it was concerning Richardson. I asked him, "What do you know about the Richardson case?" He said he didn't know anything about the Richardson case but they thought he knew something, so he said, "If you don't know anything, you can't tell anything." I said, "If you can get out of jail by telling what you know, but you say you don't know anything, how can you get out of jail by making a deal like that?" He said, "They don't know that."

So he asked me, "Have you ever been on probation before?" He said, "During probation, how many people are in the courtroom?" I said, "Well, the sheriff, judge, supervisor, and in some cases prosecutor." So he said, "I am going back downstairs and talk with the Sheriff again, because I don't want the people to put me in a trick," those were the words he used.

So he went back downstairs. When he came back up later he smiled and said, "Everything was all set." I said, "What is there supposed to be?" He said, "This is the deal, you scratch my back and I will scratch yours." I said, "I only hope you know what you are doing, because if you don't know what you are doing, you will find out later on, because you are getting yourself involved in something that you don't know what you are doing."

So on Thursday he went to court. He was released on probation. We didn't know what the statement he was going to make until James Richardson was arrested following his preliminary hearing. James Richardson came back and said, "Well, fellows, I am back. My reason for being back is the lie that Ernell Washington told and the lie that Spot told"—which is known as Weaver—so I said, "What statement did he make?" James Richardson said that he got on the witness stand and told him that he killed his children. That is when we find out just what his statement was.

Q. Did you see him after this?
A. Yes, I did.
Q. What happened at this time?
A. He came back up to the jail to visit, and he came looking for McQueen. McQueen had gone. He walked up to the bars. I told him, "I heard about what happened." He said, "I will be right back, I have to go upstairs." So I haven't seen him. Next I heard about him being deceased.

The prosecution made much of the fact that McDonald had known Richardson before he was arrested. Robinson sought to establish Johnson's relationship with Richardson and with his attorney.

Q. Do you know James Richardson?
A. Only from seeing James Richardson occasionally or going back and forth from work. I have never met him personally up to the time he came to jail.
Q. You aren't a personal friend of his?
A. No, sir.
Q. When was the first time you ever saw me?
A. Over here at the jail Tuesday or Wednesday.
Q. That was the first conversation you and I ever had?
A. That is right.
Q. Did I give you anything for testifying today?
A. No, sir, you haven't.
Q. Did I do any favors for you?
A. None whatsoever. If you did, I don't know.
Q. Didn't I iron that shirt for you?
A. That is all you did for me.

Johnson's testimony evidently stung the three prosecutors. They huddled in earnest and, some observers said, in apparently agitated conversation. Although Hill had questioned

the two previous witnesses, perhaps as an indication of the
disdain with which the prosecution viewed convicts testifying for the defense, Schaub rose to cross-examine Johnson.
There was little subtlety in his open sarcasm.

Q. You knew quite a bit about the courtroom procedure.
   Have you been in many courtrooms?
A. No more than the ones concerning myself, sir.
Q. Is that very many?
A. Oh, a couple of times.
Q. Do you consider yourself a jailhouse lawyer?
A. No, sir, I don't have any reason to do that.

Schaub, unable to get the answers he considered useful,
soon took to testifying through his questions, although, of
course, not under oath, and knowing that he could not be
subjected to cross-examination. The defense lawyers did not
object, the judge remained silent, and the black prisoner,
awaiting a ruling by the parole commission, was hardly in a
position to object to the procedure. He merely answered the
statements.

Q. You talked to my investigators since you have been
   down?
A. Yes, I sure did.
Q. Did you talk to Deputy Lee Hayes?
A. I sure did.
Q. You told them you wanted to make a deal with me,
   didn't you?
A. No, sir, I didn't.
Q. You deny you told them that you told these men that if
   we would give you a break, make a deal with you, that
   you come up here and tell some stuff about Lee Mc-
   Donald?
A. What kind of a break could you give me?

Q. Did you talk to Mr. Lee and Mr. Ostling from my office?
A. No, sir, I didn't.
Q. What did they talk about?
A. What did I know concerning the case.
Q. Did you say you wanted to talk to them—you wanted to see me?
A. To whom?
Q. Somebody from the State's Attorney's office. You didn't send word that you did?
A. No, sir, I didn't.

Displeased with the consistent denials by the witness, Schaub in one sentence accused the witness of dreaming up his testimony, of lying, and he suggested that he had discovered the motive as well; Johnson was trying to get a break from Schaub and his office.

Q. Isn't it a fact that you dreamed this whole thing up so you could get down today so you could use this information you are lying about now to get a break from us?
A. What kind of break?
Q. To get out of jail.

The answer was so obviously extraneous to Schaub's purpose in asking the question that he indicated that he had completed his cross-examination before the witness even had a chance to offer it. The trial transcript reveals that of all the testimony offered in the trial, only the cross-examination of Johnson concludes with a "question."

He was questioned on redirect for just a moment. He said that he had been telling the truth.

Q. Any reason not to?
A. No, there isn't. I would like to say I never met Richard-

son in my life and I am a father myself. If I had a doubt in my mind—I am speaking of myself—

MR. SCHAUB: Object to the speech.
THE COURT: Sustained.

Schaub's recross consisted of one question.

Q. Then you deny you asked to speak to somebody from the State's Attorney's office to get out of jail while you were down here?
A. Yes, sir, I do.

It now appeared certain that persons connected with law enforcement would be brought in by the prosecution in an effort to cast doubt upon the three prison witnesses who had testified for Richardson.

The last defense witness was Flanders Thompson, the Sheriff of Lee County. He said that in the twenty years he had been Sheriff he had occasion to supervise and make arrests of persons charged with felonies.

Robinson had one more question to ask before the defense rested.

Q. Would you please tell the court and jury what is the practice of your office in either you personally or having any of your officers either make statements to the press or give personal opinions of the guilt or innocence of men you have arrested for a felony?

MR. SCHAUB: Objected to as immaterial to the issues of this case.

THE COURT: Sustained.

MR. ROBINSON: The defense rests.

It seemed somehow properly symbolic that the last word spoken by the Court before the defense rested was "sustained." Schaub's objection was technically well taken, without doubt. Yet one is left to ponder the law that deems it permissible for a sheriff to hold press conferences and to proclaim the certain guilt of his charge while it is improper to discuss the fact that he did it.

Schaub's first rebuttal witness was John Boone, a deputy sheriff from Collier County. Boone, known as "Bad Boy," is a tough black man, used throughout Florida by law enforcers in difficult cases involving Negro defendants.

Q. Were you assigned up to assist in De Soto County?
A. Yes, I was.
Q. In the course of your investigation, did you see one James Cunningham?
A. Yes, I did.

He said that he talked with Cunningham in a bar, and then:

A. I reported to the Sheriff of De Soto County.
Q. Frank Cline?
A. Right.

He said that he had met Cunningham in a bar in November.

Schaub evidently had been troubled by the evidence that indicated the three convicts who testified for the State made their observations known in March rather than in November.

Boone was put on the stand solely to show that he had spoken to Cunningham in November. Boone said that Cunningham told him on that occasion only that Richardson had said to Cunningham that he feared for his life. "He came to jail and he started crying while he was talking to him. He asked what was the matter. He stated to him that they was going to kill him."

That testimony, limited though it was in value, was a clear violation of the hearsay rule, as the judge was to hold a moment later.

Robinson questioned Boone about his interrogation of Richardson. He said that he had talked to him many times but that he made no admissions.

Q. During the course of this investigation you have been pretty brutal with a lot of people in this case?
A. That is not true.

A little later Robinson asked, "Do you deny you had been involved with this man and cussed him and insisted he tell you the truth?" Before Boone could respond, Schaub objected. "Objection unless there is some substantiation for this. His questions are very suggestive with no basis. He is testifying himself. He has gotten all negative answers." At last Schaub had displayed some sensitivity to the rule prohibiting counsel from communicating to the jury through questions.

Q. You never cussed this man?
A. No, I had no reason to.
Q. Never did?
A. What would I want to cuss him for? I don't even know the man. That is the first time I seen him.
Q. You talked to him quite a bit?

A. I tried to.

Q. How many times were you together, the two of you together?

A. Several times.

Q. How many times?

A. I didn't count them.

Q. In fact, you talked to him about every day, didn't you?

A. Not every day.

Q. Took him downstairs and brought him back?

A. I did several times, but not every day.

Q. Quite a few times?

A. Yes.

Q. You kept trying to question him?

A. He wouldn't answer.

Q. He denied it, too?

A. Sure, the only thing, you told him not to talk to me or anybody else.

Q. Didn't he deny the fact that he killed his children?

A. Certainly he did.

MR. ROBINSON: No further questions.

Treadwell made his third appearance as a prosecution witness. He said that he had been "the prosecutor in charge of the charges pending against Ernell Washington at that time." Schaub was trying to prove through his own colleague at the prosecutor's table that there was no deal with Washington. The record does not reveal that he was entirely successful.

Q. I will ask you when you and the other investigating officers in this case first learned that Ernell Washington might be a witness in this case?

A. On March 6, myself and Sheriff Frank Cline and Mr. Norman Dezlight, the special officer from the Florida Bureau of Law Enforcement, and myself took a statement of Ernell Washington in the De Soto County jail.

Q. When was the first time you discussed with Ernell Washington the possible sentence he might receive for those charges, with him or his counsel?

A. It would have been March 7, the day after the statement.

Q. The first time you ever discussed it with Ernell?

A. Not with Ernell. I discussed it with his attorney, Mr. Walter Talley, the Public Defender.

The Richardson case was the biggest legal event in Florida that year. A press association said that it was the third-biggest news story of the entire year for the State. It is difficult to believe that in November it was known that Washington had heard admissions made by Richardson the month before, and yet was not questioned by Treadwell about it until March 6, the next year. Treadwell maintains his office in Arcadia, just a five-minute walk from where Washington was confined.

Treadwell then said that he first talked to Washington's lawyer "about possible probation" on December 9. In what appeared to be the presentation of an entirely new prosecution theory, perhaps brought on by the testimony of McDonald, McQueen, and Johnson, Treadwell then testified, "I first learned he [Washington] would be a possible witness on March 6, 1968."

The State's next witness was Virginia Nash, a nurse at the Arcadia General Hospital. Schaub called her so that she might answer one question.

Q. Would you please relate to us what if any emotion James Richardson displayed in identifying those children?

A. He had no emotion.

Whitson handled the cross-examination quite expertly.

Q. How long have you been a nurse?
A. Thirty-seven years.
Q. You are an RN?
A. No, LPN.
Q. Do you know what shock is, emotional shock?
A. Yes, sir, I do.
Q. Have you ever seen anybody in emotional shock?
A. Yes, I have.
Q. Have you seen people in emotional shock for two or three days and they don't cry and you pray they will cry so they will get rid of that shock?
A. Not that long.
Q. You have seen it as long as that boy was in that hospital before he identified his children for you, haven't you? You have seen it longer than four hours, haven't you?
A. Yes, I have.

Schaub responded with one question:

Q. Did you see any evidence of this from James Richardson?
A. No, sir, I did not.

On recross, Mrs. Nash said that she had no way of determining whether Richardson had been in a state of shock.

Schaub called one of his own investigators next. E. G. Ostling said that a deputy sheriff, Lee Hayes, brought David Johnson to see him. Johnson told him that he had "something detrimental to this case" to tell Schaub, the witness claimed. According to Schaub's investigator, Johnson wanted to be released on probation. As to what information Johnson had to offer, Ostling said, "He talked mostly in circles." As to what the information was, Ostling could only answer, "He would not tell me."

The cross-examination by Robinson was brief.

Q. He never did tell you what he wanted to talk about?
A. You are correct.
Q. You don't know what it was about?
A. No, he would not tell us.
Q. So you don't know what he was going to tell you?
A. I only know what he said.
Q. But he didn't say anything about the facts? He didn't say what he was going to say?
A. He said it would be detrimental.
Q. He didn't say what it was about?
A. No, he said he wanted to talk to Schaub.
Q. You have no idea as to what this man was going to tell you, do you?
A. No, I don't know what was in his mind, of course not.

Lee Hayes testified for less than one minute. He agreed with Ostling that the meeting with Johnson had taken place.

On cross-examination Robinson asked the deputy if Johnson was indicating that if Schaub got probation for him he might decline to testify for the defense; "The fact that he didn't testify could be detrimental to the defense; isn't that true?"

The Court sustained Schaub's objection to the question.

The Court recessed for the day.

On Friday morning, May 31, the final day of the trial began with the testimony of Norman Dezlight, a special agent for the Florida Bureau of Law Enforcement. He said that he had questioned McDonald and that "McDonald told me that he couldn't help me but he sent me to Ernell Washington, Spot, known as James Weaver, Cunningham, and McQueen."

Q. By virtue of that, did you thereafter meet Ernell Washington?

A. Yes, sir, I did.

Q. Did you talk with him?

A. Yes, sir, I did.

Q. Did you bring this information to the Sheriff of De Soto county?

A. Yes, sir, I did.

Q. Did he acknowledge he had information concerning this case?

A. On the first day he did not; on the second day he did.

Dezlight said that he notified Cline and Treadwell of Washington's statement on March 6.

Whitson's cross-examination was on another subject.

Q. I believe in response to certain questions there that you knew there was a central file, that there was a cooperation of law-enforcement officials in various places in Florida, that you were kept abreast of everything that took place; is that right?

A. More or less, yes, sir.

Q. Do you know Sheriff Rodney Thursby of Saint Lucie County?

A. Yes, sir, I do.

Q. Is it a fact that you called Sheriff Thursby and told him that the State had an extremely weak case in this instance?

MR. SCHAUB: Objection and ask the Judge to instruct the jury to disregard it.

THE COURT: Sustained, granted.

The last witness called by the prosecution was James Foy,

another of Schaub's investigators. He was called to rebut the testimony of Annie Mae Richardson regarding her observation of the defendant's actions during the evening of October 24 and in the early hours of the next morning. Foy brought with him a tape recording to prove that Mrs. Richardson had lied. He said that Schaub himself was present at the interview.

Q. Did you have the interviews transcribed?
A. I did.
Q. How?
A. By means of a tape recorder.
Q. Do you have the tape recording with you?
A. Yes, I do.
Q. How long does it take for the interview of Annie Mae?
A. In the neighborhood of 30 to 45 minutes more or less.
Q. Did you mark the portions concerning her answers to when James went to bed the night before the children's death?
A. Yes, I did.
Q. How about the part of the life insurance? Did you mark that portion?
A. Yes, sir.
Q. Do you have the tapes with you?
A. Yes.
Q. Would you set them up?

The official transcript reveals the scene that unfolded in the courtroom. "A tape-recording machine was set up and a tape was played, during which time the following proceedings were had:"

Q. Did you say that this was the time he got up in the morning?
A. Yes.

MR. ROBINSON: Back up a little bit, because that is clarified. You can play the whole tape if you like.

THE COURT: Do you have a transcript of it?

MR. ROBINSON: Yes.

THE COURT: Do you see any need to?

MR. ROBINSON: Just substantiates what Annie Mae said all the way through.

THE COURT: Would you require it?

MR. ROBINSON: No, sir.

MR. SCHAUB: Is that the last remark? We will have to play the whole tape.

"The tape was restarted on the machine, and during the playing thereof the following proceedings were had:"

A JUROR: I couldn't hear it all.

THE COURT: You might have to raise it up. Let me state there will be no leaving the courtroom during the playing of this. There will be a minimum of noise. No one will be admitted into the courtroom.

"Because of interfering noise or inaudibility, this reporter was unable to record sufficient of the tape to certify as to its accuracy."

The court reporter, or stenographer, was seated closer to the tape recorder than anyone else in the courtroom, yet he certified that the tape was largely inaudible.

The official investigation was well under way when the State's Attorney himself traveled all the way to Arcadia to question witnesses. In his presence the wife of the suspect was questioned and a tape recording of her interview was made. Schaub cannot investigate every crime that occurs within the substantial area that comprises his jurisdiction. This was the big case, as his campaign literature was later to claim. Was the State really unable to provide an adequate tape recorder for the interview?

The Court completed the record by admitting the valueless tape into evidence. There was no cross-examination of the witness. The case had ended with a decided anticlimax, but it had nevertheless ended.

Charlie Smith, Gerald Purvis and the enigmatic Bessie Reese had not been called.

Whitson moved for a directed verdict:

The Court responded with four words: "It will be denied."

All that was left of the case were the closing arguments by each side, the judge's charge, and the jury's verdict.

The rules which govern trials in Florida and prevail even in capital cases do not provide for a transcript to be made of the closing statements by either side. This odd procedure permits the prosecutor a good deal of freedom, since he may always deny that he made the prejudicial remark for which a new trial may be sought. It cannot affect the defense lawyer very much, for the State may not appeal from the verdict of acquittal, even in Florida.

Robinson's closing argument centered on the weakness of the circumstantial evidence and stressed that the only evidence against his client was offered by the three convicts who had a great deal to gain through their testimony. He stressed the fact that the parathion found on the various kitchen utensils had never been linked to Richardson. Robinson ridiculed the prosecution's argument that Richardson had put parathion in the grits when they were cooking. The children ate the grits for breakfast and would have been dead long before lunch, he said.

While the evidence did not relate the parathion to Richardson—no one ever saw him put it into the food, no one ever saw him with parathion, and no one testified that the

poison was ever in his possession—Schaub did link the parathion directly to the defendant. In his closing argument,
perhaps in response to the most telling point made by
Robinson, Schaub said that the evidence showed that the
parathion had been "in Richardson's locked refrigerator." No
witness had said that during the trial.

Schaub continued, "When seven out of seven die by oral
ingestion of parathion, we do not have an accident, we have
a criminal act. I submit to you if we have a poisoning we
have a premeditated murder." Schaub had enunciated new
juridical concepts. Poisonings are not accidental when all
die, and the very death of all is proof of premeditation as
well. Yet a minute amount of parathion in the food, a tenth
of a teaspoon, would have killed all of the children, the evidence had showed.

During the closing argument, when it was too late for the
defense to offer any evidence or even comment, Schaub
offered a surprise conclusion. "The reason for the parathion
in the talcum powder was to collect that two-thousand-dollar
insurance policy on Annie Mae." Schaub then charged the
defendant with another crime in his closing statement—attempted murder. Later Annie Mae was to tell me that the
talcum powder was her husband's and that she had never
used it. But that was later.

Schaub then talked about motive. "It's difficult for anyone
to have a motive to kill seven small children. James Richardson had two. He wanted to get out from under them,
and he wanted to collect on their life insurance." This despite
the fact that there was no life insurance and that Schaub
had refused to call the insurance salesman as a witness so
that the jury could determine whether Richardson could have
been under the impression that there had been a policy in
effect.

Schaub discussed Richardson's statement that he was innocent and that he had loved the children next. "When such

a sanctimonious hypocrite goes through such false propriety with such dramatics . . ." and then Schaub let his generally booming voice trail off either for dramatic effect or because he could not think of a fitting conclusion for such a grandiloquent start.

Richardson sat at the defense table looking totally bewildered. He understood very little of what Schaub was saying.

"He had the best opportunity to poison the children's food," Schaub continued. "He had the only opportunity, and he had the motive." Of course, Annie Mae Richardson, who prepared the food, and Bessie Reese, who helped to serve it, both had better opportunities to tamper with the food than did Richardson. If Mrs. Richardson's testimony was accurate, her husband had no opportunity at all to place the parathion in the food.

Later Schaub was to say that he did not ask for the death penalty. "I never do," he said. "That's up to the jury." That day, however, Schaub told the jurors that they must consider whether Richardson, "who murdered his own children," should die in the electric chair. Of the death penalty he said, "Neither my oath as State Attorney nor your oath as jurors permit us to take the easy way out."

Schaub stressed his resentment at the derogatory allegations made about Arcadia, Cline, Judge Hayes, Treadwell, and Dr. Schmierer. There were those who thought his appeal to be chauvinistic. Whatever Schaub meant, he did defend the white Arcadian establishment to a white jury from the largely illusory attacks made by the black defendant and his National Association for the Advancement of Colored People lawyers. True, the NAACP did not support counsel for Richardson, but the jurors had read that the organization had retained Robinson to represent Richardson.

After the closing arguments were concluded, the Judge began his charge to the jury: "As I informed you at the start of this trial, the thirteenth member of the jury will remain in the box until such time as the jury does retire for the verdict; so at the conclusion of the reading of these charges, the gentleman on the last row on the immediate left will step aside."

Schaub left the courtroom and the city as soon as the jury retired to consider its verdict. He was on his way home to Bradenton. Veteran courthouse buffs interpreted his sudden departure as a sure sign that he felt that he would have no victory to celebrate that day.

After the charge was read, Robinson approached Grant Kessler, the thirteenth member of the jury. In an important case, or in one that may require several days to try, the Court will often swear in an alternate juror. The alternate is present during the entire trial and stands ready to serve as a regular juror should one of the first twelve suffer a disabling illness. Lawyers often interview the alternate as soon as the charge has been read. In that way it becomes possible to make an educated guess as to what the other twelve may be thinking. In any event, there is nothing else to do in the suspenseful moments that begin when the jury retires to consider its verdict and that come to a conclusion only when the verdict is read. Robinson approached Kessler and asked him what he thought about the case. Kessler replied, "It looks to me like the State didn't have much of a case." He added that he would have found the defendant guilty anyway: "Someone had to do it, and he could have done it." Kessler explained, "All niggers lie, anyway." Robinson said, "But on the voir dire examination I asked you if you would give as much credibility and weight to the testimony of a Negro person as you would to a white person, and you said you would." Kessler responded, "Well, what can you do? You know how they are."

Approximately ninety minutes later, that murmur that runs

through any courtroom just before it is announced that the jury is on its way in quickly spread through the chamber. Young Negro men, wearing their hair in the natural African style, stirred uneasily. A number of blacks from citrus groves in the Arcadia area looked about, wondering what was to happen.

Robinson was not in the courtroom. He had agreed with Whitson to alternate two-hour shifts. Whitson had drawn the first one, and it now appeared that there would be no need for a second. There was no time to call Robinson before the jury entered the courtroom.

Juries sometimes return for the purpose of asking a question, having the judge read a portion of the charge to them again, or to have portions of the evidence read. Moments before the jury filed in, the unforgettable whisper, always present, often correct, was heard, "It's a verdict."

The Judge had charged the jurors that they could return one of six verdicts and that their decision must be unanimous: guilty of first-degree murder, the penalty being death; guilty of first-degree murder, with a recommendation of mercy; guilty of second-degree murder; guilty of third-degree murder; guilty of manslaughter; not guilty.

He now looked at the foreman and said, "Gentlemen, have you reached a verdict?" The foreman answered, "We have." He continued, "We, the jury, find the defendant, James Joseph Richardson, guilty of first-degree murder as charged in the indictment. So say we all."

Whitson remembers that, "A howl went up, 'Oh, Lord God,' and 'Oh, no, dear Lord.' "

Some present began to cry. A number of women half-sobbed, "No, no, no." Annie Mae wept uncontrollably. Judge Justice ordered that she be taken out of the courtroom at once. He then ordered other women who were crying to leave.

The Judge asked Whitson if he wanted the sentence to take place that day. Whitson asked for time to confer with his partner by telephone. He was given a few minutes and called Robinson at the Holiday Inn, where he was attempting to rest.

"John, the jury brought in a verdict of guilty of murder one without a recommendation of mercy. The Judge wants to know if we want the automatic sentence to be imposed now." Robinson said, "Richard, this is a bad joke. You know I don't believe that." Whitson insisted that he was in earnest and asked if Robinson agreed that the sentence might just as well be imposed now. Robinson acquiesced, adding, "I just can't come over there now. Give me a few minutes."

Whitson returned to court and said that the defendant was ready for sentence.

The Judge then ordered Richardson to stand. He did. The judge then looked down at Richardson from his bench set high above the level of the floor and said, "You have heard the verdict, that they have found you guilty of murder in the first degree. The court adjudges you guilty of murder in the first degree. Do you have anything to say why I should not pronounce sentence?"

Richardson was dazed by all that had happened around him. He was concerned that his wife was no longer near. The Judge repeated his question, "Do you have anything to say why I should not pronounce sentence?" Richardson looked at the Judge, then at his attorney, shrugged his shoulders with some embarrassment, and said, "I don't understand." The Judge repeated his question, "Do you have anything to say?" Richardson said, "Sir, I don't understand." The Judge, having dallied long enough, brought the drama back to the original legal script, but not without considerable difficulty. His normally red face (he had been a redhead before his hair turned judicial silver) blanched. This was the first death sentence he was ever to impose. Most judges prefer to start that aspect of their career with a clearly guilty defendant. He gulped, choked, drank some water, and began, "It is the sentence of this court that you be committed to the State Prison at Raiford, there to remain until such time as you shall be put to death according to the laws of the State." He half-coughed, half-choked, and sipped from the glass again.

Richardson turned sideways toward a deputy, who held out a pair of handcuffs. Richardson extended his arms, and the deputy placed the handcuffs on his wrists and then locked them. He then led him into a room near the court. Whitson told his client that this was not the end, but he did not appear to understand.

In the corridor Mrs. Richardson was silently sobbing. An elderly Negro woman walked over to her, put her arm around her, and said, "It's just prejudice. It's all prejudice."

Whitson attempted to convince Richardson that the appeal would be prosecuted quickly and diligently. By then Richardson understood that he had been sentenced to death. He turned away for a moment, then looked at Whitson and said, "It's all right, Mr. Whitson. I trust you and Mr. Robinson." Whitson said that eventually Richardson would walk out of jail, that after a new trial he would be found innocent. Richardson replied, "I trust you and Mr. Robinson. Would you thank Mr. Robinson for me if I don't see him again soon."

As Whitson walked out through the courtroom, he saw Treadwell. "He was dressed in one of those flowered Hawaiian shirts and Bermuda shorts. He walked right up to me, all smiles, stuck out his hand, and said, 'Don't you feel bad. Y'all can't win them all, and you boys did a real nice job at the trial.' He had his hand out. I never said a word to him, just walked right on by. I had never refused a man's hand before."

Robinson hurried over to a house that he had arranged to make available to Mrs. Richardson and other members of the family. He spent three hours there consoling and reassuring the heartbroken group. Then he went to the jail to visit Richardson and pledge his continued commitment to the case. He left Richardson in the jail and wearily returned to the Holiday Inn. Cline and Treadwell and some others were celebrating the victory with a party at the bar at the motel. Cline walked out of the lounge smiling broadly. He saw Robinson and stopped, then smiled again and said, "Say good-bye to James for me."

Robinson repeated the words he had just spoken to his client, "This is not the end." Cline said, "No?" Robinson replied, "I know what you've done. This case will be back, and I'll ruin you for what you've done."

Cline's smile vanished, then returned. "Take your best holt," he said.

5. The Investigation

FRANK CLINE

AFTER READING THE TRIAL TRANSCRIPT, I was anxious to meet and interview the main characters in the drama. Purvis, purportedly, supplied motive. Bessie Reese was a crucial witness, and so was Charlie Smith. Although the jury had not heard them, I was determined to.

I also wanted to meet Schaub and Cline. I planned to interview Robinson and Whitson and hoped to arrange to get into death row to talk with Richardson. Barnard and Minoughan appeared to have relevant information to offer. Finally, I hoped to get more information about the sudden emergence of the three convict witnesses for the State.

Half a year after my investigation began, I had been able to interview every relevant witness and party.

I began at the beginning—with Frank Cline. I confess at the outset that my candor was somewhat guarded in my telephone call to the Sheriff to arrange for the interview. I reasoned that if I said that the validity, not to say probity, of his methods was in question in my mind, the termination of the meeting might be too abrupt, if, indeed, the meeting ever began.

I informed Cline that I was planning a book on mass murders and that his case might comprise the first chapter, since he had solved it so quickly and neatly. He seemed pleased, and informed me that he was satisfied with the job, adding modestly that he had "a whole bushel of help from other folks."

He agreed to see me the next afternoon at his office in the jail. I arrived on time, but he was not there. A deputy asked me to return in an hour. I did, and Cline still had not returned. I told the deputy that I had an appointment with the Sheriff, that my name was Mark Lane, that I was an author, and that I planned to write a book, or part of one, about the Richardson case.

I asked if he might call to tell Cline that I was waiting. The deputy did not answer. I repeated my request. The deputy said, "You just wait there," indicating a plastic-covered stuffed couch. The deputy was concentrating on a radio broadcast of a football game.

During a commercial, about five minutes later, he called Cline and told him that some reporter was waiting. "Naw, I don't know his name. Says you said for him to come down," the deputy reported to Cline. After a brief pause he added, "He didn't say which paper he's from." Then another pause, and the deputy said, "Okay," and replaced the telephone receiver into its cradle.

He turned the volume up on the radio and during the next commercial advised me to "Just wait there like I told you. The Sheriff is coming over."

During the next hour, I had an adequate opportunity to observe the waiting room. On the wall was a guide to hunting and fishing in Florida and to the proper dates for shooting ducks, squirrels, and rabbits. A poster warned the reader to "Lock 'em up," referring to blasting caps, so that "children can't find them and get hurt."

A wall was covered with posters of wanted criminals, including one who had been reported by the newspapers to have been captured two months before. Another wall bore the De Soto High School "Bulldogs" 1968 football schedule and the same school's 1968-69 basketball schedule.

The police radio intermittently barked out intelligence, competing on those occasions with the football game.

One report stated that a man had been bitten by a rattlesnake and that he was being rushed to a hospital. Ten minutes later a telephone caller evidently was inquiring about the snakebite. The deputy replied, "Well, I don't know where that happened. It seems that I did hear something like that on the radio a while back, but I'm not too sure. We're pretty busy here."

During half-time, I was entertained by the sounds of marching bands and the deputy's nails being trimmed in time, by a pocket nail clipper, which he handled with surprising skill.

Sheriff Frank Cline arrived, shook hands with me, and ushered me into his little office. Our interview was relatively brief.

I conveyed the impression that I knew almost nothing about the case and that I was going to rely primarily upon him for a recitation of the relevant facts. Sheriff Cline took full advantage of the situation. He told how quickly he had recognized the parathion smell in the apartment.

He said that he was the first law officer to arrive there and that, although he had a lot of help from other agencies and people, he was proud of his role in solving the crime so quickly. He said that he found the bag of parathion the next day.

I told him that I had read a newspaper article that indicated that a woman, Bessie Reese, had served the food to the children. He said, "Well, that's right, but she didn't have anything to do with the crime. The jury believed her, and so do I." I asked if Mrs. Reese had testified at the trial, and he replied, "She certainly did. She was an important witness for us."

I asked Cline if there had been any charges of racial bias in the entire matter. "No, none at all," he replied. "In fact, the head of the NAACP helped us a lot in this case. He walked right up to me on the street and offered to help us get Richardson."

I remarked that that seemed rather unusual. Cline smiled, puffed on his metal-stemmed pipe, and said, "Well, we don't have the problems here, I mean with the colored, that you have in those big cities. We have none at all." I congratulated him and asked if he could share Arcadia's formula with me. "We don't have these problems, and I don't think we will have. What we do have is control. We just control the situation."

I thanked the Sheriff for the interview and asked if I might return with a photographer sometime in the future. He said that I might.

In the next weeks, I had an opportunity to learn more about the Sheriff of De Soto County. He had been a deputy in 1965 when the sheriff died. In a special runoff election, he won by securing the preponderance of absentee votes. His rough-and-ready approach to criminology, in an area where cattle rustling still constitutes the major law-enforcement problem, won him strong supporters and bitter enemies.

One summer he was involved in a gunfight with a suspect. Cline was wounded in the ankle; the suspect was killed.

Even his theory that Negroes have lower intelligence because their skulls are too small to allow their brains to grow evidently did not harm him politically in the Quarters. His use of the word "nigger" rarely distinguishes him from his opponent, in any event, so the small Negro vote often has had little choice.

On May 7, 1968, Cline was reelected, but by a rather narrow margin. He was opposed by a young man who had little background in law enforcement. Of the more than 3,400 votes cast, Cline won by eighty. The election campaign began not long after Cline announced that he had solved the murder of the Richardson children.

The strange and brutal happenings in the De Soto County jail in Arcadia had caused some concern in that small town. When Judge Hayes was alive, his unwillingness to see evil under certain circumstances was an invaluable contribution to the continuation of the events in the jail.

As one example, when a thirty-three-year-old resident was arrested for various traffic violations and placed in the jail at 12:45 A.M., it seemed mysterious to some that his lifeless body was discovered there just five hours later.

Judge Hayes, acting as coroner on that occasion, said the explanation was quite simple. The man had committed suicide, evidently in fear of having his driver's license suspended. The local newspaper explained how it was done. The deceased "had used one of his sheets to tie a noose around his neck. He then had utilized one of the cell bars to get leverage, held the sheet with one hand, and squatted or leaned down to choke himself to death."

The newspaper concluded its factual recitation: "De Soto County Coroner Gordon Hayes, Assistant State's Attorney J. H. Treadwell, III, and Sheriff Cline investigated, and Judge Hayes ruled death by suicide."

After the death of the Coroner, it began to appear that most of De Soto's crime had taken place in its jail facility, where criminals with long records were confined together with juveniles and persons awaiting certification to be sent to mental hospitals.

On March 30, 1969, the Tampa *Tribune* disclosed that "Violence among prisoners in the antiquated, deteriorating De Soto County jail occurs frequently." The *Tribune* began to look into the matter when one inmate was stabbed, almost fatally, by another.

Allegations of constant beatings by some of the prisoners and news reports of successful escapes from the institution, including one prisoner who dug his way out with a spoon, reveal that not much has changed at the county jail since the arrest of James Richardson. Yet the Sheriff has changed considerably.

Duncan Groner, the incisive reporter for the St. Petersburg *Times,* observed, "But Cline has very obviously mastered the first chapter in a primer of public relations since he arrested Richardson something like a month ago. In the long gone days, Cline liked to talk about how much the local 'niggers' loved him. Now he calls them Negroes and inevitably adds the predictable: 'We don't even call 'em chiggers round here no more. They're chigroes.'"

I arranged with Cline for another interview. We met at his office in the jail and then drove over to his office in the courthouse in order that I might see the award given to him by *Official Detective Magazine* for having cracked the case so quickly.

I asked what he considered the strongest evidence against Richardson. He replied without hesitation that it was the testimony of Weaver, Cunningham, and Washington. I asked how he came into contact with the three men, and he replied that, "Weaver gets in jail and out of jail all the time. He said something was bothering him. Then we talked to Washington and Cunningham, and after that it sort of all fell together."

I asked the Sheriff what evidence first pointed toward Richardson as the guilty party. "Well, there was a lot of head scratching going on. We talked to a lot of people.

Talked to ourselves and we come upon the information from the insurance agent, which, in itself, raised the question of Richardson's guilt.

"Then we did background on a lot of individuals, and the tests raised questions as to why certain articles contained parathion and others did not contain it. It was in the sugar and in the powder. That was 'cause he wanted to kill his wife also." I informed Cline that all of the available evidence demonstrated that the body powder was used only by James Richardson and that Annie Mae did not use sugar. The sugar was used by James in his coffee. Cline studied me for a full minute. I wondered if I had gone too far in revealing my knowledge of some of the facts. Then Cline said, "Well, he put it there to throw suspicion off of himself."

The Sheriff was facile. He had a theory for every situation.

Since the mood had altered, I told him that I discovered that Mrs. Reese had not testified at the trial. He said, "I thought the defense would have called her." When asked why the State did not, he answered that he was "not in charge."

I asked him if he had ever questioned Bessie Reese. "Yeah. I got hours and hours and hours of tapes with every witness we ever talked to. Bessie too. I got hours of tapes with her."

Cline told me that the smell of poison gas was over-whelming when he entered the apartment on October 25. I asked why Bessie had been unable to smell the poison before she served it to the children. He shrugged, "Sometimes people don't pay attention to what they smell." Had he asked Bessie Reese that question? "I don't remember if I did or not, but, anyways, I don't remember what she said."

We talked about Charlie Smith. "Oh, you all know about him, do you? Well, he is the one what found the parathion bag. It was in the shed that morning, all right, and Charlie found it there."

Cline told me that he had searched the entire area the

night before, including the shed "three or four times, and I couldn't a missed it." "Did you miss it?" I asked. "Hell, no. It wasn't there. It was put there after we was done looking that night or in the morning. And it was put there by the killer—by Richardson."

I asked why Richardson, who, according to the Sheriff's theory, had successfully hidden the murder weapon, would display it so near his own apartment, where it was sure to be found that morning. "It's simple," replied the Sheriff. "He didn't want to be seen carrying the bag." "But," I reminded Cline, "he did carry it, according to that theory, late at night, in a small town where he was known, and on the very night that his children had died." Cline said, "Yes, that's right."

Did not Richardson at the trial account for every moment of his time that night and morning? Cline looked almost disgusted, "Well, those people . . ." I changed the subject.

What led Charlie Smith to the bag? "Well, you got to know Charlie. He is a wino. Now, this shed was on his path, where he went every morning from his home to where he caught a ride to work. Well, that day Charlie goes by the building on the avenue and he meets Bessie in front of the apartment. He says to her, 'We ought to find that parathion before a lot of kids get into it.' He leads her to the shed. He starts ripping plywood off the window instead of opening the door. Then he sees the bag there, and he says, 'What is this?' And that's how he found it. Peculiar! He didn't even go in the open door. He ripped the wood off of the window."

I asked Cline if he had a theory to explain that unusual approach to an open shed.

"That's simple too. Charlie was drinking that morning. He saw someone put the poison through that window. In his mind, you know what I mean, in his mind there weren't even a door there, for practical purposes. You got to understand these people. How they think. That door is only eight inches from the window. He thought it had to go through the window. It was dropped in there that way. Parathion was on the sill, and some spilled on the floor."

I asked Cline if he was of the opinion that Smith actually saw the killer put the parathion in the shed. "It sure looks that way," he answered. I asked Cline if he had ever questioned Smith. "Sure. Hours and hours. Got it all on tape." Did Charlie ever tell you who the murderer was? "Well, he ain't exactly said he saw them put it in the shed. I know he did, but he won't say it, so he won't tell who did it. But it had to be Richardson. He's the one that poisoned the kids, isn't he?"

A good question, but one I left unanswered. If Smith actually knows who the killer is, should not he have been called as a witness by the State? Cline answered, "Wasn't he?"

Cline added, "But's like I said, that's not the important question. It was the insurance that led me to it at once. Insurance was the important question."

I asked why the insurance agent had not testified at the trial. "Wasn't he a witness either?" Cline responded. "Anyway, I talked to him, and I'll tell you what he said. Richardson thought he had insurance. That's the main thing. That's why he did it, for the insurance money. That's how they are. Sure, Richardson denied it, but who would you believe? Purvis, an insurance salesman, or something like Richardson?" Another unanswered question.

Cline continued. "Anyway, witnesses see things that weren't even there. Witnesses are always wrong. Take you. You've been here taking notes for a long time. You don't even know what's up on that wall right behind you, back about twenty foot from you, do you?"

I knew that there was a rack with enough arms to supply a small army, rifles, shotguns, a submachine gun, and various other weapons. I could hardly have missed it when I entered the room. Cline thought he won that one, nevertheless, since I was unable to identify the make of the weapons. I conceded, and asked if there was any doubt in his mind that Richardson was the murderer. "No. There is none."

I asked if he had ever admitted his guilt.

"No, he never did. He was stubborn. But there is no doubt."

By then Cline knew that I had read the transcript of the trial and began to suspect that I was not convinced by it. He went on, "If we could have just told the jury everything we knew without those rules of evidence making the evidence inadmissible, they would never have bothered to leave the the jury box to say guilty."

My curiosity was aroused. I asked if he was referring to the "lie-detector test," the substance of which he and Schaub had refused to disclose to Robinson or to me, while fully commenting about the "results" to the press. I pointed out that the jury had, in all probability, read his assertion that "Richardson had failed the test." I reminded him that Judge Hayes had also said that on many occasions.

The Sheriff said, "No, I don't mean that. There's a lot more. There's plenty more that could have been brought out. Frank Schaub has said that many times. I can't think of any of it now, but you ask the State's Attorney that question."

Cline walked me to the door and introduced me to a deputy and to one of the Sheriff's dogs. "We got trail dogs that follow a trail even four hours old; and ketch dogs that will kill or disable you. That's a ketch dog there. He's one hundred pounds." I observed that it was a German shepherd. "We call all German shepherds ketch dogs."

Then he showed me his automobile. It was a Ford LTD. "I call it a police interceptor, four-twenty-nine. You see that speedometer, it goes up to one-twenty. I've gone so fast in this car, I just run out of numbers."

Several weeks later, I read that a number of convicts had escaped from a De Soto County correctional facility and that the Sheriff and his men were unable to locate any of them.

FRANK SCHAUB

I interviewed Frank Schaub at the office he maintains at the Manatee County Courthouse in Bradenton. My concern for apparent consistency, if not full disclosure, led me to introduce myself to the prosecuting attorney as I had to the Sheriff.

Schaub was born in New York State, a fact omitted from his otherwise detailed political fact sheet. When a transplanted New Yorker seeks votes in the Deep South, he must be somewhat cunning. The fact sheet carries Schaub's claim that, "I have prosecuted at trial over one hundred homicide cases and had only three acquittals."

It also lists the cases Schaub has selected as the most important. First on the list is *State v. James Joseph Richardson* —for the parathion poisoning of his children." The *State v. Carl Coppolino* takes fifth place.

As a reason for seeking reelection, Schaub complains of the "continual erosion by the Supreme Court of the evidence and laws needed for convictions." He states that, therefore, the area needs the "services of every experienced prosecutor."

He adds that it is necessary "to continue the widespread image of our area as the most law-abiding in the State of Florida," and concludes that he must be reelected "to insure that the hard-fought and expensive convictions we obtained in such cases as the Richardson, Coppolino, and Sikes cases are not reversed by the higher courts."

I told Schaub that Cline had informed me that there was additional evidence against Richardson that would have proven his guilt conclusively that was not admissible due to the rules of evidence. I asked Schaub if he could relate some of it to me.

"Well, what convinces me beyond any doubt was his lying about many different things. He lied, and he contradicted himself when we questioned him."

I asked if he might give me an example. "Dozens of things. I don't recall them now, but there were many. Very many. Many were not too consequential, but others were."

"Do you recall any false statements that Richardson made?"

"Not offhand. It's been some time now."

"Yet this is what convinces you of his guilt?"

"Yes. There were many of them, many contradictions."

"What was the strongest evidence that connected Richardson with the poisoning of the children?"

"We never did. It was a circumstantial case. We never had any direct evidence that he administered the poison. But it had to be him or her. Either one. Things she used were saturated with parathion, and not things that he used."

"Such as?"

"Powder and sugar."

"What is the basis for that conclusion?"

"What conclusion?"

"That Mrs. Richardson used the powder and sugar and that he did not?"

"I don't remember. We were told that."

"Was Cline the source?"

"Possibly. As I said, I am not sure."

"What was the motive?"

"Insurance. And to avoid the responsibility for supporting

the children. He was on the outs with his wife. She had accused him of having an affair with the woman next door. Anyway, he was motivated by complete self-interest. He had no interest in his family or anyone else.

"He was unusual for a Negro. He didn't drink, didn't own an automobile. He just didn't spend money. He had a pathological adoration for money. Complete self-interest. He had no milk for the children. He fed them grits three times a day. Insurance was the main motive."

"Why did you not call Purvis to testify?"

"Under the insurance law, you can't solicit insurance on credit, particularly those handling debits. They frequently will write somebody up with no hope of collecting. But it is illegal. If he did make such a definite commitment, then there would have been a policy and the company would have to pay. So, I felt that this agent would not have testified that there was a policy. So, I didn't put him on."

"Why did you indicate that you were going to call him?"

He smiled at the naïveté of the question and answered, "The other side was discouraged from using him. They didn't call him, you know."

"Why was no record made of the testimony at the preliminary hearing?"

"A record at a preliminary hearing is against the interest of the prosecution. I didn't want that testimony preserved."

"Was the smell of parathion strong when you entered the apartment?"

"Yes. He put the poison in the food the night before, while it was cooking. There was testimony about that."

"Then how could Bessie Reese not have smelled the parathion in the grits that were cooked before seven A.M., when the Richardsons left for work?"

"That house had more smells. You could have anything in there and not smell it. It was filthy."

"Parathion is a deadly poison gas."

"Yes, I know. Well, I smelled it. I don't know about Bessie."

"What was the strongest evidence against Richardson?"

"Only he could have done it. Or his wife. We had nothing to prove that she did it, so it had to be him."

"Could Bessie Reese have done it? She helped serve the food."

"There was no motive for her, and no inclination."

"Did she have a record?"

"Yes. She killed her second husband. I think she was convicted of second-degree murder."

"What about her first husband?"

"I have no idea. There was a story going around that she had poisoned him, but we never looked into it. There was a suggestion that we dig up the body, but we never went into the subject."

"Did her third husband leave with Richardson, fall in love with Richardson's cousin, and decide not to return to Bessie not long before the children were killed?"

"We heard about that. We never went into it, though."

"Yet Mrs. Reese was never a suspect because she had no motive, no access to the food, and no inclination?"

"That's right. That is correct. I don't have much more time now, so we will have to conclude."

"Just another question or two please? How could the court accept into evidence death certificates that give as the cause of death 'premeditated murder'?"

Schaub laughed for the first time during the interview. "Did you see them in the record? The defense never objected. It amazed me. I never saw anything like that in a record before. I was amazed that it was admitted."

"Cline said that he had hours and hours of tape recordings with the witnesses, including Smith and Reese. Have you heard them?"

"My investigators heard them."

"What was on the tapes?"

"I don't recall what they said."

"Did Mrs. Reese feed the children?"

"She admitted that she cut up the food. The kids fed themselves." A two-year-old fed himself? "Maybe Bessie helped feed them."

"What about Charlie Smith?"

"He found the parathion. I think he knows considerably more than he said. He probably saw someone put the poison in the shed. Maybe Smith was with Richardson when he put the parathion in the shed. Smith may have been with him on that."

"Why didn't you call Smith at the trial?"

"I wouldn't put him on the stand."

"Did Richardson kill any children before October 25, 1967?"

"There was a lot of children that died at young ages."

"How many?"

"We found quite a few."

"Do you recall the number?"

"No."

"An approximate number?"

"I don't recall."

"Did you get any proof that Richardson was responsible?"

"No."

"Are you absolutely certain that Richardson poisoned the seven children?"

"Yes. Beyond any doubt. The only question from the beginning was whether the wife was involved. She is of extremely low intelligence. It had to be him or her or both. We had no proof that she was involved. So, it was him."

As I left Schaub's office, I thought of the words spoken to Robinson by the alternate juror. Schaub had placed a fine veneer upon them. But then, he was an attorney, an elected official, a man of taste and sophistication. One could hardly expect him to say, "Someone had to do it, and he could have done it. All niggers lie, anyway." Not in those words.

JON NORDHEIMER

It is difficult to know exactly what prompted the appearance of the three prison witnesses against Richardson. Yet it is not difficult to ascertain the feelings of two of the men most deeply involved in the prosecution of the case regarding the need for additional evidence before the three were discovered.

George Lane was a radio and television reporter for WINK, a St. Petersburg station. He is stationed in Punta Gorda, approximately twenty-five miles from Arcadia, and he was on the scene not long after the deaths were announced. Cline invited him into the Richardsons' apartment, although he failed to disclose that visit during his testimony.

Lane, who is not related to me, took pictures of Cline as he examined the contents of one of the Richardsons' refrigerators on October 25. Some of Lane's pictures were widely circulated by the wire services.

He developed an interest in the case and covered it closely. Much later he was in Cline's office in the De Soto County jail, taking pictures, when Frank Schaub walked in. Lane said that he heard Schaub address Cline, "You got me into this mess. Now, you better get some evidence to get me out of it." Lane states that the conversation took place after Richardson was charged with the murder but before the three prison witnesses were discovered.

The jurors evidently accepted the testimony of the prison witnesses who testified for the State and rejected as unworthy of belief the statements of the prisoners who testified for Richardson and against the three men.

If the jury had been able to hear an impartial eyewitness account of Richardson's first crucial half-hour in the cell, it is possible that the verdict might have been different.

There was such an observer, although Cline was almost successful in preventing that occurrence. Jon Nordheimer was in Arcadia, covering the coroner's inquest for the Miami *Herald*. After the verdict, when some reporters thought that the job was completed, Nordheimer went to the Arcadia jail and asked for permission to see Richardson.

After a moment's delay, Cline told him that Richardson did not want to see him. "It was clear to me that Cline did not want me to see Richardson. He was very firm about it. Of course, he said that he didn't care whether I saw him or not, but that he would not let me up to the cell because Richardson did not want to see me. I insisted.

"When he still refused, I told him that if it later turned out that Richardson wanted to see me, it might be embarrassing for the Sheriff. I said all that I want is for Richardson to tell me that he didn't want to talk to me, and that I would then leave. Cline finally agreed. He sent one of his deputies up with me to see the prisoner."

Nordheimer told me that he had interviewed Richardson before. "He was pretty uncommunicative with me that time. It was soon after the children died, and it was a black-white thing there in that ghetto, in that old cow town. I really regretted the situation. I hoped that he would relate to me then, but I understood, of course, what he had been through."

The deputy escorted the reporter to Richardson's cellblock. "Richardson shook his head slowly as the door locked behind him," Nordheimer said. "Then he started saying, 'I loved those children. I worked night and day for them.'"

The reporter told me that he offered a cigarette to Richardson. The prisoner said, "Hello," took the cigarette, and said, "Thank you."

Nordheimer said that Richardson "continued to protest his innocence." He added, "There certainly was no evidence that he had just made a confession to his fellow prisoners or was about to make one. He obviously thought that it was the most incredible thing in the world that anyone might think that he could have killed his own children. He said that he had just bought them dolls for Christmas, that he loved them."

Nordheimer told me that there were six other Negroes in the cell and that they stood there in the background "listening to Richardson protest his innocence."

It was late in the evening, and a trusty was asleep on a cot outside the cellblock. He woke up and asked what the talk was all about. Richardson said to him, Nordheimer reported, "They are accusing me of killing my children."

Nordheimer also heard a conversation between Annie Mae Richardson and her husband, but it was quite different from the version that the State presented to the jury. "Annie Mae awoke in another cell, hidden from her husband's view. Her voice was thick with sleep. 'What's the matter?' she asked. 'They got me charged with murder of my own children,' he replied. There was no answer from the other cell."

Nordheimer continued to question the defendant. "Richardson said, 'I think somebody better find out who killed my children. That's what I think.' Later Richardson said, 'I've been a working hard man. I've been down all my life. I've tried to protect my children at all times. They say I got my civil rights. Ha! How can a Negro get his rights? They are holding me here, and the judge says I killed my own children. How can I put poison in their food if me and my wife are working in the groves? How can I, huh?' "

What were the impressions that Nordheimer took from the Arcadia jail that night? "First, that Cline, for whatever reason, did not want me to see Richardson, to the point where he was not even truthful about the reason. And second, that Richardson was incredulous, there is just no other word, at the thought that he could even be a suspect."

ROBERT STANCEL

Ernell Washington is dead. Before he died he indicated to Beatrice Cosey, the woman who killed him soon thereafter, that his testimony about Richardson was false. Miss Cosey told Robinson that she "knew that Ernell was lying" and that he "practically admitted" that Richardson had made no admissions to him.

Just after Cunningham testified, he indicated to Robinson that he had been less than truthful. Robinson asked him to tell the truth. Cunningham asked if he would have to go back in the courtroom if he did tell Robinson the truth about what Richardson said or did not say in jail. When Robinson told him that he would be required to repeat the truth under oath, Cunningham stated that he would rather stick to the original story.

The other member of the trio, James Weaver, was more explicit. During the middle of February, 1969, the March issue of *Playboy* magazine was circulated. It contained my letter urging a reconsideration of the Richardson case. This brought about considerable press comment in Florida. James Weaver was back in jail. So was Robert Stancel, a white trusty at the Manatee County jail. Stancel, a practicing moonshiner, had just read about the case and began to talk to Weaver about his testimony. When he learned all he could, he wrote to Robinson.

Robinson visited him in the jail and tape-recorded the interview. Stancel explained his position and his interest. "Richardson is a dumb nigger. He is to be felt sorry for. He is not to be run over like Frank Schaub run over him. I mean, a man don't know his rights, don't know the law, there is no need to just put him down and stomp him. That's something that I feel and everybody feels about the case. Some deputies in De Soto County and a lot of people, upstanding citizens, well it's not going over good with them at all. Hell, they're all upset. Why wouldn't they be? Frank Cline has been a friend of mine. He's done me a lot of favors, but still he'll convict a damn man easy."

Stancel told Robinson, "I was reading the Tampa *Tribune*. I'd just come from court, and Weaver just started talking about Richardson. The deal he got in Fort Myers in his case, and I asked him, and I said, you know I don't think the boy is guilty, because Spot knew I knew Richardson on the outside, had acquaintances with him. And Spot said, 'Yeah; quite a few people thought the same way,' and everything, and he just went on in detail, in confidence, you know, one trusty to the other in jail."

Weaver had been in Lakeland, Florida, when he "was called back from there," Stancel said. "Frank Cline called him. The Sheriff called him. He came to Arcadia on the bus and met him. He [Cline] was down there, and he said they had some kind of discussion or something." Stancel set the date for the encounter toward the end of March, 1968, approximately at the time of the preliminary hearings.

Stancel said that Weaver began crying on another occasion. "We sat there talking, and James started crying." Weaver cried, Stancel said, because he felt responsible. "He knew that James didn't do the killing. He said that. And I asked him about going to Frank, and 'No,' Frank knew what he knew. He said, 'Don't let Frank know' that he had told me anything." Stancel said that Weaver did not expect that Richardson would be convicted. "He thought that even with his testimony there would be no case." The conviction and the sentence troubled him. "I think that's what upset him more than anything. We talked about death row, and I think that bothered him more than anything."

Robinson asked Stancel about the mechanics of the Weaver testimony, who prepared it and how it was done. Robinson asked, "Did he tell you that he had lied about his statements that he made?" Stancel replied, "Yeah. He said that he was told what to say and what not to say."

> *Robinson:* "Did he tell you who told him what to say?"
> *Stancel:* "Yes. This was specific."
> *Robinson:* "Who did he tell you?"
> *Stancel:* "The Sheriff and the State's Attorney."
> *Robinson:* "Told him what to testify to as to Richardson admitting that he killed the children?"
> *Stancel:* "Right. He said that Richardson never said anything to him about killing the children. The best I understand it, he [Weaver] did have some charges on him, whether they was good or bad, in De Soto County. When you have the Sheriff and the State's Attorney on your side, well, you know."

Stancel said that after the conviction Weaver felt "real bad. But I don't think he'll ever go to the authorities on his own. You can't just back up on a deal like that." Stancel said that Weaver was not so much afraid of a "perjury rap" for telling the truth but of far more serious consequences.

BOBBY WOODS

If Weaver was loquacious many months after the trial, it

was not without precedent. Just after he testified, Weaver gave some indication of withdrawing from his position.

Bobby Woods, a Daytona Beach resident who had known James Richardson rather casually, offered to testify on his behalf as a character witness. Robinson subpoenaed him, and he remained in the witness room for part of the trial. Just before he was to testify, however, Robinson learned that Woods was not really familiar with the defendant's reputation in the community, although he held him in high regard personally. Accordingly, Woods never was called.

Woods and Weaver met as they applied for travel expenses in the courtroom in Fort Myers. Woods had not heard Weaver testify earlier that day and did not know who he was. A conversation about the case ensued.

Woods told me that Weaver said to him, "I know that the man is not guilty. We tried to get Ernie [Ernell Washington] not to make that deal. He was talking about making that deal. He's the kind will do anything to get out of trouble." Woods said that Weaver also said, "I stand to get a lot of money out of this." Woods quoted Weaver as having said, "I've done everything—gambling, moonshining, stealing, killing, you name it and I did it. But before, I never did lie to send a man to jail." According to Woods, Weaver said, "Annie Mae never did call down to James about killing her children. This was the deal that Ernie made with the Sheriff."

Woods said that he did not know who he was talking to until he saw a picture of Weaver on a subsequent occasion. "I was surprised to see that he had two eyes. When I saw him, one eye had been so badly closed that I thought it was a permanent injury. In fact, he had just been badly beaten. I found this interesting in view of the fact that Weaver told me, 'They made sure I was here. They kept me in jail for the last two wecks.'"

Woods said that he had driven to Fort Myers from Daytona Beach. "When I passed through Arcadia, I saw that a sheriff's car picked me up and followed me for a while. In Fort Myers I was told by guys who know their way around not to drive back to Daytona through Arcadia. But I did anyway, and outside the Arcadia city limits, I was driving maybe fifty-five or sixty, a red car filled with white men came charging up on me, swerved in front of me, and forced me off the road into a ditch. I got back onto the road, sped up, and just did get away."

RICHARD BARNARD AND
JOSEPH MINOUGHAN

When I returned to Arcadia, I called upon Police Chief Barnard. He was busy but willing to talk to me for a short time. He said, "Lt. Minoughan wants to talk to you. He'll be here in a few minutes, so why don't we wait for him."

The lieutenant arrived fifteen minutes later, and the joint interview began. Much of what the two men told me has been reported in an earlier chapter of this book. My first question to Barnard began with a long narrative.

Lane: "Robinson told me that one day when he was eating at a restaurant here in Arcadia, he overheard you talking to two men and that you said, 'It's a damn shame, the prosecution of that man. They have no case against him. There is no way to tie him to the poisoning.' He told me that later he approached you, introduced himself as Richardson's attorney, and told you what he had overheard. Robinson told me that you then said, 'Well, I'm certainly not going to lie to you. I did say that. There is no case against that man.'

"My question is: What is your comment?"

Barnard: "It is true. I did say it. That was at an early

stage, and I did not see any evidence at that time."

Lane: "Is it true that the only new evidence since that time is comprised of the testimony of Weaver, Washington, and Cunningham?"

Barnard: "Yes, and I never did believe those three, and I still don't believe them. I don't believe that Richardson made any admissions. There must have been a deal there. Don't ask me for the facts of the deal, I don't know anything about it."

Lane: "Are you satisfied with the result of the trial?"

Barnard: "The whole case smells. Bessie Reese told me she warmed up the food, prepared it, and dished it out to the kids. Now they say she denies it. I searched that shed the night before the parathion was found there. Who put it there in the morning? For what reason?"

Lane: "What was Washington's reputation?"

Minoughan: "He was big, rough, vulgar, loud, and boisterous. He would like to think of himself as tough. That girl that shot him in the bar did it in self-defense. He was abusing her, he was threatening her. He had just testified, I guess a couple of weeks before, and he was feeling very big, maybe a little protected."

Lane: "When did you hear about Washington, Cunningham, and Weaver as State Witnesses?"

Barnard: "It sure was sudden. We heard about it through the newspapers when it happened. It must have happened very quickly."

Lane: "How did Boone get into the case?"

Minoughan: "Boone was sent into the case by the Governor. That's the word among

Lane: law-enforcement men, but that's hearsay. Don't quote me as saying that I know he was sent by the Governor."

Lane: "I'll quote you as saying what you just said."

Minoughan: "O.K."

Barnard: "Boone did tell me that the Governor sent him into this case. He said the Governor sent him in to crack the case."

Minoughan: "Let me tell you one thing. If I'm ever in trouble, I would not want to be tried in Fort Myers."

Lane: "Why?"

Minoughan: "Isn't it obvious?"

Barnard: "Joe is from Chicago. He may not be used to our ways yet."

Minoughan: "Yes, I was on the police force for twenty-five years in Chicago before coming down here."

Lane: "Chief Barnard, at the trial you never did get to answer the question about what you thought of Cline's reputation in the community."

Barnard: "I sure didn't."

PAUSE.

Lane: "Did Cline share any information about the Richardson case with your office?"

Barnard: "He sure didn't. He really kept us out of the investigation. I don't mean necessarily that his honor over there [pointing toward the county jail] was trying to hide something, to cover up. Maybe he was just trying to keep the publicity to himself. We don't care too much for publicity in this office anyway. We've never had a press conference."

Lane: "Lieutenant, why did you never testify? You were the first officer at the hospital, the first officer at the apartment, and the first officer at the shed after the parathion was found."

Minoughan: "I don't know. They served a subpoena on me, but nobody called me as a witness. I was in the witness room after Cunningham testified. That guy got so drunk during lunch that they had to carry him off to the county jail. They physically carried him to the jail."

Barnard: "Just before that, Robinson was talking to him, and he just about admitted that he had not testified truthfully. Robinson asked him to tell the truth, and Cunningham said something like, 'If I do, do I have to go back in there and testify?' Robinson told him, 'Yes,' and Cunningham said, 'Well, then, I'm sticking with the same story.'"

Lane: "Can we take a couple of pictures?"

Barnard: "Of what?"

Lane: "Of you and the lieutenant."

Barnard: "Absolutely not."

Minoughan: "None of me, either."

Barnard: "Why don't you go over to the county jail? I'm sure his honor will pose for you."

Lane: "I have pictures of Cline. He posed with the award from *Official Detective Magazine.*"

Barnard: "That's a great award. One day I opened a big envelope in the mail addressed to me and discovered that I had one too. For my work on the Richardson case. Can you believe that? There it is, right there. An award for me, and I don't even think there is a case."

GERALD PURVIS

Gerald Purvis no longer sells insurance. His license to do so is irrelevant to his new occupation. I asked him to tell me about the meeting with Richardson on October 25, 1967. "Were you at his home by invitation? Was there an insurance policy in effect? Could Richardson have been under the impression that there was a policy?"

He began, "I was working door-to-door, and I saw the light on in his house, so I knocked. He had not called me, and we had no appointment. In fact, he had no way of knowing that I was coming at all. I talked with him, tried to sell him some insurance, and we did reach a tentative agreement for a policy covering him and his wife and a number of children. But he had no money, so there was no insurance in effect. I knew that, and I certainly presumed that he knew that also. In fact, I told him that I could not give him a receipt until he paid the premium, and the receipt is proof that there is a policy. I did not give him a receipt that night. I never did, because he never paid and there never was any insurance.

"The newspapers have distorted all of this and blown it all up. There never was any insurance. The newspapers said that I said that I would pay the premiums, but that's not true. I might have said something like, 'I'll take care of the application and be back next week to collect the premium,' but nothing more. The newspapers made the man sound very stupid, like he just couldn't understand what I was saying to him. I've never said anything about this to anyone before because I didn't want to get involved, but that man did not seem at all stupid to me. I think that he understood exactly what was going on all the time we were talking.

"I *know* that there was no insurance written that night, and unless he was very stupid and very confused, he knew that until he got that receipt there was no insurance. Anyway, I said, 'I'll be back next week to get the money and give you the receipt,' and he seemed satisfied. He never asked me if I could get the policy written faster or anything like that. He didn't seem to be in any hurry for the insurance."

I asked Purvis if he had been questioned by the State's Attorney about his discussion with Richardson. "Oh, yes. Mr. Schaub questioned me. I told him what went on that night, and they had me testify at the coroner's inquest. They said I would testify at the trial, they called me for the trial, but then they never put me on the witness stand. I was just as pleased about that, since I really did not want to get involved, but I also felt that it would be good to try to clear up the distortion in the newspapers about this thing."

I asked Purvis if he had read the newspaper stories that said that Richardson killed his children for the insurance. "Well, I'm no lawyer or sheriff, and I don't want to argue with anyone, but there was no insurance. That's that. There was none." I asked him to comment upon various wire-service stories that claimed that Richardson thought that there was insurance. As an example I read one to him: "An investigation into the deaths in De Soto County showed the migrant fruit picker took out insurance policies on seven of his children, not realizing the policies weren't in effect until the premiums were paid."

Purvis said, "Well, maybe they're some kind of mind readers. I was there, and I couldn't agree with them."

In fact, just two men were there for the entire conversation. The early press comments by Treadwell charged that Purvis and Richardson offered conflicting stories about their discussions. Cline had said that it was the fact of the insurance that initially led him to suspect Richardson, and the State's Attorney's office said that their suspicion was first aroused by the "conflicts" about the insurance. Yet it seems that the two men were in substantial agreement. Both the salesman and the prospective client said that no insurance policy was written, and they agreed that the children were not insured.

BESSIE REESE

There were but two more witnesses to see.

It was not too difficult to find either Bessie Reese or Charlie Smith. It took two days to discover that Mrs. Reese had moved from Arcadia to Nocatee, a town also located in De Soto County. I stopped at the post office there and inquired about her.

The old man behind the counter said, "I don't know where she lives, she's a nigger lady."

I asked how I might go about finding her.

"Oh, just ask any of them burr heads."

I said, "Excuse me?"

He laughed and said, "I mean niggers. But they all stick together. Ask any of them where so-and-so lives, and they say they don't know. But tell them you got a check, and they tell you exactly how to get there."

Following the advice of the federal presence in Nocatee, I drove into the Negro community of shacks. I asked the first man I saw if he might know where Bessie Reese lived. "Oh yeah. She lives in the big white house down at the corner there." Mrs. Reese's home was more modest than the description, but it was a very substantial establishment and quite luxurious when compared with some of the surrounding hovels. Her standard of living had evidently improved since she moved from the dingy apartment building she shared with the Richardsons. No one was home. I waited in the automobile, which was parked in front of her house.

Soon I saw someone approaching from approximately a quarter of a mile away. I thought it was a man. The person was huge and was wearing dungarees.

"What do you want?" I was asked. I replied that I was looking for Bessie Reese. "Well, that's me," she replied. I asked if I might talk with her for a few minutes. She grunted either agreement or disapproval, which I at once took for consent. I walked up to the door of her house, which was partially open, held it entirely open for her, and then entered after she did. She said, "Well, what you want to talk to me about?" I told her that I was interested in the Richardson case. She became very uneasy and began to wring her hands. "I don't know nothing. It was in the papers. I don't know nothing more." It was clear that she did not want to talk with me. Yet in De Soto County, uneducated Negroes do not ask whites, even offensive ones, to leave their homes. I began to feel uncomfortable, for I knew that I was taking advantage of an historically odious relationship. But, given the circumstances, I did not feel sufficiently ill at ease to leave.

I asked if she had talked to Sheriff Cline about the case. "Yes, many times. One time he come and arrested me. It was a Sunday. They didn't give me no reason. Just put me in the jail. I say, 'What for?' and the Sheriff say, 'For a material witness!' " I asked when she was released. "They let me out that same night." On bail? "No, they just let me out. They come and got me from my house and put me in the jailhouse and locked the door. Then they let me out later. Never did say why."

Did she know that she was jailed when Robinson was in town trying to find her and interview her? "I heard that later. I never did talk to that man."

Did she believe that Richardson murdered his own children? "I didn't know anything about it. I don't know nothing, like I told you before." Was she at the trial? "Yes, they give me a paper to come to court, and they carry me to the court. But they don't tell me to testify at the trial. Just wasted them days."

What happened at lunchtime on October 25, 1967? "The kids come to my house. They were in the yard in the morning. Some were in school, some was playing round the house. The older girl, I forget her name, asked me to divide the rice. I go in the kitchen and fix the food for them." How did she fix the food? "I didn't fix the food. That was wrong. I divide it up in seven parts. Then I left before they ate. I just get right out of there before they eat."

Did she notice any smell while in the kitchen? "No." How could she explain that she didn't smell the poison? "I just didn't."

Did she know that every witness who entered the kitchen thereafter complained of the very strong smell of poison? "I just say I didn't smell it. That's all. I don't have to say no more. I talk to the Sheriff and the lawyers for the State, and I don't have to say no more except I didn't smell nothing."

Was she present when the parathion was discovered in the shack behind the apartment building? "Yes." What were the circumstances? "I was home talking to a friend of mine. Charlie come up. He say, 'You know what, three or four people told me that stuff was down there in this little house.' I say, 'Who told you?' He say, 'I can't call the name now.' So we walked to the shack. He looked in the window. I took out a cigarette lighter and helped him to look. And he found the old bag of poison." Who had told Charlie Smith about it? "He never did call the name."

Did she know the Sheriff? "Not real well. He talked to me about this." Did the Sheriff know any members of her family? "Well, I got three daughters. Almeda and Dorothy was arrested for being drunk. They was in the jail with the

Sheriff. I guess they know him, all right. But I don't believe the Sheriff talk to them about this thing."

Had she ever killed anyone? "If you mean the kids, then no. I didn't do it." Had she ever killed a husband? "They say I poisoned one. They say it cause he drinks a cup of coffee and then he just dies. But the doctor don't say he was poisoned. Say he died from stomach. They didn't prove nothing." Had there been an autopsy? "What you mean?" Did they cut open his body to determine the cause of death? "No, what for?" Had she ever shot a husband? "Yes. I shot Eddie Reese. I killed him with a rifle cause he come after me. They convicted me of murder and give me twenty years." That was less than twenty years ago, wasn't it? "I just spend four years in Raiford, then they let me out on probation."

Was she presently married? Where was her husband? "I'm married to Johnny King. He went off to Jacksonville with James. I was in Bradenton when James and Johnny went off. Then they come back. Then they went off again, and Johnny never did come back. They say he living with a girl there, with one of Richardson's cousins."

Did she ever threaten the Richardsons because of that occurrence? "You believe that? You think that's why I kill them kids?" I explained that I had made no accusation, but merely inquired if she had ever threatened the Richardson family. "I didn't kill them kids. Yeah, I told about them, that I was mad. Did you hear that from them people back there?" (Indicating north, toward Arcadia.)

Did she know Charlie Smith well? "Good enough. He come over when he was drinking. He drank with Johnny."

Did she suspect that anything might have been wrong with the food when she served it? "No." Was she in the house when the children became ill? "No. I never went into that apartment after they ate the food." Didn't she take care of them after they became ill? "Yes, but on my porch.

I did not go into that house after they eat. I never went back into the house after I cut up the rice. I am sure of that."

Did she know that the teachers testified that they had found her in the Richardson apartment, after lunch, holding one of the dying children? "Did they say that?" Yes, they did. "Well, I went into the house to get clothing for them." For the children? "Yes, the kids." Why? "Cause they was sick. That's why, cause they was sick." Then, was she in the Richardson apartment when the teachers came? "Yes."

Did she smell anything then? "No." Was she interested at that time in trying to find out what made the children ill? "Yes." And the house was filled with the smell of para-thion gas, and she smelled nothing? She was unable to find any clue to the sudden illness that all of the children were experiencing? "I didn't smell nothing."

Did she take the children to the hospital or send for a doc-tor or help of any kind? "The teachers come to take the kids away. They took them." But had she sent for any help when she saw the children dying around her? "I don't think I did. But the teachers come for them anyway. Then they told me that nothing could have been done for them anyway. Too much of that poison. It was enough, all right. Nothing could be done anymore."

CHARLIE SMITH

It took several days to find Charlie Smith. I was becoming known in Arcadia, and the official lines of communication were beginning to close. Arcadia is not exactly a tourist center. Less than three hundred visit the little town each year. My continued presence, particularly in the Quarters, an unlikely place for a visitor to sojourn to, let alone tarry, was causing some consternation. Blacks resented pictures being taken of their shacks, and a glance into the rear-view mirror too often revealed a deputy's car not far behind. As the sheriff had told me, the clue to tranquillity was control.

I did find the house, but Smith was not home. He was there on my second visit, however. The house was nondescript but of sturdy appearance when compared with some of the others. The yellow-painted boards sagged. It was set but six feet from the railroad tracks. But Smith did not exactly live there. He lived in a chicken-coop-like structure in the backyard. Chickens abounded back there. His rent was $6.50 a week for a small room, not tall enough to stand in. It housed one bed, one bedside table, and a broken chair. On the floor was a cracked bowl and a chipped pitcher half-filled with water.

I introduced myself, and he invited me in. We both sat on the bed, directly on the mattress, as there was no linen and there were no blankets. I told him that I heard that he had found the parathion. "That's right. That's what you heard. That's what everyone says." Did that mean that he had not found the poison? "It don't mean nothing." We talked for almost an hour. He assured me that he believed James Richardson to be innocent but told me that he couldn't tell me a thing. "Well, mister, that ain't exactly right, that I couldn't. I can. But I can't. Do you know what I mean?" I told him he was being a bit too mysterious for me to follow. "Yeah. You leave here when you finish. I got to stay." I said that I appreciated his predicament, but there was a man on death row who might be saved by the facts. "Maybe it's too late now, huh?" I said that maybe it was not too late.

Smith thought, rinsed his mouth out with water from the pitcher, spit it into the bowl, then said, "O.K. I'll tell you a couple of things, but I don't want no trouble. I'll tell you about how the poison was found. I saw Bessie after I heard that the children were dead. I went up there to find out who died. I ask Bessie, 'Was it your family?' and she say, 'No, the children next door.' We was there, near her house, and she says to me, 'You see that little house over there?' She points to a shed. You've been there? You know what shed I mean?" I said I was familiar with the shed and the layout. "She says, 'Old man used to live there. He had a garden there, and he had powder to kill the insects, the bugs.' Then she says, 'Maybe we should go look there. That man's been dead and gone a long time.' She starts to walk to that shed. She takes out a cigarette lighter, and I follow her. She reaches out and puts her hand on the board, right at the window there, and she tells me, 'Help me pull off this board!' So I help, and we pull off the board. We both pulled it off. Then she gives me the cigarette lighter; no, she don't give it to me exactly, she lights it and holds it down in there for me to see. She puts it this close to some old bag in there [at this point Smith held his hands out, palms extended, six inches from each other]. Then Bessie says, 'There's a bag there.' I pick it up and give it to her. She gives it back to me and she says, 'Charlie, you found it.'

"Then she walks across the street and told a lady there to call Frank Cline, 'Charlie found the poison.' A police officer come. Then Frank come. Bessie tells everyone that I find the poison. I didn't even know it was the poison until Bessie read it. She says it say 'poison' right on the bag."

Did Bessie Reese know that Cline had searched the shed several times the day before? "She knew it, all right. She was right there. She knew that the poison was there in the morning, too. She had to know it. She took me right up to that bag and showed it to me so I would be the one that picked it up first. I was the one that they said found it. It's true I picked it up first, but she took me to it. She had to know the bag was right there."

What happened next? "Then they tell the papers I find the poison. I don't say nothing, except the Sheriff comes to talk to me. I tell him what happen. Then they put me in the jail for nothing. Keep me there for two months. For nothing. Say I'm a material witness. For what? Bessie finds it, and they put me in jail. Bessie was in jail later for just a few hours, cause that lawyer comes looking for her, but I stay in two months. I don't know nothing. They don't even make me testify at the trial."

We talk about his home. What does he do for heat in the winter? "Stay with friends until it gets late. Then I jump into bed and put all the clothes on the bed. No stove in here." How are things in Arcadia? "I tell you, not good if you're poor." And if you are black? "That's what I mean. If you're black you're poor." Is there an NAACP in Arcadia? "If there is, I never hear about it. No, we are alone here." What is his income. "I make forty dollars a week for field work, farm, you know. Pulling up them stumps, you get a little more. But you only work when they want you. Just half the time."

Does he know anything else about the case? "I know. I know. I can't tell you now. Maybe you come back later. Maybe I can tell you then. I tell you this. That man didn't do it. That man did not kill his own. No, sir. I know that."

JAMES RICHARDSON

In November, 1968, I asked Robinson if he might be able to arrange for me to meet with Richardson. The defense lawyer said that he was anxious for me to talk to his client. "Just talk to him for half an hour, and I'm sure that you will know that he is innocent. I've never said that about a client before, but there is something about James. I don't want to sound mystic—if you could just talk to him, you would know what I mean. However, they won't let anyone in to see him except me. It's maximum security on death row, and the State doesn't want any more publicity about this case anyway." Robinson told me that reporters for national news magazines had requested permission to interview Richardson, as had many local news-media representatives. "Within the last few weeks there must have been a dozen requests," he said. "They all wanted to interview him for stories on the first anniversary of the deaths, just a week ago. But the State refused every request."

I told Robinson that it might be possible to insinuate me into the prison, since I had one advantage that the reporters lacked: I was a member of the bar. I suggested that Robinson might introduce me as associate counsel. He agreed to try. Two weeks later he informed me that he had made arrangements for the visit. In the hope that we might minimize conflict with officialdom, we arrived late Friday afternoon, November 29, on the second day of a four-day holiday weekend.

The attractive administration building on the sprawling and neatly manicured acreage was all but deserted. One official was present, and Robinson introduced me to him and chatted informally with him for more than twenty minutes. The official called ahead to the East Wing, which houses the death-row prisoners. We returned to the automobile and drove toward the East Wing. I remarked on the friendship that my colleague had developed with the prison official and asked him how long he had known him. "I just met him with you," he said. "I never saw him before." I asked how he knew his name, and Robinson said that he read it on the name plaque on his desk. Again I marveled at the instant warmth and informality so often generated in the South when two consenting adults of the same race meet. It was an indication, I thought, of what might one day be when all men meet in the South.

My thoughts about the future were shattered by an electrical voice that was upon us, and clearly in the present.

"Please park your car there and walk toward this tower," it commanded more than it suggested. We obeyed. A man in the tower above us and perhaps thirty yards away was then visible. He asked for our names; we gave them. He asked us to wait; we did. He did not say that we could not look around, and I did that also. The East Wing was a complex of three-tier concrete buildings, its facade regularly interrupted by blue-black bars. The connecting buildings were surrounded by a high metal fence topped with strung barbed wire. Ten feet from the fence, and running parallel with it, was another imposing metal fence, with its own lethal accouterment. In the corridor formed by the two fences were a number of rather large German shepherds. I asked the voice if I could approach the dogs, and he said I could, but he warned me not to reach through the wire fence. I took two steps toward the fence, I was still fifteen yards from it, when the dogs began barking angrily. The dogs closest to me snarled as they hurled themselves against the fence in an effort to get at me. Later one of the guards explained that the dogs had been trained to be vicious. "Even the trainer wouldn't dare go near them," he said. "They feed them by pushing food under the fence. The dogs are never let out of there." Dogs and men. Each caged. Neither free, and both trained to become less, not more, than they were before entering this place.

A fenced corridor ran at right angles to the other. It ran through it from the outside world through three large gates into the East Wing. The guards were cordial. We signed the registration book. We were then ushered into another room, through it, through a concrete corridor, through a magnetic field to determine if we carried metal objects, through electrically operated metal gates, always on closed-circuit television, and into another room, and finally into a room not far from death row.

James Joseph Richardson was there, waiting for us. He

had been brought from his cell into a glass-enclosed room. He embraced Robinson, then shook hands with him. We shook hands when we were introduced. He looked so much like James Baldwin that I was struck by the resemblance. Medium height; dark-black, close-cut hair; slight, with a head that appeared just a bit too large for the rest of him. Small talk at first. Robinson: "Well, how are you, buddy?" The reply: "Not so good, Mr. Robinson. Not so good. I gave up smoking. I spend all the time just trying to read the Bible."

I asked Richardson to talk about the case.

"I remember that morning; I will never forget; I can't forget. The night before we asked Bessie King's daughter, Dorothy, she's about twenty-five years old, to keep our children. That night we ask her; she said she would.

"You don't know what it is like to sit up there and look at the electric chair. Yes, we can see it. And at night they keep the lights up. Many are praying. Some of the prisoners cuss me out. They call me a damn rev cause they heard I was a preacher. I used to sing in a quartet in a little jubilee, and I used to preach also.

"On the twenty-fourth, Bessie came to the house and talked with my wife in the kitchen. I was looking at television. Someone knocked on the door, but the television was so loud, I'm hard of hearing in this ear [indicating his right ear], and I saw a man standing in the door. I never seen him. It was strange to me Bessie King came in four or five minutes before. He stared at me; I stared at him. I started to wonder. It was an insurance man. I had insurance, but it had relaxed. Also, I said, 'I ain't got no money.' He said, 'Insurance is very cheap, and I would like to sell you some.' So I opened the screen door and he came in.

"We sat on the settee facing the front. He sat beside me. I said, 'I ain't got no money. How much is it?' He said 'on the whole family'? I said, 'Yes. We have ten children, seven here and three in Jacksonville.' I had worked on a garbage truck in Jacksonville for five years. He said you could get it all for two dollars, or maybe he said a dollar and something. But I told him, 'I don't have no money.' He said, 'You could borrow it from the woman in the kitchen,' but Bessie said she had no money till she got paid off Friday. He said, 'Could you borrow it from a neighbor?' I said, 'I can, but I don't want to worry anyone.' So he said he would write it up, but it's no good until after you pay it. I said, 'O.K.' And he wrote up the paper. Before he left, Bessie King kept running in and out. So the insurance man said, 'I'll be back to get the money on Tuesday.' I said, 'O.K. Can I double it, pay it for two weeks on Tuesday?' I never saw him again. That was the first time and the last time.

"Just after he left, Bessie came back. I turned the TV around and looked at it. Bessie King came back in the door after I had locked the screen door and talked with my wife. I continued looking at television. My wife said you better talk to Bessie about Dot keeping the children. Bessie said, 'I will keep the children, if I be home in the morning.' I say, 'You know we don't have no money, till we catch up with the bills.' Bessie say, 'O.K.'

"I think Annie Mae and me got into bed about midnight. We went to the hospital that night to visit a man, Israel Jackson. My wife had fixed food for him. And so we lovey-dovey and everything. We laughed and talked things over about what we were going to get the children for Christmas. I felt Annie Mae crossing over me early that morning. Then I heard her call my daughter, 'Betty, you get up now. You gotta get up now.' Betty got up and began to wash her face. Annie Mae waked me up. 'You better get up now, it's getting late,' she said. 'Get up and put on your clothes.' I said, 'O.K., O.K., O.K.' She said, 'You want coffee?' I said, 'Do

I have time for coffee?' Did I have coffee on that morning or not? I don't know. I don't know that I drink it or not. She said, 'Betty, you make sure you wash all the dishes.' We had cleaned up the house the day before, and we had bought washing powder, and we got a pretty glass with it. At a quarter to seven or ten minutes to seven we walked out the door. We never asked nobody for nothing. We always worked together. You never would see one unless you would see the other. People would ask us, 'Can't you go by yourself sometime?'

"My wife reminded me to ask Dot, so I did. Dot said, 'Yes, I may not be here, but if I don't be here, my mother will.' When Bessie had no money, we went to the store and got her, oh, ten or fifteen dollars for food. We had groceries for them. We always had food to give them. They were pulling us down, in a way. We could have gone to one store cheaper, but the other store gave us credit. We had food for the next week when we spent ten or fifteen dollars, but in three or four days it was used up. They were four, and we were nine. They would use the food, and then they would borrow from us.

"They got mad at us cause when we first went there we didn't know how to work, but then we learned, and sometimes our check would be a hundred and fifteen or a hundred and twenty-five dollars for the two of us, but taking care of two families was getting us down. We borrowed from our job. We agreed to pay on Friday ten dollars to Bessie for keeping the kids.

"We went to work on a truck with a cover. Sometimes there were fifty or sixty or even a hundred people would get on the truck. We walked about five or six blocks to the truck. We stopped at a lady's house. I would carry her bag for her. It had ice water, and she would work with us. We got in the truck, and then we went out onto the field. We had to wait until the trees got dry. They told us it is dangerous to climb up into the wet trees, but sometimes I would climb up into the wet trees just to get through. We picked fifteen boxes of oranges, me and Annie Mae together. Before we did pick them all, my wife and me, we sat down on a box and my wife ate a chicken sandwich and I reached back and started to get a sandwich too; I think that was a ham sandwich.

"I was talking to another guy. He was always dreaming about a butt-naked woman, and he said, 'That was a bad dream. That meant death.' Then a man came running across the field yelling, 'Richardson, Richardson.' Then he said, 'Someone of your children are sick. So one of you come with me.' I thought about my little boy when he had been sick. We always had to keep a close eye on him, and we had asked Bessie definitely to look out for little James. The guy says, 'Hurry up. They have been calling and calling on my phone.' I said, 'We just knock off for the day.' I throw the sack on the back of the truck and jump on. Annie Mae was in the cab. I jumped off as soon as we got to the hospital, where I saw Bessie King standing there looking scared. I started back to the truck to help my wife out of the truck. I walked up to Bessie and said, 'Bessie,' and she looked like she was scared and she was going to run. I said, 'What happened?' She said, 'I don't know. Go inside and they will tell you.' I said, 'O.K., probably James got sick.'

"We go into the hospital, and people come from everywhere. I said to myself, I wonder what is going on? So about that time, a minister walked up, and he said, 'Did you have any insurance on the children?' I said, 'No, we don't have any insurance. We had some but it elapsed, then we took up some from last night, but it's no good. It's not paid, because the man said he would be coming back on Tuesday.' Then the minister said, 'You really need it.' We went out into the chapel. Bessie King walked into the chapel, and the schoolteacher was trembling. She walked into the chapel. Then the Sheriff came. He looked at me and he looked at my wife and he said, 'You have a key to the icebox?' I said, 'Yes, my wife has a key, and I have a key. We always leave the box unlocked for Bessie.' The policeman looked worried. He asked for the keys, and I handed him the keys.

"About ten or fifteen minutes later the minister said, 'All of us must get down on our knees and start praying.' I said, 'Pray for what?' He said, 'It is time to pray,' and he began to pray. The Sheriff come back and looked at us for a long time, and he say, 'Boy, all of your children are dead,' and I said to him, 'You are a liar.'

"My wife went down to her knees, and she cried. It was sad. I have never seen anything like that before. The nurse said, 'One child said, "I want to go home with my mom and dad. I feel fine," and then she laid down and died.' I didn't know what to do. They was treating us like some dogs. People I don't know come up, both white and black."

At this point James Richardson broke down and started sobbing. He looked toward the ceiling of the cell and cried, "Oh, Lord, oh, Lord, if you only knew, if you only knew what they meant to me," and he continued on almost hysterically. It took fifteen minutes before John Robinson and I could quiet him down. I finally said, "Listen, Mr. Richardson, I am here because I think maybe I can help you, but if you don't stop crying and if you don't continue to tell me what happened that day and answer some of my other questions, I won't be able to help you." He continued sobbing, but his sobbing diminished somewhat, and finally he began to speak again.

"Well, now they started coming. Two state's attorneys came, and I sat and watched them. They went in and tore up my house. They had flashing cameras. They asked me nothing. Annie Mae was like in a trance. She couldn't even answer any questions. Cline had been there. He tore up everything, people in the neighborhood told me. We got to the house from the hospital. We got out of the car ready to go into the house, and the police come up. I hollered and said, 'Don't you smell something?' We were on Bessie King's front door, and the closer we got, the stronger it smells. Police officers and Annie Mae and me went into the house, and the smell was very strong. It smelled like the stove had just been cut off. It was two-thirty, almost three o'clock. The police had been there before, and everything was all torn up since from a quarter to one, when I was at the hospital. So we went in, and I helped my wife lay down on the bed. Bessie King came, but she never did say a mumbling word.

"Same day that afternoon the police started coming from every which a way. They took us to the State's Attorney's office after they came back with Bessie and her daughter. That evening they took Annie Mae. They kept her very long. I love that woman. That woman is very faithful.

"After the funeral, they sent for us to come down to the welfare office. So we went on down to the place on Seventeenth Street, and the lady said, 'Frank Cline wants us to go down to the jail, and he wants you to go there.' She said, 'Frank Cline has maybe two or three thousand dollars,' and, 'We can't help you because you have to see him.' We went downtown to a store, and a deputy came and said my wife should go with him and I should go home, and I said, 'She doesn't go nowhere without me.' So he took us down to the Sheriff's office, and Cline ordered me, he said, 'You just sit down there, boy,' and he helped her into the office, and he was laughing.

"My wife finally came out, and Cline called me in. 'James, sit down,' he said. It was the lie-detector man. He said, 'I want you to tell me all your troubles now.' I said, 'What do you mean?' He said, 'See that thing?' I said, 'Yea.' He said, 'This thing tells me the truth or tells me whether you are lying. I am not here to hurt you, but this is my job.' Then he strapped it onto my arm and asked if I ever had a falling-down spell. Then he gave me the test. He asked if I knew where the poison was and if I did it and if I did it for the insurance. He went back into the other room, and then he come back with Cline. Cline said, 'I knew you were lying from the very beginning, and I am going to Jacksonville and I am going to find out more about that.' Then he looked down at my wife and smiled. The deputy finger-printed me. They put me in a cell.

"About an hour later they put my wife in jail. About one-thirty or two-thirty in the morning a deputy sheriff came up. Then he pushed me downstairs. Cline was there standing with Judge Hayes and newspapermen. Hayes went out the door with the newspapermen, and Cline said, 'Stand up here and hear your guilt.' He looked over the papers, read off the seven children's names, and read them again and read the warrant for the first-degree murder signed by Judge Hayes. Cline said, 'How do you plead, guilty or not guilty?' I said, 'I am not guilty,' and Cline said to his deputy, 'Take his damn ass upstairs.'

"The police were gambling there with dice and with cards. Ernell Washington was there. He would beat up the guys who would come in drunk, and he would take their money and then he could gamble with the police officers. Someone looked out the window and said, 'Bad Boy is here.' The place got silent. Everyone was afraid. Bad Boy said to me, 'You sick? Something wrong with you, Richardson?' Bad Boy had a big gun in his belt, not in a holster. He called me into a little room. Bad Boy said to me, 'I want you to tell me something.' I said, 'I don't know nothing.' He said, 'You know about that NAACP. You know about that NAACP.' Now he said, 'I want to treat you nice if you let me. If not, when I get through with you, you'll wish you told me something. You heard about them damn NAACP's gonna get you out.' I said, 'I don't know about that.' He said, 'When I get through with you, I am gonna fuck you up.' He pointed a gun at me all of a sudden. I was sitting there scared and trembling. Then he said, 'If you tell me what I want to know, I'll let them release your wife.' I wanted my wife released. I didn't want Annie Mae in a jail cell. Then I said, 'I don't know nothing,' because I didn't know nothing. He said, 'Those lawyers are not gonna get you out. They're not gonna get you out. They're gonna let you stay in.' Then Bad Boy says to me, 'I'm a preacher too.' And I says to Bad Boy, 'Oh yea, do you want to pray with me now?' He pulled out his gun. He pointed it at me. He said, 'Your Lord won't help you, you ain't got no money.' Bad Boy said, 'I can hurt your lawyer, but he can't do nothing to me, and I will get you a little later.' Then Cline come in, and he said to me, 'You ain't never seen the electric chair?' I said, 'No.' He said, 'Get your damn ass up.' I got up. Then he shoved me and I fell toward the deputy. The deputy pushed me back. Then the deputy pushed me very hard into the cell, and he slammed the door and hit my leg.

"When I was in jail a man called Sam, everyone called him Sam, I didn't know his other name, told me that Ernell Washington called up Cline and he said to Cline, 'If you scratch my back I'll scratch yours.' Ernell told me that Cline was going to kill me. Then Cline put me in a cell by myself. Weaver and Ernell told me that that was the death cell. That is where they put people when they are going to kill them.

"Then Johnny Robinson come in the case. God sent that man to help me. That is when they stopped threatening me, when they heard he was coming. Until then I was so scared I was trembling all of the time. Bad Boy used to shove me around. He pushed the gun in my face. He snapped

the trigger. I didn't know if the gun was loaded or not.
"At the trial, they said that my children ate that food cold.
That's not true. My children do not eat cold food. They
would spit it out before they would eat it. They would spit
out grits or anything else. Lunch was grits in a big pot.

"I don't know who killed my children. I know that Bessie
killed her husband, her second husband, and I took the
third husband, Johnny King, with me to Jacksonville back
in June, 1967, and I take him to my mother-in-law's house,
and he lived with my cousin. When we got back, we heard
that Bessie was threatening to get us. She wanted to know
where her husband was. I was kinda scared when I heard
that she was going to get us. But I didn't tell Johnny King
to stay in Jacksonville. He decided that for himself. I don't
think he liked Bessie very much."

Some hours after we had arrived, we rose to leave. The
lawyer and his client shook hands, at first in silence. Richardson, with his lawyer's hand still in his, turned to me and
said, "God sent this man to me. The NAACP told me that
there were three lawyers who might be willing to work in
my case. They read off the names. The last one called off
was Mr. Robinson, and I said Robinson is like Richardson,
it's my namesake, and the Lord wants me to take him. So
I said Robinson, that is the lawyer that I want, Robinson.

"And then when he came to see me in jail, and then they
wouldn't try to scare me like they was going to kill me
after that, then I knew that I picked the right man. I don't
rightly know why the Lord sent these trials to me, I loved
them children so, but he sent Mr. Robinson to save me."

Then he turned to his lawyer. "I don't know what you
can do. I know you is trying with your heart, and I thank
you for that and for bringing this man to see me who I
know will try to help me and try to tell the truth. I thank
you for everything."

Robinson said, "James, I love my little daughter, Robin. You know that. We talked about her. But next to her, I love you best, and I am going to get you out of here if I spend every dime I have, if I spend every hour that is left to me. I swear it, James. You are going to walk out of that door. And we will get you a job in Daytona Beach and you and Annie Mae can start to have a new family. You will be free."

By now tears were falling from the eyes of the client and the lawyer. They embraced for a moment. And again, in that cell on death row, as a black man and a white man cried together, I thought of a different South.

DEATH ROW, RAIFORD

Robinson and I walked through the cement and tile halls, through the steel doors, and finally into the air. A guard approached. He said that the administration building had called down, and we were to be shown the electric chair, "sort of a treat," he said. I had tried a number of capital cases some years before but I had never seen the place of execution in any state. I was not curious enough to examine one now. Robinson seemed willing, though, and we walked on the grass, made one left turn, then another, then the guard opened the door and we were there. "This is the witness room," the guard said. It was separated from the execution chamber primarily by a large glass plate. "And that is the famous chair," he said as we walked into the execution room. "About a week before the man is to be executed, they bring him on down from one of those cells there. [He indicated the two lower tiers in the three-tier building.] They put him in one of the cells right along-side this room. Then one day, he don't know which one it might be, they take him out and bring him in this room. [We walked into a small dressing room just off of the execution chamber.] In here he is dressed. He gets all new clothes, new socks, new underwear, a brand-new suit, never worn before. He is not allowed to wear any shoes. Then they take him into the room with the chair, and he sits down there. They strap him into the chair. Strap him over the chest, on the legs and arms, and a mask is put over his head. Then a helmet goes on his head. It has an electrode and a sponge which is wet with saltwater.

"You see two guards bring the man in here, and they stay in the room the whole time. We also have the superintendent of prisons in the room, we have a doctor and a medical technician both, and a priest or a minister, you know, depending on the guy's religion. Then the executioner comes into the room, after that curtain is pulled. Anyway he wears a long black robe with a black mask over his head. All you can see are two slits for his eyes. The executioner throws the switch. It really used to be terrible. You should have seen it years ago before the improvements—the body got all burned where the electrodes touched the skin. Now it is humane, anyway more humane. Now when he pulls the switch, a three-cycle operation starts automatically. The voltage goes up, and when it reaches the maximum, it goes down and the amperage goes up. When that goes up, the first shock hits the prisoner. That goes on like that three times, three shocks hit his body. You can see what those shocks do. But they don't burn very much anymore, the electricity just goes through the whole body. I don't know how they do it, but it's much better than it used to be, what with the smell of flesh burning. The whole thing takes only eight minutes from the time the executioner walks in. That guy works a number of states in the Southeast. I think five states. He gets one hundred dollars for each one. For each execution. No one is supposed to know who he is."

We walk out. The guard pauses in the witness room. "According to law, we have at least twelve other people witness the execution through this glass partition. They just sit in this room and watch."

I asked my first question. "Where do you get the witnesses from?" He answered, "People just write into the prison asking permission to watch an execution. We have a very long waiting list at the office."

Index